RUNNING AND RETURNING
Seeking Balance in an Imperfect World

By Vicki Ash Hunter, Ph.D.

Running and Returning

Seeking Balance in an Imperfect World

Cover Design and Interior Layout: Nicole Wurtele

All photos courtesy of Vicki Ash Hunter unless otherwise noted.

Published by CG Sports Publishing

A Division of The CG Sports Company
cgsportspublishing.com

ISBN: 978-1-7359193-8-6

Quantity order requests can be emailed to:

Publishing@cgsportsmanagement.com

Printed in The United States of America

Praise for
Running and Returning

"Enduring the circumstances we must surrender to doesn't need to feel miserable. In fact, often, that simple act of letting go of control can lead to just enough relief that your next steps become attainable. Having guidance and knowledge of those steps is key. Vicki Hunter, as I've witnessed, has persevered to find real relief through obstacles that most would crumble under. Her lifestyle, relationships, and inspiration are the real deal. In this book, she shares inspiring stories and lessons that could help us all stay steady under life's many pleasures and pressures."

– Eric Goodman, D.C., founder of Foundation Training

"A harrowing hero's journey where the courage of the athlete triumphs over extreme physical challenges, both chosen and unforeseen. Vicki embodies the warrior spirit of the modern woman, but it is the deep reservoir of love for family that is the true victory in this candid and captivating memoir."

– Lorraine Moller, 1992 Olympic bronze medalist, winner of the 1984 Boston Marathon, and author of "On the Wings of Mercury"

"Vicki Hunter, a wonderful storyteller and writer, has written a brilliant account of addiction in its many forms and how she turned to running as one of the ways she coped with her own demons and those of her daughter. What makes her account so riveting is that for her, a highly competitive athlete, running was both an addiction and a way to deal with her and her family's mental health issues. It is the struggle between the positive and the negative aspects of running that ties together this riveting family tale."

– Edward S. Greenberg, Emeritus Professor of Political Science and Research Professor of Behavioral Science, Institute of Behavioral Science, University of Colorado, Boulder

"Running and Returning is an inspiring memoir that highlights the value of movement to cope with the hurdles life throws in our way. Vicki Hunter's life story also shows that the highs of life are enhanced by being active."

– Benji Durden, 1980 U.S. Olympic Team, marathon, 1983 U.S. World Championship team, marathon

"I love the way Vicki writes in a real and relatable way—it makes me pay attention and understand. Between the travails that Vicki had to endure from her accident, her upbringing, and her parents' struggles, it is amazing that she emerges as this incredible human being. I have a new understanding of the person that I have known for so long. A highly recommended read."

–Mark Plaatjes PT, 1993 World marathon champion

"Running and Returning shines an honest healing light on the dark side of the athletic world: Who are we when our bodies fail? How do we learn to train for the sheer love of movement? And how do we take care of ourselves without abandoning taking care of others? Vicki Ash Hunter brings academic, clinical, and "street cred" experience to these questions, while also tackling the topics of self-worth, self-doubt, and distraction. Her experience as an endurance athlete, adult daughter, professor, wife, and mother makes Running and Returning real, soulful, enlightening, and accessible."

– Dr. Eric Dorninger ND, LAc

To my daughters, Jade and Jessi:

My reason for having children wasn't to have more friends, but you have given me that treasured gift. I am in awe of your grace, strength, character, resilience, and zest for life. I am overcome with pride and admiration for how you both give back to the world and for the unique individuals you have become.

I wrote this book because of you and for you. You made me who I am, and I have learned more from being your mom than from anything else in my life. I haven't always made the right choices, but since becoming your mother, every decision I have made was with you in mind. I would go to any length to support, protect, and defend you.

With love and gratitude always,

Mom

Acknowledgments

I could not have written this book without a team of people behind me. I have often wondered at the notion of a lone person completing anything of value. It seems to take at least two, and I have many more than that to thank.

My very first editor, Terzah Becker, helped me take a loose bunch of words on paper to a more structured document. I am grateful for the hours she spent, as well as for her belief in the project when few others had any. Sarah Schantz, writer and editor extraordinaire, came on board when the book was in its early stages and read like an academic treatise. Sarah took me under her wing, introduced me to other writers, invited me to her writing workshops, and edited the crap out of this book. She basically taught me how to write creatively, and I am forever grateful. I am also thankful for her friendship.

Thank you, Dessa Willie, Jeannine Fox, Lisa Mansfield, and Lea Carey, for reading early versions and giving valuable feedback.

The team at CG Sports, especially Holly Neumann and Elaine K. Howley, have been extraordinary. I was clueless about how publishing worked when I started this endeavor. They have allowed my dream to come true.

Dad, I did it! The book we were going to write is a bit different than what we envisioned, but you planted the seed. I only wish you were here to read it.

Mom, this book is a tribute to you. I would not have the strength and resilience I do if it weren't for you.

Truly this is my story, but my siblings came along for the ride. Linda, Jody, Jeff, and Wendi, I appreciate all of you and the unconditional love we have for each other that Mom instilled in us. Thank you for the insights you provided during the writing process.

To my daughters, Jade and Jessi, this book wouldn't exist if it weren't for you. I love you with all my heart.

Brian, thanks for your constant support and never giving up on us or anything. Life would not be any fun without you!

Table of Contents

Preface

There's a strand of Judaism that believes in the mystical path of *ratzo v'shov*, running and returning, a theme that reverberates throughout this memoir. In our case, it was running away from sadness, feelings of unworthiness, and despair.

My mother thought that having her own children would save her.

I chose running as my form of escape.

Jade, my oldest daughter, chose drugs.

The "return" for my mother was never quite as complete as I wish it could have been. She never truly found her way to safety and security until perhaps her final days.

Jade, I believe, is on her way. But only she can navigate that path.

For me, in my sixth decade, I do think I've found my middle way, one of more balance and confidence. I recognize when I need to return to myself, focus inward, rest, and be present rather than running away from my now.

I don't think anyone is born into this world with the sense they aren't enough, but once we must navigate all life throws at us, we consistently get that message. I see the dance of running and returning as finding the way back to our true selves, to the best version we can be.

It's an intergenerational dance. Like the cold sore virus I inherited from my mother—who got it from her mother—trauma (the Greek root word literally means *wound*) of various types flows through families, mine included. This is our story as we navigate the world as best we can, running and returning from the individual and generational, as well as the physical and emotional traumas we've faced as a family of Jewish women in modern America.

*The events portrayed in this book are all true to the best of my recollection. Some names and personal details have been changed to protect the privacy of the people involved.

CHAPTER 1
September 11, 1997

The soon-to-be mother smiles broadly as she drives the 40 minutes to town from the house on Magnolia Road, some 8,000 feet above sea level. She's 14 weeks pregnant and headed to a swim session in Boulder, Colorado. She's suffering from morning sickness and fatigue, but the soothing properties of water call to her. The sun sends a specter of golden light through the aspens on the secluded road as a neighbor walks by with two Brittany spaniels. The man nods at the woman and she nods back as she drives by.

The suspension of her body in the water creates spaciousness and release from the physical and emotional weight of the baby inside. The queasiness evaporates. She luxuriates in the pool for as long as she can. She should get food to nourish her body, but the water takes away the nausea and she lingers longer than she has time for. Eventually, she does get out of the pool. After dressing, she heads to the university, stopping only to get a piece of banana bread from the café on campus.

She spends the afternoon teaching her honors seminar in international affairs and meeting with students to discuss their thesis topics. At 6:30 p.m., she drives downtown to meet her husband for an event at the Boulder Theater. They find each other on the sidewalk in front of the entrance and walk in together. Some people are dancing to "Psycho Killer," as the DJ spins the Talking Heads into the mix, but mostly the crowd is talking and drinking. The only food available is carrots and celery sticks, and at 9 p.m., the mom-to-be tells her husband she's tired and hungry and needs to go home. As he walks her to the car a few blocks away, there's a chill in the air, and copper leaves from the nearby trees scatter along the street.

He kisses her goodbye before she climbs into the white Subaru station wagon. "I'm going back in for a bit," he says to her through the still-open door of the vehicle. "But I'll see you at home soon."

She wakes up in a brightly lit room; a machine next to her bed blinks lights, the green lines go up and down. Her husband sits nearby, but the tube down her throat prevents her from talking. Nurses and doctors mingle beyond a glass wall. She reaches for a pad of paper and manages to scrawl: *What happened? How did I fall off my bike?* The shooting pain along her back, like red hot embers etched along her spine, makes his words evaporate in space as the husband tries to describe what happened.

"You were in a car accident," he says. "You hit a tree and broke a lot of bones."

According to him, after driving away from the theater the night before, the woman drove up Magnolia Road with its sharp, hairpin turns that eventually switch to dirt and rolling hills, the low guard rails along the side only pretending to serve duty to keep a car from going off the edge. As he talks, she finds herself floating away, as if she is still in the pool, held by the womb-like qualities of the water she'd swum in only 24 hours before.

The story continues as he tells her what he knows. At the top where the road levels off, the car spun out and hit a crooked but massive ponderosa pine on the opposite side of the road. The entire right side of the car smashed in on her body, leaving her a broken ragdoll curled up under the steering wheel, blood streaming from her right ear. Shortly after, a neighbor came upon the scene, sometime around 9:30 p.m., and called 911. He reported she was awake and speaking at that point. Her husband doesn't know what she said, and she desperately tries to remember. *Did she ask about the baby? Did she understand what had happened?* For years, she will wonder what was going through her mind at the time.

The husband visibly squirms as he finishes. "There were cars lined up on the road as emergency vehicles halted traffic." This is the scene he came upon, a feeling in his gut making him panic. Getting out of his own vehicle, running along the road, stopping only long enough to ask an officer what happened, he heard the words, "white Subaru," and ran faster screaming to the paramedics, "She's pregnant!" as they loaded his wife into the helicopter.

The injuries: three skull fractures resulting in brain injury; ten broken ribs, six in two places; a broken sacrum; a fractured pubic symphysis; a punctured liver; collapsed lung; and post-traumatic amnesia (PTA) or, as my doctors called it, 12-hour amnesia, resulting in no memory of the hours right before and after the accident. Maybe that last injury is a blessing.

At first, the collapsed lung is the hardest sensation to deal with: it's like being smothered with a pillow, yet every four hours a nurse makes her breathe into a respirator to expand the organ. She makes fists with her hands and grimaces and even turns away as the nurse approaches with the tube.

The brain injury is the next hardest. The world is murky, like looking through a piece of gauze. Nothing is clear. The pregnancy seems like it's living outside of her, in another form, separate from the wreck that is now her body. Blurry vision like she's underwater adds to the sense she's in a dream. Sounds are muffled as if she's in a deep well and can't get out.

This can't be real, she thinks. Just hours ago, she was planning for a perfect future. But the broken ribs remind her this is all too real. She has what they call "flail chest," meaning the ribs have separated from the chest wall. Her right shoulder blade tells the tale of a knife being shoved into it again, and again, and again. There is no relief.

The baby floats deep inside, protected by the warmth of amniotic fluid, seemingly oblivious to the chaos outside the womb.

Her pain is beyond manageable, so she is given morphine. Although, like other opioids, it is highly addictive, it is deemed the safest option for the baby.

But her goal from the outset is to get off the morphine as quickly as possible. At first, she needs the relief it provides, but soon, it becomes another burden. At times, she gets agitated, and it's impossible to tell if the drugs are causing it, if it's the brain injury, or if it's the lack of control she has.

The nurse returns with the respirator tube, and the injured woman cries when the ball barely moves as she tries to inflate her lungs. She cries when she's alone at night. She cries when her husband tries to comfort her. She cries when the doctors talk to him as if she isn't in the room.

On day four, her hospital room overflows with visitors, and the waiting room is so crowded with friends it's standing room only. The nurses decide it's too much and limit the number of people who can be there. The flow of visitors starts to level off, but her mother comes for a week, and the woman experiences the strange dichotomy of comfort and more pain in front of this older woman she has tried to please her whole life.

A cold sore forms on her lip as if the trauma is oozing out of her body.

It's exhausting to try to be strong. Her mother's presence seems to magnify her weakness. With the pain at white-light intensity, bolts of electricity course through her body. It's hard to hide the truth.

The husband becomes the buffer, and while the mother sits in the recliner by the bedside, he makes small talk and tries to keep the mood light. Although the mother goes to a hotel each night, she's there 12 hours straight during the day. She reads magazines and watches TV when the woman in the bed manages to nod off. Whenever her daughter's pain becomes too much, the mother doesn't hesitate to yell for a nurse to up the morphine dose. The mother silently prays for the grandchild that she never thought this daughter would give her.

The days begin to blend, each a mixture of doctors' examinations, breathing into the goddamn tube, and the major ordeal of getting out of bed to go to the toilet. Her husband helps her to the bathroom where he must wipe her ass. Talk about true love.

She tries to walk but can only make it a few steps. She winces in pain as she attempts to put one foot in front of the other using a walker. She can't sleep, so she watches reruns of *I Love Lucy*, trying to put herself in the comfort of the TV living room where she sits with Lucy and Ethel on the couch while masterminding a way to trick Ricky once again. The husband manages to sleep on a cot by her bedside, oblivious to the noise coming from the TV mounted on the wall.

Ten days have passed. Something is wrong; the pain is even more severe than what's become normal. Lying in bed, crying, she sees a white light and the tunnel no one wants to see when they're young, especially when they're also in love and pregnant.

Beams of white light pierce the grayish tunnel, illuminating the darker portions of an opening, almost like a train tunnel. But the white light is

BRIGHT. It pulls her, and when she drifts toward it, the pain lessens in her body. She feels pulled and repelled at the same time. A voice behind her lures her back away from the entrance to the tunnel.

"It's all going to be OK," her husband is saying. "Hang in there. The doctors are on their way, we'll figure this out."

The woman had been given a spinal epidural to help with the pain, but an infection had ensued, and her pain level had spiked.

It's a tug of war, but she returns.

Then, I return to my body. And I start to fill in the blanks: I am the pregnant woman who's been in a terrible, life-threatening car accident. I am the patient in this hospital room who just glimpsed the infamous white light so common to anyone who's had a near-death experience.

I am the woman at the center of this story of trauma, running from my mother straight through to the daughter growing inside my now broken body.

 Heritage

The cliché, *money doesn't buy happiness*, could not be truer in my family's case.

My mother, Joan, grew up privileged, the granddaughter of Philadelphia real estate mogul Jules Mastbaum. As an art aficionado and wealthy man, he spent a lot of time in Europe with his wife, Etta. They were intrigued by sculptor Auguste Rodin and bought many of his works. In 1926, after Jules' death, Etta gifted the Rodin Museum to the city of Philadelphia, in honor of Jules.

Jules and Etta's daughter, Peggy Solomon, whom I called Nana, was a strong, independent woman who became a master bridge player at a time when few women were permitted a seat at the table, literally and figuratively. She played bridge with Omar Shariff, and she married Congressman and lawyer Ben Golder in 1930. Family lore states that Ben represented some unsavory characters in the course of his law practice; one day Peggy opened the door at their summer home in Atlantic City to find the infamous gangster Al Capone standing there.

My mother grew up in a luxury, downtown Philadelphia penthouse apartment overlooking the very center of high society in the 1930s—Rittenhouse Square. She never wanted for anything financially as a child; I remember visiting my grandmother and her second husband, Charlie Solomon (my mother's father, Ben Golder died years before) in their palatial, skyward apartment. The doorman with his red jacket and jaunty cap made an impression, as did the obligatory trip to Bookbinders, Philadelphia's poshest seafood restaurant, for lobsters. Nana and Charlie's kindly butler, Adolph, always greeted me as "Miss Victoria," and I'd hug him, despite his always smelling of cooked cabbage.

Adolph would show us into the Trophy Room, where Nana and Charlie awaited us. The mirrored walls and shelves accentuated the glinting, overwhelming display of silver bowls and enormous trophies they'd won at bridge tournaments. To my young eyes, it all seemed like actual treasure. Nana was the third female in the United States to reach the level of bridge Life Master. Charlie was a professional, who wrote a bridge column for *The Philadelphia Inquirer* and had authored four books on the game. In

1960, the year of my birth, they were featured in a newspaper article, "The Solomons: Top Married Bridge Team."

The Trophy Room was reserved for entertaining, and Charlie would serve us drinks from the fully stocked bar, which meant a Shirley Temple for me. When the maraschino cherry burst in my mouth, I wouldn't want to be anywhere else. While waiting for the adults to finish their cocktails, we kids would play the slot machine that stood in the corner by the windows overlooking the square. I always had a sense of being grown-up while at the same time getting to play at an amusement park when I visited Nana and Charlie.

For the most part, my mother had what any observer would call an advantaged start in life. However, the drawback was that her parents were gone much of the time; Ben was busy with work, and if Peggy wasn't with him she was occupied with her social life and playing bridge, leaving my mom and her sister, Norma, to their own devices much of the time.

My father, Larry Ash, had a different upbringing.

In the early 1900s, his grandparents, Rose and Isadore (Isaac) Potash, escaped the pogroms of Czarist Russia. They fled to the U.S., bringing my father's father, Joseph, and his sister, Leonora. They settled in Newark, New Jersey, where a lot of Jews landed after leaving Ellis Island. They joined a Conservative synagogue, instead of continuing in the Orthodox tradition they had followed in Russia. They continued to celebrate Jewish holidays and Shabbat, a ritual on Friday night that leads to a day of rest on Saturday. Isaac worshiped Rose. He went into real estate with his brother, and at first found some success, enough so that Rose could go to school and learn English. She graduated high school and went on to write poetry, some of which was published in leading periodicals of the day.

The Great Depression did not leave them unaffected, and Isaac and Rose lost almost everything, which contributed to my grandfather's intent to pursue financial independence. He made it his life's mission to become a successful businessman. Joe studied Dale Carnegie's books and dedicated himself to becoming a good salesman. He shortened the family name to Ash to facilitate his business dealings and perhaps minimize the Jewish association.

Pop-Pop, the name I used for him, started Active Amusements, which sold pool tables and pinball machines for home use. In addition, the company owned several arcades in the Philadelphia area. Once video games came on the scene, he attained exclusive distribution of Atari for Pennsylvania, New Jersey, and Delaware. Around this time, he also made a connection with a Holocaust survivor, and they went into business on a property in Ocean City, Maryland. This relationship continues to this day, and the arcade still occupies prime real estate on the boardwalk.

My mother's father died when he was 54 and she was just 15. She stopped participating in sports and became determined to have a family of her own. Prior to this, she had been active, playing tennis and basketball at school and spending summers outside at her grandmother's farm in rural Pennsylvania. During my childhood, she never spoke of Ben's death, or of his life. It was like he never existed. Before she passed though, she did tell me one story about his funeral.

"Norma and I were sitting in the mortuary with Nana as the mourners came in to view the body when Aunt Clara, Dad's sister, came in and threw herself on the casket, crying, 'Don't leave me, don't leave me!'"

She didn't go into details about how her own mother reacted, but knowing my Nana, I'm sure there wasn't much emotion displayed. My grandmother was a very controlled person; I have no memory of her ever laughing, let alone crying in public.

I could only think about how that must have affected 15-year-old Joan—her dad's sister completely losing it over her brother's death while her own mother sat there stoically.

Before Norma passed, I asked if she and my mom ever spoke about their dad's death, or anything else that may have contributed to Mom's lifelong sadness, and her response was adamant.

"No!" She told me then, "Your mother never shared her feelings with me. When she told me her first marriage was ending, I asked why she'd never said anything to me about the problems she'd obviously been having. She answered by telling me, 'You're always on cloud nine so you wouldn't have understood.'"

Saying I was surprised by this revelation is an understatement. When I was growing up, Mom and Norma were best friends. It made no sense to me that my mother didn't share her feelings with her sister. But Mom was self-deprecating, constantly putting herself down about her weight, and when someone doesn't love themselves, they have trouble confiding in others.

Mom yearned for a family life based more on a fairy tale than any reality she'd ever known. She went to junior college for a year, her only goal at that point to be a wife and have children. When Bud Isenberg proposed, she dropped out and married him.

However, Bud wasn't the family man she thought she'd married. When they divorced, he moved to California, where he sold insurance to Hollywood stars. He didn't make an effort to stay in touch with his children as they grew up and didn't contribute much financially as far as I know. This left the door open for someone like my father, Larry Ash, to walk into my mother's life.

For Mom, Larry represented stability. As an elementary school teacher, he was someone who loved kids. In the beginning of their relationship, he seemed to relish helping raise Linda, Jody, and Jeff. He tried to be a positive influence in their lives, spending time with them, taking them to play tennis, and helping with homework.

Many years later, after this second marriage had failed, I persuaded my mother to come to therapy with me. I was in my 20s and trying to understand why she married Dad in the first place—by then, she had only serious animosity toward him.

"Well," she said, "I married him because I knew he'd be a good father figure for Linda, Jody, and especially Jeff." She sat beside me on the loveseat, the afternoon sun spilling in through the ivy-cloaked windows and I finally understood: She had subsumed her own needs for the needs of her kids, even after her first marriage failed for similar reasons.

In the beginning, though, it appeared that my parents had the ingredients needed to make a marriage work. And I think my mother really tried to make it so.

My parents met through mutual friends, and from the start, they were enamored with each other. They both loved art and travel and they frequently vacationed in Europe and the Caribbean islands. When they returned, they'd walk through our front door into the entryway that seemed so massive to me, with its high ceilings. As my mom opened her black-and-red-plaid travel bags, that space became a cathedral of gifts, making me curious to see the world for myself as parts of that great unknown seemed to tumble out of the suitcase.

The perplexing part for me was that despite appearances, Mom's unhappiness hung over our house like a gray fog. If we moved through that atmosphere either too fast or too loudly, she'd lose her temper and yell. We'd be cowed into putting on our best behavior.

The most visceral memory I have of this is when friends would sleep over. We'd be wrapped in our sleeping bags on the floor of the living room directly below her bedroom, giggling as girls do, when from the top of the stairs we'd hear a booming, "Shut up!" that reverberated throughout the house. These shouts always caused me to cringe from embarrassment. I knew something was wrong because when I slept over at friends' houses, their parents never yelled like that.

I understood from an early age that there was trouble in the marriage. My parents' relationship was like a big empty room they never seemed to occupy at the same time. When I was 8 and fighting with my younger sister, Wendi, my dad lost his temper. "Why can't you two get along?" he yelled. I shouted back, "Why can't you and Mom?"

Yet, I don't remember them fighting. In fact, there wasn't much interaction between my parents once those initial honeymoon years ended. Dad came home from work in the late afternoon and went to his study until we'd eat dinner as a family in the breakfast room, as we called it. I don't remember much about what happened after dinner, except for Dad helping Jeff with his homework. Mom would retire to her bedroom to watch television and go to sleep. Dad still slept in the same room, but I don't recall them going to bed together.

The breakfast room was next to the kitchen and was the central point of activity in the house. It was cluttered with school books, my mom's lists, shopping bags from the grocery store, and a phone hanging by the bulletin board, while our school artwork decorated the rest of the wall space. In many ways, this scene of normal family life was all a masquerade for what my mother wanted. Really, we were disconnected like puppets on different strings all going their own ways.

The age difference between the two sets of kids might have contributed to the feeling of division that defined the family. Eleven years separates Linda, the oldest, from Wendi, the youngest, and there were five years between Jeff and me.

It was not for lack of trying on my mother's part, at least not initially. However, some of her tactics may not have been ideal, particularly when it came to blending the family, painted in stark relief one day when I was 8.

I recall wearing a white, pinafore dress with black velvet around the collar and waist. The air smelled of lilac, and the sky shone robin's-egg-blue. I felt special, skipping school. But I was also nervous; I couldn't remember ever getting to miss school when I hadn't been sick, but this was to be a very special day for the whole family.

We kids assembled in the house's entranceway, Mom and Dad buzzed about. She anxiously tried to hustle us out the door, but I could sense he was worried—his eyes twitched as they only did when he was on edge. Like me, my siblings were also dressed up—plaid skirts and white blouses for the girls, and a tie for my brother.

I didn't understand all the fuss. Linda stood off to the side looking bored. Jody followed Linda's lead, rolling her eyes when my mother told her to get in the car. Jeff was smiling and practically jumped out the front door. He was always like that, easy-going and easy to please.

At the courthouse, we walked into a majestic room with rows of wooden benches and people in uniforms standing by the door. A large man in a black robe sat behind a big desk at the front of the room and spoke in a booming voice, as if through a megaphone. I didn't understand most of what he said, until the end when he told Linda, Jody, and Jeff to come closer.

He talked to them in a serious voice, and then, one by one he told them that they each had a new title. As if putting a crown on their heads he said, "your last name is now Ash."

I remember thinking to myself, *Hey, that's my name.* An odd sense of pride and ownership rushed over me.

To celebrate, we went to a Chinese restaurant for lunch where we sat around a circular table and ordered egg rolls and wonton soup. I drank tea out of the small white porcelain cup wondering why everyone was so quiet.

When I look back, I can see the dynamic playing out. The day we went to the courthouse my parents had been married for over eight years. But in another two, they'd tell me they're separating.

But that year, my mother had decided to give my father the kids to adopt for his birthday.

When he married my mother in the late 1950s, divorcees were not looked upon kindly. Divorced women with young children fell even lower on the list of desirable mates. But my dad loved my mom, and he took the job of parenting my older siblings full-on. However, when they split, he essentially gave up on the children as well.

To this day I don't know exactly what they fought about or couldn't resolve, partly because they never fought in front of us. And also, no one ever talked about it. They tried therapy, but it didn't help them get to the root of their problems.

I can only assume the vicious cycle of my mother's depression played a role and the fact that my father felt helpless in every way. He couldn't make her happy, and I'm certain he wasn't all that content either.

But he got to go to a job every day that he loved. He had a purpose. My mother, on the other hand, was searching for fulfillment, and kids and marriage didn't provide it.

CHAPTER 3
Mom

Mom started an affair with Pat, the mailman, when I was 9 or 10.

Almost every afternoon when I came home from junior high, Pat would be sitting in the breakfast room drinking a cup of coffee in his blue uniform. He was like an uncle who was always there—I never questioned why.

Their relationship ceased to be intimate years before she died, but I recall being with Mom at her Florida home when my own children were small. Pat would call frequently. After she finished talking to him, usually casual gossip about the folks on his mail route, she'd hand me the cordless phone as if it were the most natural thing in the world and I'd have a conversation with him.

The truth is he was the great love of my mother's life. But the fact he would never leave his wife, a woman she and Pat referred to as "Mother" like she was the evil matriarch from the movie "Psycho," led my mom to be angry and spiteful on top of her already moody blues.

If Pat had left his wife and married my mom, I wonder whether that would have resolved her cycle of depression. But I doubt it because I think it was the idea of romantic love that Mom was in love with, not the hard work of being in a lasting relationship.

The one place Mom was happy was at her estate sales. It began when a friend of hers was moving and needed help getting rid of her belongings. My mom offered to help by placing an ad in the local paper, and the rest is history. Eventually, everyone in the area knew that if Joan Ash was having a sale, it was worth going. While these estate/garage-style sales are now common, 55 years ago, Mom was a pioneer. She was good at it and the business was thriving.

At 10, I started working for her on weekends, collecting money from the shoppers. She'd smile, laugh, and chat with all of them. If they were repeat buyers, she would remember their names. Mom was everywhere at once, moving around the house like a butterfly—full of zest and light as a feather—a different person compared to when she was home, either in bed asleep or watching television.

I remember my parents being liberal and open-minded when I was young, but Mom became more and more negative and critical of the world around her as she got older. It was devastating to watch.

As she became more depressed, she slept more, and I rarely saw her in the mornings before I left for school. She used pharmaceuticals to deal with her emotions; while I knew she took Valium, I had no idea how much the drug affected her emotional state, and I don't know what other drugs she might have taken to cope with her lingering sadness. I also know that at that time doctors were prescribing Valium to women like it was a cure-all. The Rolling Stones even wrote a song about it called "Mother's Little Helper."

When I was in high school, I didn't think twice about the fact she was never awake when I got up for school. I was getting up to run before class, tiptoeing by her bedroom at 5 a.m. on my way downstairs just to get out the door. The house was eerily quiet at that time of day and I always felt like I was doing something clandestine. I followed a set route that snaked through my suburban neighborhood, past the houses with their white picket fences and perfectly manicured lawns. When I'd get back from my two-mile run, I'd again tiptoe by her closed door, grab the lunch I'd made the night before, and head out the door.

Mom also struggled with her weight and was always dieting. I'd go with her to the local Weight Watchers and watch her weigh in. We'd arrive at the strip mall in Abington, a suburb about 20 minutes from our home, and meet in a small room where they weighed the clients. The dirty, off-white walls and the claustrophobically low ceilings magnified the dreaded scale in the middle of the room.

Each adult waited their turn to be called to the scale, to then endure having their number broadcast across the room. Standing nearby as my mother climbed on the scale, I'd think, "I am never going to do that."

While she was always dieting, she stocked our house with every snack food you could name.

Every kid in the neighborhood knew that the Ash house was the place to come for the best treats. She'd buy bags of Snickers and Milky Ways and put them in the freezer because everyone knew they were best like that. She did the same with the chocolate donuts from Entenmann's. She continued doing this my entire life—whenever or wherever I visited her, I would find those donuts in her freezer.

"I have them there for the kids," she'd say, meaning either me and my friends when I was young or her grandkids later. The problem was she couldn't resist eating them, especially the chocolate donuts.

I wanted to be as different from her as possible. This desire grew as I got older. The last thing my mom was ever going to do was run, so I ran miles and miles. She slept all the time, and when she was awake, she was sullen and moody. So, I just avoided her. I ran instead, doing it to make myself feel good, awake, and healthy.

Many of my early running experiences transpired at Alverthorpe Park, close to our house. Mom took us there when we were young to feed the ducks in the pond, so it evoked fond memories even though I was going there to escape my current home life. There was a running trail marked with mile signposts—1.8 miles for the entire loop. The first time I made it around without stopping felt like I had conquered Mount Kilimanjaro.

Running also allowed me to avoid Mom's issues with food; quickly, I discovered I could eat whatever I wanted, no Weight Watchers required. On top of that, I knew she didn't like my running, which was more reason to do it.

"Vicki, do you really need to run again?" she'd ask, then state the obvious by saying, "You ran yesterday." As if running one day meant you didn't need to do it ever again.

I was also becoming interested in nutrition and wanted to eat healthy food that would help my running. My weekend morning meal consisted of yogurt, wheat germ, and molasses because I had read that these foods were full of nutrients that runners needed. This was when my understanding of food as fuel first took hold.

Like any teenager, I did sleep in on Saturday mornings and would eat this after my run so sometimes Mom was up and about by that time. She'd take one look at my bowl and say, "That looks disgusting."

But instinctively, I was starting to identify that if I ate healthy food, I felt better. So, while I indulged occasionally in the treats she had in our kitchen, I knew how to stop before I made myself sick on junk food. My mom, on the other hand, never really learned this lesson and was perpetually eating to illness.

When my mother became an adult and started having babies, she basically stopped moving her body. She wore her sedentary lifestyle like a badge of honor.

"See, Vicki?" she seemed to say. "I'm not going to do anything that anyone says is good for me. Instead, I'm going to eat donuts and watch TV."

This may sound like an exaggeration, but truly, this was her life. There were times when she joined a gym, walked with neighbors, and even tried a water aerobics class, but she hated the obligation of exercise. She never stuck with any effort long enough to feel or see the benefits.

All the energy she did have went toward shopping. She loved flea markets and dragged us kids along when we were younger. When she visited me as an adult, the only thing that would motivate her out the door was going shopping or eating at a restaurant. She could spend hours in a mall while I would be exhausted after visiting one store. She gave me a hard time about this on shopping expeditions, saying that if I "didn't spend so much time running" I wouldn't be so tired.

Part of her love for shopping was the thrill of a deal, even if it wasn't something she needed. It also didn't matter if it was a valuable antique she found at a thrift store or a plastic bowl at the dollar store. A deal was a deal. The sad part was how fleeting her euphoria was.

Mom lived until her mid-80s, but her later years were filled with pain from bad joints and chronic inflammation. On my family's last visit to see her in Florida, she was limping so badly that we'd have to drop her off close to our destination. On one excursion to the beach, Mom was struggling as she got out of the car. I asked her if she was alright or needed a doctor.

"I'm fine," she replied. "My foot just aches a bit. It isn't a big deal." A few days after we left, she finally went in to have it looked at and it turned out it was broken. It had probably been that way for months, but she had no idea how it happened. Her lack of awareness around her body was painfully obvious.

Six months before she died, I visited Mom and convinced her to go to the pool at her apartment complex. This was daunting for her since it was a quarter-mile away, and at this stage in her life too far for her to walk. She used a walker to get around, something she hated because it made her feel old. The idea of getting out of bed, going down the elevator, and getting into the car to go to the pool was almost too much for her. She said 'no' many times before she finally said 'yes.'

It took a while to help her get her suit on and take off her jewelry, which as usual, included bracelets and necklaces and many rings. Mom wouldn't go anywhere without her bling, but she took off most of it to go to the pool.

At long last, I had her in the car, but when we pulled up in front of the pool and I started to help her out, she said, "Vicki, I don't think I can do this. Let's go back."

"Mom," I replied, "I'm as stubborn as you, and I know you can do this. It's not much farther. Just take one step at a time."

She sighed and said, "OK."

With each step, she had to take a deep breath. The wheezing in her lungs sounded like she was close to drowning on the liquid that had collected in her chest. Deep down I knew she'd feel better once she was in the water, so I ignored my doubts and tried to stay positive. We took about 50 steps, and then she rested on a nearby bench before we could make the final push to the door.

Though the pool was inside, it was surrounded by glass windows, so it felt like we were outside. Slowly, slowly, we made our way into the water. Originally, I thought she might last 15 minutes, but she relaxed as I held her and gently swayed her back and forth. Time lost any meaning as the sun glistened off the surface and we allowed the warm water to soothe us. A half-hour later she was still moving and didn't want to leave.

"Vicki," she said, "this feels like heaven."

The next time I went to visit, Mom was back in the hospital again and after that she never fully recovered.

The last few years of my mother's life, until her passing in 2016, we spoke almost every day on the phone; we talked about our television shows, my girls, and mostly just the simple things of life. It wasn't always smooth, but we were able to be open about how we felt, allowing us to work on accepting each other for who we were. The one thing I chose not to share with her was Jade's struggle with drugs. Knowing she was so close to the end of her life, I didn't think it would serve any purpose to tell her.

She was never one for any fanfare and had requested no funeral and to be cremated. Once again, the incongruencies of her life became apparent. In Jewish tradition, cremation is historically associated with pagan practices and therefore rejected, but Mom didn't care about that and wanted as little fuss as possible.

My siblings—Linda, Jody, Jeff, and Wendi—and I decided to meet at her apartment a few days after she died to go through her things and reminisce. We spent an entire day looking at old photos, laughing, and eating cold cuts we had ordered from the local deli, which is what she would have wanted to eat had she been with us. There was lox, kippered salmon, bagels, and cream cheese, everything we'd eat on Sunday mornings after Hebrew school during the years my dad lived with us.

In looking through her clothes and jewelry in her bedroom, Jody, Linda, and I came upon a box of papers and old letters. As we started examining them more closely, I found all the newspaper listings of my race results she'd collected and saved. I had sent some of these to her, never believing she'd read them, let alone keep them. I knew then that she had been my cheerleader all along, even if she couldn't show it for fear of encouraging something she didn't quite understand.

Some of what she saved were full articles, but mixed in were some small, two-by-two-inch scraps of race results with my place and time listed. I was shocked and touched that she had thought these were worthy of saving. It further reinforced that all the time I thought I was running away from her, I was really returning.

CHAPTER 4
Sporting Life

Mom told stories of all the sports she played as a child, and she came to every sporting event I participated in. But during my youth, she practically lived her life in bed drugged on Valium. I saw her in the stands for basketball in junior high and tennis in high school, but as an adult, she refused to move her own body.

After watching me play basketball once, she told me that when she was in school, girls were not allowed to dribble. "They could only pass," she said, which sounded awful to me.

"That seems so unfair," I said, and her response was simple: "That's how it was back then," her lips a thin line of dismay. "You're lucky, and you need to take advantage of playing as many sports as you can."

When Norma started beating Mom at sports back when they were young, my mother got discouraged and quit. She was a good athlete, but because her younger sister could beat her, she gave up before she even gave herself a chance to succeed. Women weren't encouraged to be athletes, so it was easy for my mom to stop being active and focus on starting a family. On the other hand, Aunt Norma defied the norm and went on to be an avid golfer and tennis player and taught lessons in both for many years.

My mom shrank back into herself and essentially ceased moving, cutting off access to one of the body's own great ways to combat stress, depression, and all the other issues she was coping with.

The difference in the way these two sisters handled their experiences might be at least in part attributable to genetics. It's now known that there's an actual tendency toward happiness in our DNA. The latest research tells us that the inheritability rate for many characteristics hovers around 50 percent. A good portion of personality and the way we react to events are beyond our control. However, this isn't to say we can't make choices that lend themselves to happiness.

Choosing to move is one option that's been shown to positively affect mood. My aunt was a great example of this up until her death in early 2019. She was physically active her whole life and forever upbeat and cheerful. Even when bad things happened, she seemed to move on with little fanfare.

Her husband, my uncle Ted, whom we called Mole, died from heart failure in 2008 when my aunt was in her 70s. Norma and Mole always seemed so in love. They laughed with and at each other. I loved being around them as a kid because they were both so happy and energetic. He would look at her with these adoring puppy-dog eyes.

On our family trips to Mexico, when Mom and Norma would haggle with the beach vendors, Mole would smile with his crinkly eyes and gaze at Norma lovingly, even as she spent money on the junky tourist fare.

After he died, Norma was left on her own, no easy task, but especially when two of her children died—one of cancer and the other of liver disease. Yet, she continued to live a full and vibrant life, playing tennis and golf almost to the end. Whereas her sister, my mother, chose a path of stagnation and negativity that would have suggested their lives were the opposite. Mom was able to have her own children and ostensibly the life she dreamed of while Norma couldn't bear children and then lost two of the ones she adopted. Norma's drive for perpetual motion made a lasting impression on me.

CHAPTER 5
Finding My Footing

My addiction to running first became apparent on a sheep farm in the cold January of 1981 when I was 20 years old. The only source of heat in the Western Pennsylvania farmhouse I was living in was a wood-burning stove. At night, I would put on my pajamas, wrap myself in a blanket and sit in front of the stove for five minutes before running upstairs to the tiny bedroom in the attic, where I'd climb under the bedcovers to fall asleep without freezing.

I was a college sophomore at Mount Holyoke, and this sheep farm was my internship for the month. The college set up internships so students could try out different experiences for credit, and I chose this remote ranch because I had always wanted to live on a farm based on a romantic notion of what I thought it would be like. Once I realized what a difficult life it was, the attraction faded rapidly.

My days there started at first light. There were two other student interns, and we were tasked with the following responsibilities: get the fire going, make breakfast, and see to the sheep. When I arrived, I told June, the farm's weathered and cranky owner, that I ran and wanted to continue to do so while there. "Fine," she said, "so long as you get all your chores done." But I know she assumed that once I realized how hard all the physical work was, in addition to how cold the weather was, I wouldn't be able to find the time or energy to follow through with this.

She was wrong.

Each day before dawn, I'd do my morning chores, which included stoking the fire and putting out feed for the sheep. Then, I'd bundle up in long underwear and sweatpants (no technical clothing back then), and head out to run during the small window of free time before the next batch of work needed to be tackled. I was struggling with a knee injury, but it didn't stop me from this morning ritual. I only know this because I kept daily journals of my running and have records dating back to 1976. During the month I was at June's farm, I ran every day. There was no race I was training for, no start line to get to. I was not trying to run a certain pace or even a certain number of miles. The only goal was to get out the door to move my body in that rhythmic way running mile after mile lends itself to.

I ran on roads where I saw almost no one, through a landscape with nothing but hayfields by the roadside, layers of frost on the grass that looked like crystal, and when I'd finish, heading back to the farm, the sun would only just be starting to rise. The whole landscape would glisten before the grayness of the day would settle in. I'd wear a ski mask against the cold as the temperature hovered around 5 degrees Fahrenheit. That, and the fact that few people ran back then, especially women, led to some strange looks from the rare drivers who saw me out there in the pre-dawn hours of the rural countryside.

Running did something for me that nothing else could. We were working all day, chopping wood, gathering hay, cleaning up after meals, feeding the sheep; June had been right, it was hard work, but I still needed a steady run every day. If I ran, I could settle; if I didn't, I felt anxious. I don't remember much about the other two interns, but I do recall they had no desire to do more than the workload June assigned. I am certain they thought I was insane for going out to run before it was even light out, but they never said anything about it to me. In fact, it was as if I was doing something no one wanted to acknowledge, and I certainly didn't want to talk about it. All I knew was that something inside of me pushed me out the door every morning despite the frigid temps.

I've battled anxiety my whole life; it's the legacy I carry of my ancestors. The conflicting messages I got at home also contributed. My parents seemed to barely talk to each other, and this left a young Vicki confused. On the one hand, my mom could be very loving and on the other, distant, hidden inside her bedroom where she avoided the world via a self-induced, Valium-assisted coma.

Some of my happiest memories from my childhood stem from the times I frequently woke up with a bellyache in the middle of the night and went into my parents' room to gently tug at my mom, who'd roll out of bed without complaint and walk me downstairs to the kitchen.

"Sit here," she'd say, placing me on one of the breakfast room chairs. "I'll make you buttermilk."

It was her own concoction of whole milk, butter, and sugar that she'd simmer on the stovetop. It was the best-tasting thing ever, and sometimes I'd even pretend not to feel well just to get her to make it for me. The best part of the whole ritual, though, was having her to myself in those middle-of-the-night hours.

However, there were other times, when Mom seemed so far away that I feared upsetting her—I never really knew which Mom was going to show up.

Getting sent away to camp when I was 10 brought my increasing anxiety to a crescendo. Both my older sisters had gone to Camp Danbee, and it was an accepted fact that going to overnight camp was a rite of passage for East Coast Jewish girls from families of means. My Pop-Pop, my father's father, paid for it, and I was supposed to be grateful. I was, but my parents also never actually asked if I wanted to go. They didn't even inquire as to whether I was nervous about being so far from home for eight weeks, and because we didn't have this conversation, I wasn't given a chance to mentally prepare or be taught some coping skills.

Besides summer trips to the Jersey Shore and Maine with my family, I had not spent much time away from home. But I was put on a plane, by myself, and sent off to Massachusetts for eight weeks. I still wonder why my parents and so many others thought it was a good idea to send their kids away for that long. I found out at some point that my father was sent to camp when he was 5. Maybe it had something to do with teaching children to find their own way, and ultimately camp did help serve that purpose for me. But at such a young age most kids just want to be around their parents.

That first summer I was the youngest camper to be picked to play in an intercamp tennis tournament, and I was proud of that. But there was a nagging feeling I could not escape: Why had my parents sent me away? Did I do something wrong? I started having severe stomach aches, the kind that doubled me over in pain, and as a result, I ended up in the camp infirmary every week. They couldn't find anything wrong with me, so finally the camp director decided to take me to the hospital for further tests. I remember having to drink barium, which tasted like cement, before they took x-rays.

The diagnosis: a nervous stomach. Essentially, they were saying nothing was wrong with me and attributed it to homesickness. I went back to camp and continued to have stomach aches, but in between bouts, I managed to have fun playing tennis and being with my bunkmates.

I'd only been home from camp for a couple of days that first summer when my parents sat Wendi and me down in their bedroom. My father was standing in the corner and my mother was sitting on the bed while we sat on the floor. They didn't seem upset and in a very matter-of-fact way, they told us they were separating. My mom spoke first. Then my dad explained that while he wouldn't be living with us, he would always be available.

For me, all the pieces of a puzzle fell into place. My stomach aches were real. They'd been telling me something was wrong, but at 10 years of age, I couldn't put words to it. I wasn't surprised my parents were splitting up; if anything, it made sense as they didn't seem to even like each other. After they told us, I said, "OK, can I go outside now?"

About three weeks later, my stomach aches were a distant memory. I was in school, being noisy and interruptive, bothering other kids who were involved in art and science projects. It was the late 1960s, so an open classroom was commonplace, as was such independent work.

Because I was a straight-A student who usually took school seriously, one of my four teachers, Mr. Kirchner, was suspect of my behavior. I can still picture his kind face, how it was devoid of facial hair, and his short brown hair that made him look like an older Paul McCartney. He was six feet tall and always wore a jacket and tie, and when he spoke you listened even though his voice was quiet, and he never yelled. He took me out in the hallway at the top of the stairwell.

"What's wrong?" he asked, a question as simple as it was straightforward. I burst into tears. My parents had informed all my teachers of the situation, so he didn't need to voice the question, but by asking, he allowed me to feel the pain and begin to let it go. I never cried about it again. But I made a promise to myself I would never get a divorce. I'd wait until I met the right man and I told myself I'd know. I'm not quite sure how I came up with this at that age, but I knew in my heart that I was going to make different choices than my parents, especially my mom.

At 14, I ran to escape the sadness of my household and deal with puberty and the subsequent insecurities caused by raging hormones. There was also a sense of being able to disappear. No one saw me running in those early mornings, and I wasn't on the track or cross-country team. It was something I could keep for myself. It also allowed me to keep my feelings hidden from the world even though at the time I couldn't have articulated that.

Early teenage years are tough for everyone, but I was dealing with a mother who was depressed and a father who wasn't living with us. It was most noticeable in the mornings when Mom tended to sleep in. This wasn't unusual, but without Dad around, his absence was further magnified by her absence. In junior high, I would get ready for school, grab a brown sugar cinnamon Pop-Tart and eat it on the walk to school.

In those early years of my running, my mother worried about me. I was always small in stature and running accentuated my musculature. In my mother's eyes, I looked too thin. At just five feet tall and less than 100 pounds, I was tiny, but I ate. In fact, one of my favorite foods was carrot cake and I could eat half a loaf in one sitting. Mom always made sure to have some on hand as she knew I liked it. I wonder now, given her weight issues, if she wasn't jealous that I could eat half a cake and not gain weight. She wasn't obese by any means, but she was still watching her weight, and I'm pretty sure taking diet pills to control her appetite.

One evening, she sat me down to talk in her bedroom. "I made a doctor's appointment for you," she said as she looked me in the eye. "We're going tomorrow."

"For what?" I asked. "I feel fine."

"You don't look healthy," she replied. "I don't think running is good for you."

I went because I thought I had no choice. Getting in the car, I was annoyed and barely spoke to her as she drove us to this doctor that I didn't even know. She and I sat apart from each other in the waiting room until I was called, and then she accompanied me to his office. He didn't even examine me. As we sat in chairs next to each other in front of his desk, he simply asked me why I ran.

"It makes me feel good," I responded. "It helps me with all my other sports."

He turned to my mother as if I weren't there and said, "This is a phase and she'll grow out of it."

I could tell this was not the response she was hoping for as she narrowed her eyes at him, pursed her lips, and squeezed my hand to let me know it was time to leave.

After that, she'd do her best to belittle my running. "Running makes no sense," she'd say out of nowhere. "You're going to get hurt."

I was already angry about the appointment, and her snide comments made me want to run even more. Running made me feel better than anything else in my life, so when she disparaged it, I wrote it off as her just trying to control me. I never stopped to consider she might have been right about some of the health consequences of being that thin. For example, at 17, I became amenorrheic and stopped having a period for almost four years. I'm so fortunate that my fertility wasn't affected, but I'll never know if there were other health effects that occurred from that time in my life.

This is the conundrum: For the runner's family, the activity can be a source of tension and resentment, and even worry; for the runner herself, it is an essential part of being.

That winter at June's farm, on those lonely roads with long days of manual labor ahead of me, I articulated all of this to myself for the first time. June's disbelief that I would follow through reminded me of Mom's inability to support my running during my teen years. Now in college, establishing my identity, I felt compelled to defy June and Mom's doubts. If only to prove to myself that I could do it, despite the odds.

To me, running is healing. I have spent my life defining and redefining all the things running means to me. I also now see that people will find something that soothes them to escape uncomfortable feelings. My mother used food, drugs, and even sex to make herself feel better. I used running. But both of us were running away from unsettling feelings and our true selves.

CHAPTER 6
The Anger Within

I have always been competitive. From my youngest days, I hated to lose. At first, it was in neighborhood games. We had a tetherball court in our backyard, and I prided myself on never being beaten. I was ruthless; at a mere 6 years old, I'd go to any length to win. If a bigger kid challenged me, I'd steal myself to attack the ball as it came around the pole and hit it so hard, I'd almost fall over. The other kid would be ducking because it was going so fast, and before you knew it, I had wrapped the rope around the pole. Having secured my winning streak, I would walk away with a little skip in my step.

In fifth grade, all my friends stopped talking to me. The event leading up to this happened on the school playground during the month of October when the leaves were starting to fall and the air had a crisp feeling of the cold temps to come, but the sun was still warm on our bare arms. I lived for recess, so when the bell rang, I ran outside excited.

"Let's pick teams for kickball," I yelled, but it was like I was surrounded by a brick wall and no one could hear me. The other girls walked by me like they couldn't even see me. I was dumbfounded, but I wanted to play so I joined the boys' game instead. At that point, I was more motivated to play the game than to find out why my friends were acting that way.

In retrospect, I can return to that fateful day and recognize that this was one more attempt for me to ignore my feelings. In my mind, it didn't have anything to do with something I might have done. I played hard, attempting to show everyone that I could keep up with the boys. When recess was over, I felt satisfied from running hard around the bases but was still stung from the earlier rebuff.

Later, Helen, the only girl who didn't completely reject me, told me Sarah had instructed all the girls in our class not to talk to me. I was confused and asked Helen to explain. "Sarah says you're mean and no one should play with you," she told me.

My inability to lose, even in playground games, made me come across as an angry person. This anger, one of the poisons identified in Buddhist philosophy I'd come to study years later, was something I couldn't control. Where did it come from? It seemed to bubble up inside of me, and then I'd lash out.

Maybe it stemmed from my parents' struggling marriage and my not understanding the tension at home. But it's also clear to me that I was born with a predisposition to be competitive which can lead to anger if not managed. In biological terms, competition results from limited resources with two or more parties fighting for them and all getting harmed. In our culture, competition is generally seen as something positive because it seems to end in success for the person who wins. We reward the winner. It's always been interesting to me that when a person comes in second, they're deemed a loser.

But wanting to win and needing to win are two different things, and it took me a long time to figure that out. The day after Helen told me what happened, I approached Sarah in the classroom. I went right up to her and asked if we could talk. She looked at me with her blue eyes, long brown hair flowing to her waist, and with a shrug of her shoulders agreed. We went out in the hallway.

"Why are you so mad at me?" I asked.

"You try to control everything," she responded.

"I'll try to stop," I said. "Can we be friends again?"

As she waved her hand in dismissal, she said, "OK."

In the long run, she remained aloof, and we never really resumed our friendship.

I'm thankful to this day for Sarah's actions. Yes, it hurt at the time, but it made me start to examine who I was. Even at 11 years old, I was able to do some self-reflection and realize anger was going to chase people away. I learned how to control my temper and not show it. But that didn't mean I was never angry again. It simply meant hiding some of those feelings.

Starting when I was 11 and into my teens and 20s, I mostly learned to hide my true feelings from others. Running helped because it was where I could go and just be myself. It also reduced my feelings of anger—the very act of running made me happy. At the time I didn't know that my body was producing chemicals during exercise that act as natural painkillers and antidepressants. All I knew was running made me feel good.

When I was young, we were members of the local swim club, Lynnewood Gardens. Mom sat around the pool with the other mothers, while Dad played handball with the fathers. She was in a bathing suit, but always with a cover-up which was often a white, short-sleeved lace gown that opened in the front and went down to her mid-thighs. Some of my earliest memories are of the times I would wander up the hill to the handball courts at the far end of the pool, where I volunteered to fetch the balls for the men while they played.

Conflicting messages around exercise and religion dominated my childhood. Dad was active and always doing some sport–handball, tennis, squash, then jogging. Mom encouraged me to be active but did nothing herself. We belonged to Rodeph Shalom, the Reform synagogue that was right across the street from our house, behind a tall row of hedges. My friends and I made little passageways from my side of the street that led to the vastness on the other side where there was a huge grassy field and we played flag football and games like home free and hide-and-seek.

I remember going to preschool and then kindergarten at Abington Friends, a private Quaker school, before switching to the neighborhood school, Shoemaker, in third grade. The preschool was in a small white building, with a playground outside, and one of the most vivid memories I have is a picture of a man with white hair and a white beard on the wall above the doorway. You'd see it on your way in and out every day. "Who is that?" I asked one of my teachers. "God," she responded. This made no sense to me. How could God look just like a person? The picture looked like someone's grandfather. Wasn't God supposed to be more than a human?

Around the same time, Dad made me start going to Jewish Sunday school along with my older siblings. Jeff was going to have a bar mitzvah which typically occurs at age 13, while Linda and Jody had to go until confirmation, which in the Reform tradition happens at 16. I hated going and I'd try to get out of it every single week. All I wanted to do was play outside. Having to walk across the street to the long, one-story white brick building where my siblings would drop me off at my classroom felt like going to prison.

When I was 5, I demanded my father prove that God existed before I would go back. In response, he set up a fruitless discussion where he had my grandfather talk to me. Pop-Pop sat me on his lap and said something to the effect that God is what we believe in because we're Jewish. When that failed to convince me, Dad arranged an equally pointless meeting with our rabbi.

I remember holding Dad's hand on a fall day, leaves lining the sidewalk as we walked up the hill to the entrance of the synagogue. I knew I was heading toward my freedom. As soon as I spoke to the rabbi, I'd be done with this place. I went into the rabbi's office while Dad waited outside. The rabbi circled the office as I sat on his couch against the wall across from a huge mahogany desk covered with books and papers. I felt like Lily Tomlin playing Edith Ann on Laugh-In, sitting on the big chair where her legs didn't go over the edge. He started talking to me about philosophy and asked if I knew who Plato was. Thinking he had said, "Playdough" I nodded my head yes, only to become utterly confused by our ensuing 30-minute dialogue, more a monologue than an actual discussion.

When I walked out of the office in a daze, Dad asked, "So, now do you understand?"

"No," I responded, "and I still don't want to go to Sunday school."

"Well," he said, "you still have to go."

From that point on, I would find a way to run away from Judaism, either by pretending to go to Jewish class held on Monday evenings when I was in junior high but sneaking out instead with friends or just tuning out anything the teacher rambled on about. I never made the return to Judaism, or any other organized form of worship, because it never made sense to me to look for God in a certain place or time. Going inside one day a week to worship didn't satisfy me and was terribly stifling to my childhood self who yearned to run free in the great outdoors. I realized early on that any form of prayer had to hold meaning for me and make me feel good, so running and nature became my religion.

When my parents split up, one of the first changes Mom made was to put up a Christmas tree, which my father had always forbidden. At 10 years old, I couldn't help but brag to my mostly Jewish friends that we celebrated Hanukkah and Christmas, how I got presents for both. But now I know that it furthered my alienation from any form of organized religion as any possible meaning was watered down by this blatant contradiction.

When confirmation day finally came, I went through the motions of the ceremony only because I knew once it was over, I'd be done. It was held at the downtown Philadelphia location of Rodeph Shalom, a much more formal, imposing building than the two-story, modern one across the street from our house. I had to wear a dress, which was the first aspect of the day I hated. Then I had to get up on a stage with my fellow classmates and profess a belief in the Jewish traditions I held no affinity for. We stood on the stage as a group and when the rabbi asked us questions, we answered as a group, and I just mouthed the words.

The only confirmation I received was that I was done with Judaism and would never force my own children, that is if I had any, to go to synagogue.

As I was growing up, the emphasis on physical movement came from many places, but there was still a lot of misunderstanding around girls and women being active. I came of age as an athlete just as Title IX—the landmark anti-discrimination bill—was being signed into law. Title IX made it illegal for educational institutions to discriminate based on sex and ensured that these institutions offered equal opportunities for both boys and girls. But there were still few female role models for young athletes. As a kid, my tennis idol was Arthur Ashe—the first Black player to win the U.S. Open and Wimbledon. The deeper I got into running, the more I admired Bill Rodgers, the Olympic marathoner who won Boston three years in a row. Later, I'd learn about Joan Benoit, who earned gold in the women's Olympic marathon in 1984, but that didn't happen until I was in my 20s.

Early on, it was all about male role models in sports. And my dad partially fit that bill. When I was almost 13, Dad came to the house one day wearing running clothes.

"An American, Frank Shorter, won the gold medal in the marathon," he told me as we got in his car to go to a local park. I didn't know what a marathon was, but Dad was excited and joined the jogging craze that erupted after the 1972 Olympics.

The first run we did together was on the Schuylkill River in Philadelphia, near the steps of the Philadelphia Art Museum later made famous by Rocky. We'd run by the boathouses that held the crewing boats for all the clubs and universities in the area. The area was well-known for crew races, and as we'd run, the rowers would stream by, passing under the many bridges that connected the east and west sides of the city. This became one of my favorite places to run and I would return multiple times, even after moving away from Philly.

At the same time, my dad's emphasis was always on what career I would choose. From a young age, he repeatedly told me, "Vicki, you can be anything you want to be in life." He downplayed the importance of relationships and almost ignored my boyfriends when he met them. I think he didn't want me to rely on a man.

This was one idea my parents shared as exemplified by my mom's insistence I learn to pleasure myself without the assistance of the opposite sex. When I was 12, my mother called me into her bedroom one late afternoon and asked me if I knew what masturbation was. "No woman should ever rely on a man to satisfy her," she said, and then added, "Now go up to your room and practice."

After they separated, my parents vowed to remain amicable; they got along so well and co-parented so easily, sometimes I asked myself why they ever split up. My mom even invited my dad to dinner so Wendi and I could stay home on school nights. Linda and Jody were out of the house by this point, and Jeff was in high school, so he often wasn't around.

One Friday afternoon when I was 12, Dad came to pick Wendi and me up to spend the weekend at his apartment. He only had a one-bedroom, so Wendi and I would sleep in his bed when we were there, and he would sleep on the couch in the living room. On Saturday morning, he told us we were going to meet a friend of his and her daughter. We took a short drive to another building complex, but here the units were townhouses, and there was way more space than in dad's tiny, one-floor apartment.

A woman with wild, brown, curly hair that framed her smiling face opened the door. Maggie wasn't very tall, but she was a big presence in the room, energy emanating from her. She had olive skin and looked like she'd just spent a month on the beach. Her daughter, Laurie, hid behind her. Nine years old, with long blond hair hanging down her back, Laurie had lean limbs and pale skin.

"Girls," Maggie said, "it's so nice to finally meet you. Laurie, do you want to show them your room before we eat brunch?" I went to Laurie's room and spent the next few hours trying to be nice, but deep down I told myself it wasn't that important because I'd probably never see these two people again.

I did see them again. Maggie became my dad's second wife, although they waited until Laurie, Wendi, and I were out of high school to tie the knot. By then I had accepted Maggie and Laurie, but in my teen years, I was not so gracious. I could be downright mean to Maggie, as she revealed to me one day in my 20s when I was talking to her on the phone.

"Do you remember the time we went to Longwood Gardens, and we were walking and you placed yourself between me and your father?" she asked. Longwood Gardens, with its rows and rows of plants and vegetation, was one of Dad's favorite places to take us.

"No," I responded. "Did I really do that?"

"Oh, yes," she continued. "You weren't very happy about me back then."

I didn't remember doing that, but I did recall the feeling of not wanting her around. How dare she come in and take so much of my dad's heart and energy? That was supposed to be for me. This was when I thought he could do no wrong.

In all fairness, Maggie was an amazing woman. She made every effort possible to include Linda, Jody, and Jeff in family get-togethers and events. But it didn't even have to be a special occasion for Maggie to include all my siblings. Sometimes it was just having lunch and walking their Doberman, Fifi, around the neighborhood. Vivacious, loving, and caring, Maggie was also highly vulnerable and needy. When she was diagnosed with breast cancer at age 50, she took it hard.

I flew in from Boulder to visit family for a long weekend. I was in grad school at the time. I always stayed with Mom when I went back, so I only got to spend one afternoon with Dad and Maggie. I hadn't realized how bad it had gotten until Dad greeted me at the door, utterly defeated. We hugged and he held onto me for much longer than normal. Then he ushered me into the bedroom where Maggie was lying in a bed that took up almost all the space in the room beside a dresser covered with books and magazines. Her head was wrapped in a vivid red and gold scarf, and I noticed that she had lost weight since I'd last seen her.

"Oh, Vicki," she said in a hoarse voice. "I'm so happy to see you." Then she started crying.

"Maggie," I said as I went to sit by her side, "I love you and I'm sorry." I had no idea what else to say. I sat awkwardly on the edge of the bed as she continued to cry.

"I don't want to die," she almost wailed.

I felt utterly incapable of comforting her and after hugging her, I left the room seeking my father.

As much as I resented Maggie when I was 12, I loved her deeply by my 20s. A couple of years before she died, we developed a ritual of talking on the phone every Thursday evening, a date we both kept until she became too sick. Maggie embraced everything about life, including Dad and what he brought with him, which meant all his children.

I recently corresponded with her daughter, who now goes by Laura. We reminisced a bit, and I told her how much it meant to me that her mom made the effort to include all my siblings and always treated us as one family. She responded, "Thanks for saying my mom was amazing. I feel the same about your dad."

Then Laura continued, "I also have some nice memories about your mom. She gave me a pewter Doberman that I love, and it still sits in my living room."

My dad had embraced Laura as his own, and he continued their relationship until he died. While I admired this, it magnified how he'd abandoned my older siblings—the children he'd legally adopted.

Throughout my adult life, Dad was there in the background, but he receded from view because he was a chameleon and would basically morph into whatever his current wife wanted. He had a total of three marriages in his life. I talked to him on the phone regularly though, and his voice was always full of love and energy when he heard from me.

"Vicki," he'd say with such joy. "I need to share this with you." Then he'd read whatever article he had found in *The New York Times* that day that had resonated with him. I'd picture his crinkling eyes and his fervent enthusiasm as his voice resounded through the phone. It was our own special ritual and he did this almost every time we spoke.

When Dad died in 2014, it was sudden. He went into the hospital on Wednesday, November 5, complaining of stomach pain, and died two days later. The official diagnosis: a bleeding ulcer. He was on medication that most likely caused complications, and there was nothing the doctors could do.

I knew he wasn't doing well on Thursday, but Jane, his third wife, kept insisting he was OK. When I found out on Friday morning that he was gone, it was a shock.

When I spoke to my brother, Jeff, who lives in Connecticut, he said he was flying out to Arizona for the funeral.

"Why?" I asked. Jeff hadn't spoken to my dad in years and owed him nothing as far as I was concerned.

"He raised me," Jeff replied, "I want to be there."

That Saturday we all met at the mortuary for a viewing, which is not common practice in traditional Judaism, and Uncle Frank, my father's younger brother, turned to me and in a whisper said, "This is weird." But seeing Jeff, with his crooked grin and quiet good looks, like a young Robert DeNiro, was comforting.

That evening, Uncle Frank took us all out to dinner. Eight years younger than my father, Frank couldn't have been more opposite from him. Besides being six feet tall, as opposed to my dad's five-foot-eight inches, he was also funny and very outgoing. He entertained us that evening and kept us laughing.

Back at the hotel, I attempted to write a eulogy. I read what I wrote to Brian, Jade, and Jessi. I had tried to write something that felt honest. What came to me was Dad's unerring belief that I would be successful and have a profession, his undying feminism that pushed me to achieve. It was a message I wanted the girls to hear. Jade, at 16, could be surprisingly sensitive and said, "Mom, that's great, you'll be awesome when you read it."

Jessi, on the other hand, while sad about Poppi, was most concerned with the funeral and what she had to wear. "Mom," she said, "do I really have to wear a dress?"

"Jes," I responded, "on this one day, I'd really appreciate it, and I know it would make Poppi happy."

"But he's not even here," she countered.

Jessi hadn't worn girls' clothes since she was 5, and I knew how uncomfortable they made her. But somehow, I got caught up in how it would look if she didn't wear a dress, and I let that take over. I can't believe I did this, given how much I hated wearing dresses when I was her age. At that moment, I didn't even recall my own confirmation ceremony when I squirmed in my dress, willing the ceremony to be over so I could take it off.

As we walked through the desert air of Scottsdale, Arizona, to the site of Dad's burial, the mood was somber. When it was my turn to speak, I talked about my Dad's belief in me, and it dawned on me that perhaps that push was more about him than me. But in that moment, standing before people who knew him, I only spoke of my gratitude for his support and love. Tears came as I stood there, but they held as much regret as they did loss.

One of Dad's stepsons from his third marriage also said a few words. I wasn't really listening when he began, but then my ears perked up when I heard him say, "Whenever I spoke on the phone with Larry, he'd recite from the latest *New York Times* article he thought I'd be interested in."

I felt my whole body tighten and then actually shake with emotion. I had always thought this was something he only did with me, so to find out he was sharing this with at least one other person, not even one of his own children, made me realize how much I didn't know about him.

Once the service was over, we walked the short distance to the gravesite. The pallbearers carried the casket over to the burial plot and lowered it into the ground. Then those who wanted to used a small shovel to throw dirt over the casket, symbolizing the return to the earth. This isn't unique to Judaism, as it's also common in Christian burials, but it felt staged, following all the protocols so that everything looked good.

I was transported back to the rabbi's chambers when I was 5. "Prove to me there is a God," I'd asked then and was still asking years later. Back then it was my father who'd insisted I attend synagogue, and now I was watching the façade of his beliefs unfold before my eyes. Jeff and I took our turns tossing dirt into the grave and then slowly made our way back to the car.

"Are you upset the rabbi didn't mention you?" I asked.

"I didn't come to be acknowledged," Jeff answered. "I came because I wanted to be here."

We all went back to Dad's house for the shiva, the mourning that can go on for up to seven days in a Jewish household. As we entered the house, Jessi turned to me, and asked if she could get changed.

"Yes," I said, with a realization that she was just being Jessi, and that was fine.

As a teenager, running allowed me to separate and distinguish myself from my mom. At the same time, it helped me connect with my dad, something that can be hard for many girls.

I wonder now whether my mom's abhorrence of my running was one more reminder of my father.

Part of growing up is seeing your parents as human beings, not as the myths you make of them when you're young. I no longer see my mom as wicked; nor do I see my dad as a prince. Because of them both, I am who I am—a runner and a strong independent woman.

But it wasn't until they both left this earth that I could start to make sense of the mixed messages I got about family and religion. Growing up, the only thing I knew for sure was that I felt good when I moved.

CHAPTER 7
Burnout to Athlete

When we were in the seventh grade, all my friends started smoking pot. We had a core group of five boys and five girls and were the dominant group in our junior high. I remember the powerful feeling that came from this social superiority. Together almost constantly, we roamed the streets of our neighborhood on foot.

After school, when we didn't have to be at a practice or a game, we'd all go to the local drugstore at the base of the hill. We'd buy a snack—I almost always bought Tastykake shortbread cookies—then head over to the nearby train tracks and smoke pot for the rest of the afternoon. My peers were all that mattered to me at 13, and being accepted by them was seductive.

Mom had no idea I was using pot through junior high. I was getting good grades and was one of the top players on all the teams I played on. She assumed everything was fine. One winter we took our annual family trip to Acapulco, hosted by Nana. Our whole family, along with Norma's, went on these trips, so sometimes we had over 20 people in our clan.

One night, Linda, who was 24 at the time, asked Mom if she could get me high. Linda knew I was already smoking pot, but she wanted to ask to see what she'd say. Her response: "Only if I can watch."

So, Linda, Jody, Jeff, me, and my mom gathered in Linda's room and my mom sat on a chair off to the side while we all shared a joint. All I remember afterward is riding up and down the elevator with Jody, laughing our heads off the rest of the night. Mom thought that was my first time trying it, and she assumed it would be a one-time event.

Then, that spring, I got a D in my ninth-grade history class and Mom was beside herself. "Larry," I heard her say to my father on the phone, "you need to talk to her. This is unacceptable." He came over that evening and they sat me down in Mom's bedroom, which is kind of weird thinking back on it, but it was the place for all family meetings.

"Vicki," Mom started, "you've been miserable around the house, and now you have a D in a class you got an A in last term. What's happening?"

Dad leaned against the wall listening while Mom ranted. I guess she wanted him there to back her up, but he barely said anything.

I was getting high all the time by then, so I just lied and said the teacher was giving surprise tests and I was caught off-guard. "I'll try harder," I told them. The truth was, I hated this teacher and it was my first-period class, so I was either stoned or exhausted from staying up late the night before. I did manage to bring my grade up to a C, but at that time, I didn't really care about my grades.

All I cared about were my friends and Danny, my boyfriend. We went out and broke up about nine times during those three years. When we were together, everything seemed right in the world, but when we weren't, I'd cry myself to sleep. Once asleep, I'd have dreams about the ideal man. He always looked like the Marlboro man, dark hair, a mustache, and wearing a cowboy hat. He'd fall off his horse, and I was there to pick him back up.

The image of me on my knees holding his head up is still so strong in my mind's eye. How stunned he'd look while he lay on the ground like that. This dream started right around the time my parents separated, so I'm sure there was something in my subconscious that saw my father as the victim.

The summer before high school, I went to camp and was thrilled to see my best friend Karen, whom we all called Zucky. We had been best friends for several years. Zucky was beautiful with long, dirty-blond hair and a body that made grown men do a double-take when she passed by. Flat as a pancake, I couldn't help but feel a twinge of jealousy regarding her abundance in the chest department, but she always made me feel confident, telling me how cute I was.

"I wish I was as small as you!" she'd say. She also made me feel like she only wanted to be with me, which is one reason I loved being around her. Together, it felt like we could conquer the world. She and I had made plans to each bring a stash of pot, excited to be in the oldest bunk and therefore rule over the younger campers.

Despite that first summer when I was 10 and I got sick, I came to love camp. I loved living in bunks with my friends and doing sports all day. I loved sleeping in on Sundays and eating two glazed donuts for breakfast. The owners joked that we were not competitive, yet everything we did was competitive, from color wars to games versus other camps. I loved playing in tennis matches and racing sailboats.

The oldest bunk was known as WBY for "well beyond," and it was separate from the rest of the camp, across the road and secluded. Zucky and I were confident we could get away with a lot more than if we were still over in the main section where the bunks for ages 4 to 12 were, or even in the area across the road where the junior girls slept. The owners expected the oldest girls to set examples for the younger campers, so our plan to share our stash with the other girls in WBY was in complete defiance of this trust.

There were 16 of us in the A-frame log cabin that served as our home away from home. It was luxurious as far as bunks go. Our cots were in one large room on the top floor that we reached from a wide ladder in the middle of the lower level. There was a rustic feel because it was all wood, but we had running water, showers, and even a small kitchen.

Our counselors trusted us, and we were often left unsupervised. The area was wooded, so when we got back to the bunk, Zucky and I would lead some of the girls to the surrounding forest where we'd smoke a joint. Almost every girl in WBY joined us at least once.

There were some holdouts, though, and someone must have snitched because after a few weeks of this, Dan, the owner, got wind of what was going on. It was in the middle of the afternoon, so when we got called to the office, we all knew something was wrong.

In the six years I'd been a camper, I might have been in Dan's office just one other time. The air was humid outside, but inside his office at the back of the small white building that stood at the camp entrance, a small window air conditioner cooled the room. We huddled on the floor in front of his desk sitting shoulder to shoulder, all 16 of us shaking as Dan looked down at us with glowering eyes, his easy-going laugh gone. There wasn't even a glimmer of his usual wide grin. He didn't raise his voice, which was almost worse than if he had yelled.

"I'm going to ask you girls to tell me who was smoking marijuana, and

I want the truth," he said. "I'll let you talk amongst yourselves first, then I'm going to meet with each of you individually."

Dan left us in his office. At first most of the girls were crying, and all of us talked at once.

"What are we going to do?" Stacy asked, while Tina whined, "My parents will kill me if I get sent home."

I decided to take charge. I stood up and said, "OK, you guys. If everyone admits to it, there's no way he'll send us all home. Let's confess and take whatever punishment he doles out."

"Yeah," Zucky added. "Our best bet is to stick together!"

We all agreed and soon we took our turn with Dan alone. One-by-one, each girl was called in while the rest of us waited outside. I tried to keep everyone calm by telling them it was going to be fine. But as each one of us came out, there was palpable tension in the air, and everyone looked nervous. I chalked it up to people being scared, confident it would all work out.

I was the last to be called in. I sat on the couch next to Dan's desk and looked around at the walls where a montage of maps and pictures of different campers from past years were displayed.

Danbee's legacy hung heavy as I told Dan I had smoked a couple of times and apologized. He was an imposing man, and as he leaned against his desk, arms crossed over his chest, I felt a twinge of regret that I had betrayed him.

At the same time, I was still certain the punishment would be minimal because I'd come up with the perfect plan. He didn't say much in response, and I saw no change in his face from the grim look he had when I first came in.

He dismissed me from his office, and I went to stand with the other girls awaiting his judgment. Almost immediately Dan called only Zucky and me back in.

"Girls," he said, as we stood in front of him, holding hands. "You were the only two to confess. I'm sorry, but you'll be going home tomorrow."

She and I looked at each other like we'd both been kicked in the stomach. When we went back out, the other girls could barely look at us, and Zucky and I were so shocked we had nothing to say to them.

When they tried to apologize, Zucky and I walked away, our arms interlocked, consoling each other. I had never been as let down by friends as I was then.

The next day, my father picked me up at the airport and drove me back to the house where my mother was waiting. As I gazed out the window trying to avoid talking on the drive home, he said to me in a solemn voice, "Vicki, everyone makes mistakes. The key is learning from them."

Once home, we congregated in my mom's bedroom, as usual, to discuss my transgressions. Mom conveyed how disappointed she was with her eyes only. She was a master of this look, a simple combination of downcast eyes and a frown that always made me feel guilty of a cardinal sin. Nevertheless, they told me they were proud of my honesty and I knew they really meant it.

I thought to myself, *Wow, I'm lucky they aren't punishing me.* But I was still immature. That first week back, I managed to go out with friends and get massively drunk on whiskey someone had stolen from their parents. We mixed it with lemonade thinking we were making whiskey sours, but it tasted like shit until it didn't. Then it went down like water.

We wandered the streets drinking out of clear plastic cups. It was a warm August night, and I was wearing shorts and a skimpy halter top. There were at least 10 kids when we started the evening, but more joined as the night went on. We were strung out across the road, arms interlocked as we sang, "You're My Best Friend" by Queen and "Tonight's the Night" by Rod Stewart.

By my midnight curfew, I was so drunk I didn't know where I was, even though I was less than a mile from home. A neighbor must have called the police because suddenly, a dizzying array of red and blue flashing lights interrupted our joyous march. Some of my friends went running, but I was way too out of it. I was more concerned that the spaghetti straps of my halter top were falling off and exposing my chest. I got caught.

The cops escorted me home, though I don't recall getting in a police car. I don't remember any of the conversation they had with my mother when she answered the door. I have a vague memory of her putting me to bed, then of waking up later in my own vomit.

The next morning, I heard her on the phone arguing with Nana about what to do with me. I could only hear Mom's side of the conversation: "No, I don't think it's a minor mistake, and I think she needs to be punished."

Then there was a pause where I could imagine Nana trying to calm my mother down and then Mom continuing, "I don't agree. She needs consequences."

I was grounded for the three weeks left of summer before school started.

"Vicki," Mom said, "I don't trust you anymore. You're going to have to alter your behavior for that to change." Then she went to her bedroom and closed the door.

I was devastated. All I really wanted was her approval, which meant her trust. She had always emphasized honesty, so that very day I decided to forgo any substances. Mom's disappointment in me was worse than not being accepted by my friends.

For the rest of the summer, I'd get up and go for a run, then ride my bike to the local pool, swim laps, come home, and repeat the next day. When I started 10th grade a few weeks later, I separated myself completely from my junior high friends and focused on tennis and school.

From that point until my early 20s, I didn't drink or use any substance of any kind.

But that didn't mean I couldn't find that high elsewhere.

During my junior year in high school, while I was playing lacrosse, I first started getting that runner's high people often talk about. After running around for an hour during the game, a sense of elation would overtake me. It helped block out any negative feelings lingering from school, friends, or my mom. It didn't take long before I wanted more so I started to sneak in miles after practice.

Ms. Lonsinger, the coach, saw me one time and said, "What, you didn't run enough? I can fix that." She added more running to practice the next day, which didn't bother me in the least. But my teammates whined, and I think she decided it wasn't worth hearing the complaints from the other girls. My teammates thought I was crazy, but mostly they just worried that Coach would make us all run more in practice because of me.

Although I was captain of the team my senior year and got along with the other girls, I never bonded with my teammates. In my mind, anything that didn't contribute to my progress as an athlete or a student was a distraction. I can only think of one girl ever inviting me to do anything. When I said I couldn't, she never asked again.

At the time, I was focused on my own individual athleticism and didn't see how hanging with my teammates might help improve my performance and contribute to the team. I used running to establish my independence. At first, I sought separation from my family. But because I needed to figure out my own identity, I also used it to distance myself from almost everyone around me. I was the lone wolf.

Despite my general competitiveness, running in those high school years was my one athletic endeavor that wasn't about winning or losing; it was about doing something that simply made me feel good. I was protective of my running, so I never shared with friends that I was getting up before school to run. They probably would have thought I was nuts, but it was a secret I coveted.

For me, running is spiritual. From my youngest days of being forced to go inside to worship a God I didn't believe in, religion never made sense to me. But being outside, with the sky as my cathedral and the ground as my shrine and moving my body, I always felt like I was closer to a higher power. It made me feel more alive. In juxtaposition to my mom, who seemed barely awake most of the time, this was my revelation. If I moved, I was going to live.

In my 20s, when I started doing longer runs, I knew I'd found my religion. My early resistance to organized worship was the beginning of my journey to find peace and meaning on running trails, in watching sunrises and sunsets, in pushing myself in competition because whether it resulted in triumph or disappointment, it always ended in growth.

The year after I graduated college, I had a job teaching reading at Kent boarding school in rural Connecticut. I found a local running group there that consisted mostly of men who did a long run every Sunday. We'd meet at a small resort tucked away in the woods that had an indoor pool with a sauna and tanning machine that I'd use after the runs (it was the '80s, after all).

One Sunday in early fall still sticks in my mind. A few of us waited in front of the lodge for the run to start, chatting a bit, but mostly focusing on our own pre-run rituals. We did lots of calf-stretching and toe-touching—the kind of movements I now know aren't that helpful.

We left the parking lot as the sun began peeking through the branches of the maple trees. Leaves covered the ground like an offering of red and gold. It was cold that morning, in the low 40s, and a slight coating of dew clung to everything like frosting.

Most of the guys were in their 30s and 40s. They seemed ancient to me as they lamented about their latest injuries and bragged about how much mileage they did that week. But as we made our way through the forested trails, I was barely aware of time. It felt effortless.

When we circled back to the lodge, one of the guys said, "Well, we got our 20 in," and I stopped in my tracks. I couldn't believe I had run 20 miles. I was utterly complete and whole, connected to the world around me, but also independent, knowing that under my own power I had covered those miles.

I stood there feeling the hot blood running through my veins, the sacred drum of my heartbeat knocking against my breastbone. The sun was now high in the sky and as I gazed upward, I realized I had found my God.

I never saw marriage as a life goal after watching my mother's experiences as a wife and two-time divorcee. Rather than focus on getting married young, I went to Mount Holyoke College, an all-women's school. This male-free environment gave me the confidence and concentration to pursue a career over romance.

In fall 1979, my father drove me to South Hadley, the small western Massachusetts town, about a five-hour drive from Elkins Park, to the school that would change the trajectory of my life.

I was as idealistic as a young woman coming from a privileged background could be. I thought I could take on the world. I was concerned about injustice and inequality, but my naïveté around these issues was soon exposed.

I was one of the first students to arrive on campus, and when my dad left after dropping me off, I felt alone for the first time. With tears in my eyes, I went back to my room, put on running shorts, tied my shoes, and proceeded to run around the entire campus.

As I ran around Upper then Lower Lake, I marveled at the tapestry the trees provided over the dirt trail surrounding the lakes. The path was still clear of leaves, and I relished the expansiveness before me. With almost no one on campus yet, I felt like I owned the place.

When I called my mom that evening, I told her how amazing the campus was and that I couldn't wait for her to come to see it. We only spoke briefly. She wished me well, but she seemed less than interested. It was clear: This was my journey, not hers.

One evening during that first winter in South Hadley, while I was trying to decide what to do for summer break, I went to the house phone in my dorm to call my mom. The phone hung on the wall at the end of the hallway, so there was no privacy. Girls wandered by on their way to the communal bathroom as I spoke with her.

"Mom," I asked, "what do you think I should do this summer?"

She barely took a breath before responding, "Vicki, I have no idea, it's completely up to you."

My mouth hung open. All my life she had been telling me what I could and couldn't do. I thought for sure she'd give me a concrete answer. A world of freedom opened, but my tether to the earth was also severed. For a short while I had the sense I was floating off into space.

I ended up spending the summer in Boston with DeeDee, a sophomore who lived in my dorm and had become a good friend. We thought it'd be fun to live in Boston because of all of the colleges in the area and the social life we imagined we'd find if we weren't at an all-women's college.

We lived in a total dump of an MIT frat house that cost $25 a week. The three-story ramshackle building on the edge of Cambridge boasted a shared kitchen in the basement. DeeDee and I were the only women living there. Leftover pizza and beer cans covered the counters almost every morning, and the cockroaches had a field day.

We spent the first week wandering around Boston looking for work. We saw a sign outside one of the government buildings downtown advertising a job transcribing and preserving colonial documents. We were both interested, but somehow, I was the one who jumped on it.

Every weekday morning, I'd wake up at 5 and go for a run by the Charles River just across the street from our apartment. Those early mornings, running the path along the river, watching the rowers glide by, became a ritual that revived me no matter how late I'd stayed up the night before. Occasionally, I'd see other runners, but often I was out by myself. I never worried about safety, and as I look back on my running, one of the hallmarks has always been my lack of fear and willingness to run alone. I don't take this for granted now, especially knowing of many women who have been attacked while running in the years since that time.

Even though I could have taken a bus to work, I'd walk the 45 minutes to get there by 8 a.m. At lunchtime, I'd wander to Quincy Market and buy homemade falafel and a salad from one of my favorite vendors, then sit on a bench and people-watch. Families on summer vacation were common, as was the young professional crowd—men wearing ties and button-up shirts with rolled sleeves, and women in skirts and heels.

On the one hand, I was intrigued by this business set, but on the other, I wondered if I could manage the traditional 9-to-5 workday schedule for the rest of my life.

The following summer, I interned in Washington, D.C., and developed a similar pattern. My mornings started with a run, then I'd take the bus toward the Capitol. I would get off early to walk the last mile or two along the Mall to start my days at the Congresswomen's Caucus.

I arrived in D.C. an inexperienced college student thinking I would be able to influence policy. I quickly learned that almost everything in D.C. had to do with who you knew, not what you knew, and I gave up on my goal of becoming an elected official.

My love of academic discussion did not dissipate, though, and by my junior year, I had decided I wanted to get my Ph.D. and teach at the university level. Upon graduation, though, I wasn't quite ready to go to graduate school.

So, in April of 1984, I asked Wendi what she had planned for the summer and if she wanted to go to Hawaii with me. I was 23 and ready for an adventure.

Nana had spent a lot of time on the island of Oahu when we were younger, so there was something unknown and mysterious about it that called to me. Wendi was heading into her senior year at Tufts, and she didn't have other plans, so she agreed. I bought a one-way ticket.

Hawaii was appealing to me because it was about as far away from home and Mom as I could go and still be within the United States. In one way, I was running away again, but it also was a return because of Nana. Her connection there gave me a sense of returning to my roots.

My time in Hawaii was one of exploration. My first job was at a retail store called Thongs and Things, which mostly sold sandals and beachwear. I quickly worked my way up to manager. But it was boring, and the hours kept me from playing during the day so ultimately, I ended up waitressing at TGI Friday's. While I hated the actual job, I loved the hours because I had time to run and go to the beach. The pace at work was frenetic, and I had a hard time keeping up without "getting in the weeds."

I'll never forget Angie, one of the more capable waitresses. She had short black hair and porcelain skin. She never seemed frazzled, no matter how busy it got, whereas I was a wreck every time I had more than two tables to cover. She could handle 10 as if she were only serving one, low-maintenance customer. The upside of both the retail job and waitressing was I earned enough to pay for my expenses, yet the work itself made me even more committed to going to graduate school.

Restaurant life can be one of late nights and partying, and I will attest this became part of my Hawaii routine. Without school to worry about, my relatively sober life went by the wayside. I was drinking regularly, enjoying the mai tais and frozen concoctions the bartenders would make for us at the end of our shifts.

Everyone seemed to have cocaine and would offer it freely. The first few weeks, I occasionally indulged, but I never went out of my way to find it. And amidst all this, my first commitment was always to running. Cocaine was energizing while I was high, but it was a letdown when I came off it, so pretty soon, I stopped.

I only had a bicycle for transportation, a brown Schwinn 10-speed I had gotten for $50 from someone I'd met at a local gym where I went to lift weights. I knew that strength training was important and had been going to the weight room since high school, so it's not as if this was the first time, but I was still learning and always hungry for more.

I'm not sure what caught my eye about this gym, but the very first day I walked in, there happened to be a very large Black man walking in at the same time. When I say large, I mean, this guy was 7 feet tall. He started talking to me, and when he found out I was a runner, he offered to show me some exercises he thought would help.

It turns out this guy was none other than Wilt Chamberlain, the basketball star from the Philadelphia Warriors and later of the '76ers, who my mother had met years prior when he fell in her lap as she sat courtside at a game. Later that day, I called Mom. "You'll never guess who I met today."

Wendi left to go back to school and I found a roommate, another waitress from the restaurant. But I spent most of my time outside of work commuting on my bike, running every day, and swimming in the ocean. I decided I was ready to try some of the multi-sport events they had at Ala Moana beach in Waikiki. Every week, it seemed, there was a run/swim competition. I did a few of them and loved the combination of running then swimming, or vice versa. It was all very casual, I don't even recall how I did. But I do remember the feeling of finishing the three-mile run and then emerging from the ocean after the mile swim with wobbly legs and a smile on my face. I didn't even know there was something called triathlon that included biking with running and swimming, but when I found out I knew I had to give it a go.

It was May 1985, and the Tinman Triathlon was coming up. Many of the people I had met on the island were doing it. Triathlons involve different distances depending on the race. The first Ironman race took place February 18, 1978, on Oahu and covered 140 miles. It had spawned many shorter, multi-sport races like the run/swims I was doing in Waikiki. For locals, these races were now just part of island life. For me, I felt like I had found a new family of like-minded people.

Tinman was basically the baby version of Ironman with distances about one-quarter of the full race. I was dating a few guys at this time, no one exclusively, but one of them had already done some triathlons. Jim was very wealthy and had an expensive bike. When I told him I was planning on racing he said, "Well, don't expect much for your first race."

I know he thought he was going to be faster than me, and I thought so, too. But it turns out I beat him—even using my crappy commuter bike. When I finished, I was elated. I waited for Jim in the finish area and when he crossed the line, he bent over and looked down at the ground. "Nice job," I said as I went over to him expecting him to be happy for me.

"I had a bad day," was all he said and then he walked away from me. Shortly thereafter our relationship petered out. I didn't care too much, as I'd tapped into a drive to succeed in individual competitions and it fed me as much if not more than team sports ever had.

One of the relationships that continued for a while after I left Oahu was with a gentleman I met one night at work. He was at one of my tables with another guy. As I brought over their drinks, he looked up at me. Tanned and fit, with silver hair and a smile that twinkled, he asked me my name and where I was from. He seemed quite a bit older than me, but at the time, I found that intriguing.

Before they left, he asked if I wanted to go out sometime and handed me a piece of paper with his name and number on it. It simply said, Sandy, with a phone number. Little did I know it was Sandy Koufax, the famous baseball pitcher who played for the Dodgers from 1955-1966.

I really had no idea who he was, but Mom did. Sandy was famous, not only because he was one of the best pitchers of all time, but because during his career, he refused to play on the Jewish High Holy Days, and Jews loved him for that.

At the time, I had been applying to graduate schools to study political science, which made my father happy. I had received offers from several, but the best one came from the University of Colorado-Boulder. I decided to take it with the assumption I would get my Ph.D. and then move back to Oahu to teach at the University of Hawaii, Manoa campus, because I felt so at home on the island. Moving back to the mainland was only supposed to be temporary.

I went home for a few weeks before moving to Boulder. I stayed with Mom in a townhome she had moved into now that Wendi was graduating from college. A few days after arriving, standing in her new kitchen with its light-colored tile and sun streaming in the windows, I said, "Mom, is it OK if I have a guy come stay for a few days?"

"Yes," she replied, "of course."

"OK, well, just so you know," I casually responded, "it's Sandy Koufax." I think she almost fell over. Then she proceeded to call all her friends. The hot August day he arrived, she was buzzing around like a bee, like a teenager going on a first date. We sat out on her patio, and Sandy sat patiently while Mom's friends streamed through the door nonchalantly as if they just happened to be in the neighborhood. Sandy graciously gave them all autographs and tolerated their gushing. He and I went to New Hope, a tourist town not too far from Mom's house, for a couple of days as a getaway. When we went into a restaurant the first night, the waitress and other people at the bar stared at us, and I knew they recognized him. It was a thrill.

He left after the long weekend, and I went to Boulder to start school. We dated long-distance for a few more months, but the relationship died after I went to visit him and realized we had little in common. This had become even more apparent to me once I started grad school and was deep in the throes of academia and hanging out with people my own age.

When I moved to Boulder, I was entranced by the beauty and fitness-oriented lifestyle the town exuded. The first time I drove over the hill on Highway 36, a couple of miles southeast of town and saw the Flatirons—literally flat faces of sheer rock hugging the mountainside—it took my breath away. When I saw the campus with its signature orange rooftops and the beautiful brick buildings practically kissing that stone mountain, I knew I had found a new home.

My focus in my Ph.D. program was political philosophy, and there was something luxurious about having the time to discuss questions like "What constitutes the good life?" "What is the basis of a democracy?" and "What are human rights?" There was a sense among my cohorts that we were doing something that mattered. I relished the political discussions we had on our own and in our small graduate seminars led by professors I admired.

My friends and I often met at the graduate student offices in the early evening to study, and some nights around 10 p.m. we'd head out dancing at Tulagi's or The Fox on The Hill until 2 a.m. We'd shut down the bars, and, yes, I was drinking. But it didn't get in the way of school or running, so I didn't think it was a problem. Plus, there were plenty of times we'd be out and I wouldn't drink at all.

At 26, with hopes of writing a dissertation that would solve the Middle East crisis, I remained unreflective about my running. Even in Boulder, which in the mid-80s was already a mecca for great runners, I was still running for running's sake. I had no real ambition for something more. Even in the one marathon I'd run in 1984 in Hawaii, my only goal had been to finish.

When my mother came to visit me in Boulder, I'd wake up early to go run before she was ready to start the day, but it always seemed like I was just behind the eight-ball. One visit, I was out running with a friend. We'd been laughing because I told her what a hard time my mom had given me when she arrived a few days earlier when I didn't have orange juice in the fridge. According to Mom, I should have prepared better because I knew she liked juice in the morning. But did I really? It had been eight years since I lived with her.

My friend was nodding in agreement. We had slowed our pace a bit but when I looked at my watch and realized I was going to be late, I practically sprinted away. Not that we had a specific plan, but I knew my mother would want to go out to eat. If I wasn't back in time, she'd be mad.

"What's going on, Vicki?" my friend asked, pushing to catch up to me.

"My mom will kill me if I'm not back when she's ready to go get breakfast," I said.

This was the essence of my relationship with Mom at that time. I was always on edge when she was around, worried about disappointing her.

I'd been struggling with iliotibial band syndrome off and on for many years. The IT band is a thick ligament running along the outside of the thigh. When it's inflamed, it can cause knee pain. It finally got bad enough that I knew I needed help.

Boulder was still a small town, and I was taking a stretching class at CU that several professional runners also attended. This was where I first met Lorraine Moller, an elite distance runner, and Colleen Cannon, a professional triathlete. Both would become close friends. When I shared with them the details of my injury, they suggested I see a massage therapist and rolfer (a type of alternative, hands-on healing practice), who treated many of the professional runners and triathletes in town.

I'll never forget the first day I went to see Joe in his small garden-level apartment on Fourth Street where he lived and worked. I knocked on the door and was greeted by a tall man with salt and pepper hair, a chiseled face, and muscular arms. I was immediately transfixed.

The entire apartment was one room with a small kitchen in the back and a bedroom separated by a curtain from the living area. A massage table stood in the middle. I told him I was struggling with my right leg and how it'd always been problematic. He had me lie on my back on the table. When he first put his strong hands on my body, a bolt of electricity pulsed through my muscles.

"Your quadricep muscles are overpowering your hamstrings, creating an imbalance," he said. "Strength work will correct it." Remember, this was 1985, and few people in the running world were talking about strength and muscle imbalance. Joe was greatly influenced by the work of Ida Rolf, the creator of rolfing, and he understood how the body is a complex web of muscle, tendon, and bone, and how these parts are all connected by the fascial system.

As he worked on me, he asked questions about my running. He wanted to know my goals and seemed deeply interested in not only healing me but helping me to be a better runner. I felt nurtured and cared for in a way I had never experienced. After he'd worked on me for about 30 minutes, he said, "OK, let's see you run." We went outside and he watched as I ran on the street out front. Then we went back inside, and he had me lie on my belly while he continued the treatment.

"Have you ever thought of trying to qualify for the Olympic Trials in the marathon?" he asked as he guided me to flex my right foot.

I was shocked because for one, I didn't even know that was a thing and, two, the word Olympics and me in the same sentence seemed ridiculous. But he didn't seem to be joking when he told me he thought it was within my reach. I was on cloud nine when I left his apartment.

Joe had told me to try running the next day, which also made me more attracted to him as a healer. Often you go to a doctor or therapist with an injury and the advice you get is to stop running. That's the last thing a runner wants to hear. As I laced up my shoes, I couldn't get him out of my mind. When I started to run and felt no pain, I was even more in awe of Joe and his ability to heal. I felt cared for, and that was seductive.

Joe and I quickly started dating. That spring, I was signed up to run the Denver Marathon and Joe worked on me a lot before the race. Despite my initial belief that his hands were magic, my IT band was still acting up.

By mile 16, I'd been reduced to a hobble. Not wanting to disappoint Joe, I struggled to the finish in 3:50, faster than my first marathon, but still not a time I was proud of. Right after the race, my knee blew up to the size of a grapefruit and I couldn't run for a month.

Joe insisted I try deep water running. "Give it a month and you'll be stronger and healed by then," he said.

He was one of the first people to use water running as a recovery tool. He even had one of those weird bodysuits designed to aid floatation and resistance. The royal blue suit went to his knees, and I was embarrassed to be seen with him wearing it. But at that point, I was willing to give anything a try.

This was my first introduction to the warm water therapy pool at Boulder's Mapleton Rehabilitation Center. There, the pain of my knee injury literally washed away. The movement combined with the warm water made it feel like a miracle bath.

Rather than harsh chlorine, Mapleton used hydrogen peroxide to treat the water. I didn't feel like I'd just been bleached and my skin didn't itch or smell incessantly either. For a month following the race, I went every day. I was 26 years old, surrounded by a geriatric clientele, but I was ecstatic to be able to move without pain.

As I watched some of the patients in wheelchairs get pushed down the ramp into the pool, I was thankful to be young and strong knowing that my injury would heal. Right on cue, after one month I could run again.

By the end of my second semester of graduate school, Joe and I moved in together. We rented a house in North Boulder, a spacious ranch house sitting on a corner right across from Columbine Elementary School. He used one of the rooms as his office, and the home was conveniently situated on the course of the Bolder Boulder, a 10k race that today attracts 50,000 runners each year.

Joe's business was thriving, which meant we had a stream of professional athletes walking through the living room daily. I became transfixed by these runners, their lifestyle, and Joe's healing hands. There was the diminutive Rosa Mota from Portugal, eventual three-time winner of the Boston Marathon and five-time winner of the Bolder Boulder. She was a fierce competitor, and I loved how she could be so quiet and humble in person, but a total fireball in a race. I was in awe of her.

Joe and I started putting together a plan for my attempt to qualify for the 1988 Olympic Trials. I would need to run a sub 2:50 marathon— running just over 26 miles at a 6:29 per mile pace. Did it matter that I had only run two marathons prior, each over an hour slower than the qualifying time? No, according to Joe. "You can do it!" he said, and I believed him.

It helped that I had Olympian role models like Rosa, Lorraine Moller, Rob DeCastella, and Priscilla Welch. Lorraine was from New Zealand and had been running at an elite level since her teens. She ran in the first women's Olympic marathon in 1984. A few years after my qualifying attempt, in 1991, Lorraine and I traveled to Europe together. We started our trip with the Berlin Marathon where we both dropped out due to injury. The main goal, though, was to go to Barcelona, where the 1992 Olympics were to be held and see the Olympic stadium. Lorraine believed strongly in visualization, and she knew if she could run the last mile of the marathon course before race day, it would help during training. Sure enough, Lorraine won the bronze medal in 1992.

Rob was the recognized leader of the professional runners in Boulder. Hailing from Australia, he moved to Colorado with his family because he believed it was the perfect place to train due to the climate and altitude. High-altitude training is believed to help with oxygen uptake—when you train at altitude, but race at sea level there's a perceived advantage. The science is still uncertain whether this holds true for everyone, nevertheless, many runners like to train at altitude.

When I met Deek, as people called Rob, he was at the top of his game. He'd just won the Boston Marathon, so it would be reasonable to think he might have an ego. But he was one of the most generous, likable people I'd ever met. Every Sunday, runners would meet at his home in North Boulder near Wonderland Lake for the long run, which forms the central pillar of marathon training.

Deek always started out his runs super slowly so almost anyone could keep up. Of course, after a few miles, the pace picked up, and I'd be dropped like a hot potato. But I appreciated having a group to at least start with. It was a boost to know everyone was out there at the same time, suffering in their own way. After the run, everyone would meet back at Deek's house to have some refreshment, usually just fruit and whatever drinks anyone happened to bring. There was a feeling of camaraderie that I attribute to Deek's leadership.

Priscilla and Dave Welch, originally from Great Britain, were also instrumental in my development as a runner. Priscilla didn't start running until the age of 35. Prior to that, she had been a pack-a-day smoker, but under Dave's tutelage, she not only quit tobacco, she became one of the top female marathoners in the world, winning the New York Marathon at the age of 42. Dave eventually became my coach after several months of running many miles with Joe.

Based on Arthur Lydiard's model of training, which starts by developing a base through running long, slow miles, I worked up to 120 miles per week. It was all done at an easy pace, and I had a hard time believing it was going to result in me getting faster, but I listened. I did what Joe said. We'd run the dirt roads in North Boulder, weaving our way through spacious fields and the occasional farm that still existed inside town boundaries. A decade later these would be swallowed up by development, and today all these roads are paved. But, back then, we ran those once deserted rural roads only a few miles from our house.

I had one loop off Broadway where I always seemed to feel good, so we called it Magic. It was about five miles of flat, dirt road that meandered through neighborhoods. The route bordered on being rural, with many yards dotted with barns and even horses. There was almost no traffic, so it felt safe. I'd often go there for my second run of the day. I had mixed feelings about the days I had to run twice, because by mid-afternoon, I'd be tired from running early, going to class, and studying. The thought of another run was daunting. I'd start thinking about it as soon as I finished my morning run.

Walking through the door at 3 p.m. after a full day of school, my goal was to run as soon as possible so I could eat, because by this time I was starving. I was always worried about getting cramps from eating too close to a run. Later, when I started doing ultras (any distance longer than a marathon) this ceased to be an issue because I needed to be able to eat and run. But I wasn't used to that yet, and food in my stomach during a run was uncomfortable.

Still, Joe would say, "Let's go run Magic," and somehow, I knew I could get through it. The other trick he used was to finish the run by 5 p.m. and then take me to happy hour at various restaurants, like the Elephant Bar or The Walrus, at the time two of the more popular hangouts in downtown Boulder. I didn't mind a drink or two, but by this point, I didn't enjoy it much. But, Joe drank beer every night.

In January 1987, Joe and I decided to go to Phoenix for six weeks to escape the winter weather in Colorado and so I could get more miles in.

By running slowly for months, I trained my tendons, ligaments, and muscles to handle the strain running put on them. Training in warmer weather, and the luxury of being able to train nearly full-time, contributed to a healthy stretch that lasted way beyond our time in Arizona.

In Phoenix, I'd run twice a day. After the second run of the day, which we always finished before 5 p.m., we'd do our happy hour routine. Joe loved eating wings and drinking beer. I hated spicy, fried food but tolerated it because it's what Joe wanted. I made up for it by eating foods I liked at other meals.

Intuitively, I knew I needed fruits and vegetables, so I always made sure to compensate for Joe's cravings. Joe was a creature of habit, though, and he needed his happy hours. I came to see how the food was always secondary to the beer.

When we got back to Boulder in late February, I continued the high mileage for a bit, but even Joe realized I needed more stimulus to get faster, and this is when we asked Dave to come on board to help coach me. I don't think he even charged me, which I realize now was the epitome of generosity. He gave me similar workouts to the ones he had Priscilla doing, which meant hours on the track.

When I switched to this faster training, my times started dropping in huge amounts. One of the standard workouts Dave had me do was a 3K time trial on the track. This is the equivalent of 1.86 miles. I did my first one in mid-March in about 12 minutes. A month later my time had dropped to 10:30. It all happened gradually. Seeing my times drop, almost on a weekly basis with no added effort, was nothing short of miraculous.

I also found that by getting in the pool almost every day, my body recovered from workouts quickly. I'd emerge from the pool with a feeling of warmth coursing through my entire being that went straight to the center of my soul.

That's not to say it was easy. I'd spend up to three hours on the track doing workouts. It was physically hard, but I loved that part. Often, I was on the track with Lorraine, Rob, Priscilla, and the rest of the pros. Even though I was running much slower, it was energizing to be with them during a workout, and they never treated me like I didn't belong.

Tuesday was usually track day and we'd all show up around 8 a.m. at Potts Field, the official track for the University of Colorado. The warm-up was a two-mile loop around the perimeter of the area, and once everyone had completed that, there were drills to be done: skipping, high-stepping, quick feet, and side-stepping. Then we'd start doing our personal workouts for the day. Because I was the slowest, I stayed in an outside lane while the faster runners used lane one. There was a protocol to track running that I was learning, and it included a deference to speed.

With blue sky as a backdrop and the Flatirons visible as I turned the far corner of the track, it was impossible not to see how lucky we were. Times were different then, and there was an expectation that public institutions and their facilities were open to the community. This has obviously changed, and years later, the university closed the track to the public except for two very limited windows during the week. I remember the first time I showed up at the track to find it closed and wondered what Deek would have thought.

Track sessions aside, the truly difficult part was Joe. If I didn't achieve the times he expected me to run for interval sessions or races, he would stop talking to me. The first year we were together, I ran the Bolder Boulder 10K. I had run it the year before for the first time in 45 minutes, and then set a huge PR (personal record) running 41 minutes. But for Joe, this was far off what I should have run. Afterward, he said, "Vicki, that wasn't fast enough. You need to work harder. This afternoon, you need to do a track session."

I was tired and I knew I'd run as hard as I could during the race. At the time, I still believed Joe had the answers to how I could run a fast marathon, so I did what he told me. That afternoon we went to the neighborhood track at a middle school close to our home. He watched while I ran quarter-mile repeats.

The next day I mentioned this to Lorraine. "That's nuts," she said. "You didn't need to do that, Vicki."

I didn't understand training well enough at the time to know that after a race effort, the body needs to recover to get the most gain. There are times when running two hard sessions in the same day might be worthwhile, but I had just run my fastest 10K ever and another workout made little sense, physically or emotionally.

Later that year, Joe and I had another disagreement about running. I wanted to run an informal race called the Basic Boulder, a clandestine race held on the Boulder Mountain trail system. It was technically illegal because you're not allowed to congregate with more than 50 people on open space without a permit. Two of the guys in the local community, Neal and Kevin, had started this race because they were top mountain runners and wanted to have a race on the Boulder trails. Neal and Kevin were friends with some of the people Joe knew as well as Lorraine and some of the other pros. I had started to get friendly with some of them, including a couple, Paul and Mary, who were gifted athletes in their own right. They participated in events I didn't even know existed, including burro racing where you race with a donkey over long distances in the mountains. I was fascinated by this group and their athletic endeavors, but even more because they always seemed to be having fun.

Neal and Kevin had explained prior to the race that everyone needed to quickly separate once on the trails and to avoid any rangers out on the trails. Joe told me he thought it was a bad idea because he didn't want me getting injured. I decided to do it anyway.

It was like a big party and one of the most enjoyable running experiences I ever had. The best part was the actual party held after the race where we danced for hours. Joe wouldn't go with me. He rarely joined me for any social event that involved groups of people, so it was no surprise.

In the first two years of our relationship, I'd often forgo social engagements to stay home with him. This time, though, I went to the party without him and had my first taste of the trail running community that would later become a big part of my life.

Later that fall, Joe and I went to Winter Park to spend the weekend with Paul and Mary. There were several people staying at their cozy cabin in the center of town, including Lorraine. I was new to the group and fascinated by this eclectic collection of athletes. When we arrived late Friday afternoon, everyone was already enjoying their first beer and settling in to make dinner—chili, cornbread, and salad. I offered to help, but Joe disappeared. I wasn't sure where he went, and, caught up in the group conversation, I didn't take much notice.

Joe came back in time for dinner. We all sat around the small living room, scattered on chairs and the sofa, wherever we could find room. As everyone else got more and more talkative, and slightly drunk from all the wine, Joe got quieter.

After dinner, Lorraine suggested we play a game. We started with charades. We broke up into teams, but as this was happening, Joe slowly moved toward the back of the room as his discomfort became even more discernible. It was as if he literally shrank in front of my eyes. Before the game even started, Joe slipped out of the room. I felt bad for him, but I also didn't want to miss out on the fun.

Joe and I had picked the Twin Cities Marathon in Minneapolis-St. Paul for my qualifying attempt in the fall of 1987. It was a point-to-point course known for fast times. We had shared my dream of qualifying for the Olympic Trials with the local running community but very few people, besides Dave, Priscilla, and Lorraine, thought I could achieve this goal knowing that my marathon PR was 3:50. It was unheard of to take an hour off your time.

I was apprehensive of the expectation I had set for myself. But on the other hand, I knew so little about marathons and was too new to racing to be concerned. Besides, Joe seemed confident that I could do it and I relied on his belief to get me to the start line in one piece.

When we arrived in Minneapolis, Joe and I checked into our hotel and then wandered over to the expo that all big races have before race day. There were tons of vendors there. The Nike booth featured a computer program that predicted your marathon finish time. You told them your fastest 10k time and from that, they projected your finish time. My fastest 10k at this point was still my time from the Bolder Boulder so that's what I provided. When I got my print-out, I almost cried to see 3:08 in big bold print. That was 19 minutes off what I was hoping to do.

"Don't pay any attention to that," Joe scolded. "They have no idea how hard you've been training." I tried to put it out of my mind, but the seeds of doubt had been planted.

Joe suggested we take the bus tour of the race. We left downtown Minneapolis, passing by numerous lakes with names like Bde Maka Ska and Nokomis. The point-to-point course meant we had to drive to the start to only turn around and come back. My heart continued to sink as we got further and further away. I had never previewed a course before, so I thought it might help to know what to expect. But the drive plus the 3:08 prediction only made me more apprehensive.

By the time we got back to town, we had been on the bus for several hours. In my mind, the course took on the magnitude of the drive. What might have seemed doable if we'd just driven one-way became an impossibility by the time we got back to the hotel. My only thought was: *How would I ever run 6:29 mile pace for 26.2 miles?*

My alarm went off at 4 a.m. so we could catch the shuttle for the 8 a.m. start. It didn't help that it was below freezing, and I was shivering at the line. My body felt as rigid as a board.

The gun went off and at the three-mile mark, the clock read 21:00. Joe, who was also running and was slightly ahead, looked back over his shoulder and practically yelled, "What are you doing? You're running too slow! Pick it up!" I was startled by his words, but they must have done something to get me going, and I started running faster.

At halfway, the clock read 1:25 and I realized I might actually be able to get under 2:50. The rest of the race was one of those out-of-body experiences I've only felt a handful of times since. I was floating over the ground. I crossed the finish line at 2:49:24 and bent over out of shock and exhaustion. The announcer read my name as one of the qualifiers, and Joe hugged me.

I was ecstatic and called both my parents to tell them. I don't recall either of them shouting out in joy, but they did congratulate me. I think they were worried I had become obsessed with my training. They never said anything, but I'm certain they were concerned about Joe's influence over me and if they were too enthusiastic about my running successes, I would only go further in that direction, and neither wanted to encourage that.

I was hoping to just relish qualifying, but Joe insisted we do a shake-out run the next morning. This was common practice for many runners, so I went along with it. But I was tight and had doubts it was a good idea. But of course, I did the run because I still didn't trust my own intuition.

It was another cold morning, and my knee rebelled. After a forty-minute jog, my knee had locked up and I couldn't even walk. "It's fine," Joe said as he turned away from me as we returned to the hotel. "You'll get over it."

When we got back to Boulder, I once again returned to the warm water therapy pool for comfort. I found solace in the healing waters for the next month, going every day, to soak my body, but also to escape the noise coming from outside and within, the voice that said, *Well, sure you ran 2:49, but can you run any faster?*

CHAPTER 9
Falling Apart

At just 27, I had a hard time understanding Joe's struggles. He never identified himself as an alcoholic, but I believe that his drinking served to numb him to whatever demons stirred inside him. It also ended up forming a barrier between us.

Joe had a thriving business, and his clients loved him. I loved him. But my not understanding how much drinking meant to him, especially in social settings, and how that would affect our relationship, led to many painful moments for both of us.

Joe had a hard time being in groups, often seeming self-conscious. He was most comfortable in his massage room with one person. I know now that I was attracted to Joe because it seemed like he could take care of me and I hoped to take care of him in return. He was my Marlboro man.

While Joe was instrumental to my success at Twin Cities, he was never happy with my performances. The Olympic Trials took place in May of 1988 in Pittsburgh, about seven months after I'd qualified. I ran 2:52, placing 101st out of about 200 women. I went out way too fast, a rookie mistake in what was only my fourth marathon.

After the race, Joe gave me the silent treatment, and I was devastated and humiliated. Many in my family, led by Uncle Frank and including some of my siblings and cousins, had come across the state from Philadelphia to watch me. After the five-mile point, I labored the rest of the way. But, about every four miles I'd hear people calling my name and there was my family cheering by the side of the road. I had no idea how they kept showing up, but I later found out Frank had hired a driver to take them to various points along the course. This was the highlight of the day for me because I never found my groove the whole race. It was the opposite of Twin Cities where it all flowed.

That evening, Frank treated the whole family to dinner. We sat around a big table, and Frank, all six-feet, wide-grin and wisecracking-him, sat in the middle, making us laugh. Joe sat through the entire meal without saying a word to anyone. I was so embarrassed by his behavior, that while Frank continued to be his jovial self and I smiled, inside I was crying.

We flew back to Colorado the next day. It took three days for Joe to talk to me. I was in the kitchen getting ready to leave for campus. When he came in, he leaned against the wall next to a calendar of Rocky Mountain landscapes with our schedules scribbled in the squares, and looked at me.

"Vicki, you blew that race. You should have run 2:37," he said.

I was shocked. He and I had spoken about the possibility of me running six-minute pace for the race and I had given it my best going out at that pace (I hit the five-mile mark in 30 minutes). But it was clearly too fast for such a hilly course. I simply couldn't hold it. I had told Joe this right after the race, but he wouldn't listen. Joe wanted to make me into a running superstar.

Since he didn't believe I had raced the Trials to my potential, Joe decided I should run another marathon right away. I dutifully registered for Grandma's Marathon, held every June in Duluth, Minnesota, named after the chain of restaurants that'd been one of the event's first sponsors. This was only a month after the trials and I got sick before the race from classic overtraining. I was coughing and hacking at the start line.

At the halfway mark, I met a runner named Teri. She had brown hair, tanned skin, and toned muscles. She looked more like a bodybuilder than a runner, but she was clearly fit. We ran side by side for about 10 minutes. She heard my labored breathing and asked if I was OK.

"I feel horrible actually," I gasped, "but I'm trying to finish." She was a few years older than me, I found out, and from Las Vegas.

"I'm not feeling great either," she said. We tried to help each other as the miles ticked by. Grandma's is a point-to-point course that skirts Lake Superior, and as we ran by the shore, I told her about Joe and how angry he'd be if I didn't finish. Teri exclaimed, "That's ridiculous, you're clearly sick."

When I continued to cough, she convinced me to stop. She had decided it wasn't her day either, so at 20 miles, we got on the bus that was taking runners back to the finish.

On the bus ride, I shared how Joe had been treating me. Teri turned to me with wide eyes and a scowl and said, "Vicki, no one has the right to treat you that way."

When we got off the bus and she met Joe, she told him to his face, "Vicki is sick, and you need to be nicer to her." I never forgot that she stood up for me. It only made Joe angrier, and he barely spoke to me after she walked away. But her words stuck with me, and my doubts about the relationship started to grow deeper.

Things continued to deteriorate as Joe retreated into his own world and I went the other way. My desire for a life outside of our relationship started to grow stronger, and I no longer considered staying home from social events he didn't want to attend. By the end, I wouldn't even ask if he wanted to go.

At home, we were literally two ships passing in the night. We barely spoke. Joe was drinking more, and I was avoiding him by staying later at school during the week and going straight to my study after dinner. I was miserable, and friends were telling me I needed to end it.

Finally, one afternoon in mid-December 1988, Joe came into the kitchen after finishing with his last client of the day. I was starting to prepare dinner but I turned to him and said, "We need to talk. I'm not happy, and I want you to move out."

He had no response. His tall frame seemed smaller as he stood hunched with his head hanging, not even able to look me in the eye. He didn't ask for forgiveness or if we could try to work it out. He just said, "OK," and within 15 minutes had packed a bag and left. To this day, I'm not sure where he spent that night.

I felt empty but relieved. The next day was one of those cold, gloomy winter days that we don't often get in Boulder, the land of 300 days of sunshine. I went for a run, anyway, because a run could always make me feel better.

I sometimes wonder if running just numbs me or if at a deeper level it changes me. I think it's probably some combination of the two. I know exercise has a chemical effect on the brain, and I also know that if I run long enough or hard enough, I can erase bad feelings.

As I ran that day along the foothills of North Boulder, past frozen

Wonderland Lake, a loop that I had done countless times with Joe, I relished my freedom and thought about what would come next.

A few weeks after the break-up, I flew to Florida to meet my siblings at Disney World. I'm not sure why that was our chosen destination because only Linda and Jody had kids at the time. But it sounded like fun, and I wanted to be with my family.

I had signed up to do a 5K race, but was feeling feverish the night before. In fact, my running log from the week prior to the trip has notes about fever, nausea, and fatigue. I had ignored these signs and continued training. But on Saturday, January 12, the day of the race, my log reads zero miles and "sick—fever, diarrhea, vomiting all night."

Jeff convinced me to skip the race. I was upset to miss it but was so sick, I knew I couldn't do it anyway. But on Sunday I ran 14 miles on the golf course near the resort before flying home. My log simply states "6:30 a.m.: 14 miles, golf course, Orlando." This was the compulsive part of me; I'd missed the race and felt compelled to make up for it by doing a long run.

When I got back to Boulder, I was feeling a little better, so I continued to ignore my symptoms. Then, a few days later, I woke up around midnight with excruciating pain in my abdomen, like someone was taking a knife and jabbing it into my right side and then twisting it. I didn't know who else to ask for help, so I called Joe.

"Where do you feel the pain?" he asked.

"On my right side."

"I'm coming over and taking you to the hospital," he said without hesitation.

I was lying on the gurney, metal bars surrounding me—as if I might try to escape—looking at the drab, off-white walls. They held nothing to distract me. Finally, the doctor on duty in the emergency room came in to examine me. He didn't say much but told the nurses to prep me for surgery. Then he turned to me and said, "Your appendix is about to rupture. It's already leaking, and we need to remove it now." I couldn't believe I was that sick, but I was also delirious from fever and pain, I just wanted it to stop.

It all happened quickly. The next thing I remember, I was in the recovery room and the doctor was standing by my bed with his white lab coat and a stethoscope hanging from his neck. He had dark hair and stubble around his face and looked as if he must have been up all night. "I'm guessing you're a runner," he said in an earnest tone.

"Yes," I responded, gleeful inside that he had recognized me as such because that must have meant I really was one. But then his eyes went downcast, and he wasn't smiling.

"I'm concerned about your weight. You seem dangerously thin."

"Doctor," I said, "I've been sick for weeks, with diarrhea and throwing up. I had no idea it was my appendix. I'll be fine."

He just shook his head, "I hope so," he said, "but if you need help there are places you can go."

I'm not sure how much I weighed at the time, but I know I was thin. I've always been small, but with the break-up and all the running, I was not taking care of myself the way I should have, but I certainly wasn't trying to starve myself.

The whole topic of weight can be a tricky one for runners. There has been an approach that says the lighter you are, the faster you run. Runners often have an ideal racing weight that can be lighter than their normal, everyday weight that happens when they reduce mileage. My weight had always been consistent. Until I started running 100-mile weeks. I'll admit, I liked feeling lean and fast. But there's a tipping point where if you get too thin, you run the risk of injury. I knew I needed to gain some weight to get back to my full strength.

By spring, my running was feeling effortless. I ran a few 5Ks as summer approached and slowly worked my way back to fitness. I ran one that was for elite women only, and although I placed 13th out of 16 women, I wasn't discouraged because my time was fast for me (18:20) and I was preparing for a fall marathon.

Lance, a friend from grad school, had told me about the Taylor Wineglass Marathon in upstate New York. He'd recently moved back to that area to finish his degree and invited me to stay at his parents' home near where the race took place. He and his parents even escorted me to the start. That race was an especially effortless one; I ran with another woman for the first 20 miles, chatting much of the way, and then I took off. Breaking the tape at the finish line in 2:56, my biggest win to date, was thrilling. The announcer called my name. "Here comes our first lady finisher, Vicki Ash, from Boulder, Colorado!" I had a smile on my face from ear to ear and floated five feet off the ground with joy.

At the awards ceremony, they gave me a magnum of champagne and a check for $1,500. The feeling of winning something for running was otherworldly. I called both my parents to tell them. Mom sounded underwhelmed when all she said was, "That's nice."

Dad was distracted by the latest article he'd read in the *New York Times* about George W. Bush and Margaret Thatcher. I thought for sure he'd be excited because I'd actually won money, but it barely registered. It was nice to be with Lance and his family because his parents, at least, seemed happy for me. They took my picture and treated me like a mini-celebrity, gushing about how they wanted my autograph.

When I began running it had nothing to do with being fast, so when I started winning races it felt like I was someone else who was fooling everyone. I won't lie though, I loved winning, and it added fuel to my already compulsive need to run.

I completed my Ph.D. in political science in May 1992 and secured part-time teaching positions at the University of Colorado, both the Denver and Boulder campuses. This meant commuting twice a week to Denver to teach a class on the U.S. presidency while also teaching an introductory class to freshmen in Boulder twice a week. I had plenty of time to run.

I soon began to tire of racing road marathons. The pressure from Joe to try to run faster was like punishment, and that negative input lingered, even though we'd been apart for over two years. It seemed like a good time to give trail racing and ultrarunning a try. After all, many of my friends in

Boulder were trail runners and would go out for daylong adventures in the mountains. I wanted to be a part of that.

My first run up high was with Paul and Mary. On a beautiful summer day with clear skies and not much wind—unusual in Colorado high country—we ran up Mount Audubon, a 13,000-foot mountain in the Indian Peaks above Boulder. The trail starts at 10,000 feet, but I barely noticed the altitude as we ran through a forested trail. Once we emerged from the trees, I could see the top of the peak off in the distance, a half dome rising toward the sky.

I wasn't fazed by the rocky, technical trail and was able to easily keep pace with Paul. My legs felt like springs as I bounded up the mountain. On the last pitch, Paul turned and casually said, "You should think about doing the Pikes Peak Ascent."

I didn't know much about this race that climbs from the town of Manitou Springs to the top of Pikes Peak at 14,000 feet, but in 1992 I signed up. I had no idea what I was doing, but my fitness from road racing paid off, and I finished third overall for women. It only struck me later how hard mountain running could be. The feeling of floating over the high mountain terrain became more and more elusive as the years went by.

I started spending almost all of my weekends with a group of friends that included Paul, Mary, Neal, Kevin, Becky, and a few others. We spent Saturdays in the mountains running up peaks and playing in waterfalls. Some days we'd meet on our bikes and ride 15 miles to get to a trailhead, run to the top, and then ride back to town. There were no GPS devices back then and certainly no social media, so no one recorded these adventures. We did them for the sheer joy of being in nature and moving our bodies, the intoxicating sensation of muscles spent, brain cells dormant.

I can only liken it to being high without the hangover or depression that can result from a drug or alcohol binge. It also seems similar because both the drug addict and the runner have the desire (possibly need) to duplicate the feeling, even when the consequences might have a negative impact on the person's life. It makes me think of my mom who would take Valium, which would have the immediate effect of numbing her. Later, she switched to Prozac, which helped at first, but eventually drugs ceased to make her feel better. She'd look for the next best thing, which was often food. She would eat too much, looking to fill herself up, hoping to just feel better. But it always had the opposite effect.

Running was a priority for me, but I was also thinking more and more about starting a family. I'd never really considered the concept before, except to think it was something I didn't want. In fact, while in college, I thought anyone who brought children into this crazy world was selfish and misdirected. The world was already overpopulated, so reproducing seemed misguided.

But when I turned 29, it was like a switch turned on inside of me, and the desire to be a mother became an overwhelming urgency. It's a cliché, but my "biological clock" was absolutely ticking. More precisely, it felt like a time bomb would go off inside me if I didn't get pregnant.

As a result, I was actively dating and seeking a partner to start a family with. My sister, Linda, set me up with a doctor named John. The first time he picked me up, I opened the door to find a dark-skinned, handsome man with black hair looking back at me through circular eyeglasses.

After dinner at Laudisio's, a local Italian restaurant, we started dating. That summer our relationship seemed to be going well, and I invited him to go on a bike ride with Paul and Mary, thinking two couples would be a nice balance. I should have thought twice about taking him on a ride up Logan Mill Road, which starts in Four Mile Canyon at the edge of Boulder.

The first few miles are rolling hills, and Paul, Mary, and I chatted about our other friends and upcoming adventures we might do as John followed about 20 feet back. Then we came to the start of the climb. Switchback after switchback took us 1,000 feet up toward the base of Switzerland Trail, an old railroad grade converted to trail. John fell farther behind, so we waited for him at the top. He was soaked with sweat, his breathing labored when he finally caught up to us.

"How much farther?" he asked. When I told him we were only halfway, he slumped over his handlebars. "I'm not in shape for this," he said.

"Oh, you'll be fine," Paul said with a smile. "It's mostly downhill from here." Of course, that wasn't the case, and when we got back to my place after the ride, instead of staying, John said he had to go home to take care of some stuff around his house. Now that I think about it, I never even saw where he lived. Nonetheless, we continued to date sporadically, but the relationship stayed casual. While we had kissed, that's as far as it had gone.

It was later that summer when I decided to enter the Golden Leaf Half-Marathon, a point-to-point trail race that starts in Snowmass and ends in Aspen. Thinking he'd decline, but to be polite, I asked John if he wanted to go. I was surprised when he said yes. He even offered to reserve lodging.

It was September, which in Colorado means the weather could be anything from 80 degrees and sunny to snow and freezing cold. I knew I was in for a tough race when we drove over Independence Pass the night before in a snowstorm.

I was excited though, imagining a romantic B&B. As we pulled up to the hostel he had booked, I quickly realized we were not on the same page. As we walked to our room, I noticed the shared bathroom at the end of the hallway, and when John unlocked the door to our room there was a bunk bed. I left early in the morning to catch the shuttle to the race, and he wished me luck, giving me a peck on the cheek to say goodbye, as if I were his grandmother instead of a girlfriend. I was too concerned about making it to the race start to give it much thought.

Rain mixed with snow as at least 100 runners huddled at the start to stay warm. "This is the worst weather I've seen since we founded the race," the director said. He was a small wiry man who owned the most popular mountain sports store in Aspen. "I'll give the entry fee back to anyone who wants to bail now."

As I shifted from one foot to the other, a murmuring erupted from the crowd before someone yelled, "No way, I'm running no matter what!" followed by an echo of everyone shouting the same thing.

Soon we were all lined up raring to go. Everyone was willing to pit themselves against the elements for better or worse. Although I had run a few mountain races by this time, I had not faced such grueling conditions, not even during my days on June's sheep farm or the days running in the cold at Mount Holyoke. I didn't fully realize my own toughness until that day, standing on the start line.

The trail was technical and muddy, and I took to it like a pig in a trough. As I ran, I got into a zone—what some might call "the runner's high." I approached the finish line in a small park at the edge of town where John stood in his rain gear, holding an umbrella. He cheered for me as I sprinted across the grassy field to cross the tape in first place among the women. I was covered in mud, and while he seemed impressed by my win, he also looked aghast at my appearance, grimacing when I got close to him.

That was the end of the relationship.

"I like being active," John confessed on the phone later that week, "but, I'm overwhelmed by you and your friends and frankly don't even want to try to keep up."

His comments weren't a surprise. Naturally, I was a bit sad, but I didn't dwell on it.

The next year I won the inaugural Colorado Trail 50K. That race marked another milestone—the longest race I had yet completed. Achieving this kind of success was something I never anticipated. I loved trail running and continued to race at a high level for several years. I'm proud of what I was able to do, but I also know that I put a lot of pressure on myself to keep up that level of success. Once you start winning, you want to keep winning, because in competition, you're only as good as your last race.

At the time I was having fun and didn't spend too much time self-analyzing. I continued to play with my friends on weekends, spending hours in the mountains. It was time well spent—I didn't even consider it training; it was simply what we did for recreation. I also loved other activities, and swimming was high on the list. We didn't call it cross-training back then, but between swimming and water running, I think I was already onto the magic of doing other activities to recover from running.

With the advent of triathlon and its growing popularity in the last couple of decades, cross-training has become more common in the endurance world. But typically, runners run. Even now, most runners will only get in a pool or on a bike when they're injured. But varying activities can prevent overtraining, a common culprit in running-related injuries. I was committed to maintaining this routine.

One winter morning I was headed to the 5:30 a.m. swim workout at the East Boulder Recreation Center. Except for the lights in the parking lot, it was almost pitch-black out. I was hurrying toward the entrance to get away from the cold when I noticed a guy had waited to hold the door for me.

"Good morning," he said, as I hurried into the warmth of the lobby. Following me inside, he asked, "How's your day going so far?" I turned around and, in the light, saw one of the cutest guys I had ever seen. His long brown hair was almost a mullet, but I was a sucker for men with long hair. His smile lit up the entire entryway.

"Great so far," I managed to stammer back. Then we both went to our respective locker rooms.

As I swam back and forth in the pool, only half-hearing what the coach was saying, I kept thinking about the cute guy with the bright smile. I decided I was going to get him to ask me out. After the session ended, I saw him ease his ripped body into the hot tub. I headed right over, hoping to strike up a conversation.

Once I'd positioned myself across from him, my body acclimating to the hot water, he smiled at me again and introduced himself as Brian. At the time, I considered myself an expert at flirting, so when he didn't ask me about myself or try to get my number, I figured he wasn't interested.

The conversation drifted to include the other people also in the tub and after 10 minutes I realized this was not going to result in a date. I saw him a few more times that year, and we'd chat, but I didn't get any romantic vibes. I kept dating other people and didn't give Brian much more thought.

As usual, I also threw myself into my running, and having had some success in local trail races decided to focus my energy on the FILA Sky Race to be held in Aspen later that summer. It was part of a race series put on by the Italian company FILA. The races were difficult, super-technical, and invitation-only. The first race on U.S. soil was set for Aspen in 1994, and the top three men and women got to compete at the FILA Sky Race in Europe later that year.

I put everything into training for that race. I spent countless hours running at altitude and devoted almost all my waking hours to thinking about the race. I'd contemplate the different possible weather conditions, as well as my race strategy and whether I'd go out hard and attempt to stay with the leaders or be more conservative and run my pace hoping to pick people off as the race progressed. I'd visualize doing well and crossing the finish line.

Race weekend arrived, and I decided to take a nap before the pre-race dinner. When I tried to wake up, I was so groggy I could barely get out of bed. I took a shower to revive myself, but deep down I was worried. A short nap can do wonders to revive and restore an athlete, but I had slept for two hours and was still exhausted. I knew something wasn't right, but I brushed it off and went to eat.

That night I again slept hard, another sign I was overtired. Often the night before a race, my nervous system is already in a sympathetic state, getting my body prepared to run hard, and my sleep can be restless.

Turns out I was in for a long, hard day on the mountain. When the gun went off the next morning, I fell behind right away. My legs felt like steel blocks I could barely lift off the ground. I quickly lost touch with the race leaders, and as we gained elevation, it only got worse.

I couldn't understand what had happened. I dropped out at 18 miles, utterly disappointed in myself. My log simply says, "yuck" for the day.

But I should have seen it coming. I had classically overtrained, and all the telltale signs were there. The weeks before the race I'd felt lousy in workouts, but instead of resting, I just ran harder. The nap fiasco the day before was the final clue I'd gone over that tipping point every athlete tries to avoid. Train hard, but not to the point that you burn out. It's as much an art as science and requires paying attention to the many signs your body is sending. We get messages all the time, a niggle here or there, being unable to wake up in the morning without a struggle, feeling cranky—all of these are signs of overtraining.

Fast forward to May 1995. I had just finished running the Bolder Boulder and was wandering the race expo at Farrand Field, located on the University of Colorado campus next to the football stadium. There were hundreds of vendors and thousands of people. I was about to leave through a small gate at the far end of the field when I bumped into Brian, the guy from the pool. I hadn't seen him in a few months.

Somehow, I had blocked him from my brain, but there he was, cute as ever—brown eyes twinkling, a huge smile plastered on his face. I turned up my flirting dial, getting as close to him as possible without touching him so as not to come off as too pushy. We spoke about the race and what a nice day it was for running. When he acknowledged he wished he'd run a faster time, I confessed the same while looking him in the eye to amplify the connection.

Just when I started to think there was a chance he would ask to get together, he started to look around.

"My wife, Tammy, also ran the race, and I need to go meet up with her," he grinned as he went off in search of his wife. I felt completely deflated in that instant. But I smiled back and gave a light wave goodbye. The runner's high and the happiness from seeing him again quickly dissipated. I wandered back to the expo to find my friends.

Rather than thinking about dating and guys, I focused my energy on training for the second annual FILA race coming up later that summer. One of the limiting factors in sports performance has been shown to be the mental aspect. Put two equally talented runners on a start line and it's often the one who stays the calmest and most focused under pressure who will win. I was still upset about my performance the previous year and was looking for any advantage I might add to my training. A friend of mine was a sports psychologist, and I started seeing him once a week as part of my preparation.

FILA had put a lot of money and marketing into the SKY series and the prize money was significant—a $10,000 purse. However, a much bigger portion went to the men's winners. I was upset by this. Backward and chauvinistic, this was apparently standard practice in Europe at the time, but I thought we needed to take a stand.

I started talking to some of the other women competitors, and while they were annoyed, no one wanted to ruffle any feathers. I didn't care about that and wrote a letter to the race directors asking that they reconsider and change the prize money structure. They wrote back, only to refuse.

When race weekend arrived, I was much more energized than I had been the previous year. I was not at all overtrained, so when it came time for the pre-race dinner, I was ready to do battle. My main concern was the uneven prize money. It wasn't that I thought I would win or even be on the podium—it was the principle.

Race headquarters occupied part of a small hotel at the base of Snowmass Mountain. A buffet was set up in a nondescript meeting room with 10 round tables draped with white tablecloths. One side offered large windows overlooking a cement plaza surrounded by shops and other restaurants. Almost all of the athletes entered in the race were there, and once everyone had gotten their meal of pasta, bread, and salad, we settled into groups to eat.

I don't recall any race directors being there initially, so once everyone had eaten and people were waiting for the pre-race meeting to start, I decided to bring up the issue of uneven prize money with the entire group. I went to the front of the room, stood between the tables and the buffet and called for everyone's attention.

The top male mountain runner, who was favored to win, stood glaring at me, arms crossed over his chest as I broached the topic. "Women don't work as hard as the men," he had the nerve to say. "There are fewer women in the field, so it takes less effort to win."

The women had taken up the space behind me and the men were scattered throughout the room watching as the drama unfolded. I was dumbfounded that anyone believed this and was actually willing to say it out loud. It was chauvinistic, and for 1995, out-of-step with where I thought we'd come in terms of equal rights. He and I proceeded to have a shouting match in front of everyone as I fruitlessly tried to convince him that women work just as hard even if we don't run as fast as the men.

"It takes just as much effort for us to compete as it does for you," I said, as the women behind me murmured their affirmations. None of the guys said anything, afraid to speak up since they didn't want to contradict the golden boy for FILA and mountain running in general at that time. But I did notice a few of them shifting uncomfortably in their seats or moving toward the back of the room as he spoke. I would see him many times over the next decade at other races; he never spoke directly to me again.

In the race, I redirected my anger toward him and the race management and used it as fuel to run up the first snowfield. When the running got hard, I smiled knowing I was where I belonged. I finished in ninth place among the women—some of the strongest mountain runners in the world—and felt satisfied.

Afterward, we were standing around the plaza soaked in sunshine when I spotted Brian, leaning up against the wall of the hotel, sitting on the ground with his back against the wall. A red-haired woman and another couple sat nearby. I decided to go say hi even though I was sure the pretty redhead was his wife. Brian lit up when he saw me. Smiling, he introduced me to his wife, Tammy, and their friends Tom and Karen. We chatted a bit about the race which Tammy had also run, and how hard it was.

"That was tough," she confessed, and I agreed. After a couple of minutes, I said goodbye and went back to my group of friends.

Life continued to alternate between teaching, training, and dating. It was no longer a question—I needed to have a child, but, in my hunt, I met a long line of wrong men.

There was the swimmer who was a bit older and seemed experienced and stable until he told me the apartment he'd said was his actually belonged to one of his friends. Then there was the mogul skier who rode motorcycles. Befitting this, everything with him was fast and furious, including when he cheated on me with a woman I considered a friend.

When July 4, 1996, rolled around, I was at home getting ready for the next guy, Mike, to pick me up. We had plans to golf and then watch fireworks. He and I had met years before through mutual friends in the running community. He was still a runner, and we were having fun together. The relationship wasn't too serious, but I had convinced myself there was potential for it to grow.

The thorn in the relationship was his drinking. Mike had loads of money, and he spent it freely, taking me out to dinner and on weekend getaways. But he never went anywhere without drinking; I still hadn't learned my lesson.

I was hanging out in my living room with my yellow lab, Remy, when he called. I assumed it was to tell me he was running late, but instead, he said he wasn't coming, and said, "I need to end things with you." He was slurring his words and I knew he was drunk so I just hung up, too stunned to even ask why.

I laid on the floor with Remy by my side for the rest of the afternoon and cried. I thought back to when Mr. Kirchner called me into the hallway to ask how I was doing with my parent's separation, and I cried my eyes out for 10 minutes before pulling myself back together and returning to my classroom. Wiping my tears away, I decided to do the same thing. *Vicki,* I said to myself as Remy looked at me like I was talking to her, *you're way better off without him.*

Fortunately, the holiday fell on a weekend, and a friend of mine was having a party up in the foothills above Boulder. The house was on a steep hillside and the driveway angled sharply up from the road. To keep my mind off Mike, I was pounding down the wine that kept appearing in my glass as if by magic. I was feeling light and loose, and I began flirting with a guy from Australia I'd just met.

We decided to leave the party with a few of my other friends, but as we headed down the driveway, I fell behind, weaving slightly from the alcohol. Everyone was already inside the vehicle when I went around to the passenger side, slipped in the gully, and landed on my arm. I knew I had broken my wrist by the way it hung limply. The Aussie offered to take me to the emergency room and stayed with me the whole time. Then he spent the night with me just to make sure I was OK. But when he left the next morning, reality set in.

I had no boyfriend and a broken wrist. The juxtaposition of Mike breaking up with me and this guy who I'd just met staying with me and being kind and considerate was all I needed to reframe the breakup. Why would I want to stay with someone who didn't want to be with me and who'd also choose to leave me alone on the 4th of July?

A week later, on a Sunday night, my phone rang.

"Hi, Vicki. This is Brian Hunter. How are things?"

Shaking inside, but keeping my voice steady, I responded, "Fine, Brian, how are you? Is Tammy alright, does she need anything?"

I couldn't imagine why else he'd be calling. Tammy and I knew each other as friendly competitors, but I doubt she'd reach out to me, and I never doubted that their marriage was solid.

"Oh, no, that's not it. Tammy and I are splitting up, and I thought I'd see what you were up to."

Jittery and excited, I was also worried about becoming the rebound.

I said, "What you need is to go out and have some fun."

"Oh yeah?" he said, a question more than a statement as he fell silent to give me a chance to invite him out.

"A few of us are going to the Rio on Tuesday night," I said. "You should join us."

The next two days, during my normal routine of running in the morning, swimming afterward, and writing and preparing for classes in the afternoons, I found myself inwardly smiling with just the thought of seeing him. But then I'd remind myself not to get carried away. I didn't want to experience another painful letdown.

CHAPTER 10
Life with Brian

Tuesday night arrived, and when I opened the door, I knew I was in serious trouble. Brian was even better-looking than I'd remembered, with long, brown hair tied back in a ponytail, brown eyes glistening, and a smile that killed.

The Rio was packed, as usual, and the hostess pointed us to the bar. Brian and I found stools to sit on while we waited for my friends.

Over the noise, Brian said, "I don't drink." I almost couldn't hear him over the cacophony around us. But when I realized what he'd said, I had a moment of confusion and then angst that I had invited him to a place where the only reason to go is to drink their margaritas.

Once everyone else arrived, we hung out at the bar, but I didn't even order a cocktail not wanting Brian to feel left out. At one point, a friend whispered in my ear, "He's cute." I just smiled and mouthed, *I know.*

After 15 minutes passed, Brian looked at me and said, "Do you want to go get some food?" I quickly agreed and we said our goodbyes.

As soon as we emerged from the loud space, we both looked at each other with a sigh of relief.

"Let's go somewhere we can talk," he said. "Do you like Thai food?"

"I haven't had much Thai," I answered. "But I'll try it."

At Siamese Plate, the host greeted Brian like an old friend. I didn't know many men who liked different kinds of food, so I found this appealing. I was intrigued that Brian was already more adventurous than anyone I had previously dated.

"Can I order for us?" he asked. I said sure but admitted I wasn't a fan of spicy food.

"Trust me," he said before ordering something called jungle curry. When he told the waiter to make it "Thai hot," I flinched.

Perhaps it was the fact that he spoon-fed me because I was still in a cast, but this dish tasted so good I didn't mind how spicy it was, even when it made my eyes tear up. Brian's appetite was voracious, and he ate everything I left on my plate plus his own.

For hours, we sat and talked about our families, running, and jobs. He also explained more about his sobriety—he'd been sober since he was 18, but we didn't dwell on it that evening.

It was obvious we were both huge endurance athletes. He had done several Ironman races as well as marathons and ultramarathons. Since Joe, I hadn't dated anyone who came close to running as much as I did, so it was enticing to me to know we had that in common.

We finally had to leave when the waiter came to check on the bill for the fourth time and told us they were closing. Brian drove me home. At the door, he kissed me goodbye and told me he had a great time, but he didn't come in.

The next night he did come in, and we spent every night together for the next three weeks straight.

Months later he told me he had made a list of all the women in Boulder he might want to date once he knew his marriage was over.

"You were number one," he said as we cuddled together on my couch in the living room late at night. A rerun of "I Love Lucy," played so softly we could barely hear it.

He spent most nights at my house after that first date and on weekends we'd head to his house in the mountains. He had two Dalmatians, Norman and Jake, whom he shared with Tammy, and I had Remy.

Often, Tammy had the dogs, but when Brian had them, it was like a canine circus in my house. I never witnessed the transfer of the dogs between the two of them, and I wouldn't let my mind go to imagining what they talked about or how they acted together.

When we had all three of the dogs, it felt like we were a unit, so I focused on that and allowed my fantasies to wander into the future where our children were part of the picture. Ultimately, Tammy got Jake, and

Brian kept Norman.

In August, I ran the Pikes Peak Marathon with a cast on my wrist. I didn't even think twice about whether this was a good idea or not. Lance had agreed to be my support, and he drove me to the race.

As we drove past the skyscrapers dotting downtown Denver, he asked how it was going with the new guy. In the first semester of grad school, before I'd met Joe, I had a huge crush on Lance that was totally one-sided. But our friendship became one of the deepest I made in school. Being able to talk to him about Brian came naturally.

"I like him a lot," I responded. "He's fun and very active so we're having a blast. He's not divorced yet though, so who knows. It's still so early in our relationship."

Lance shrugged and said, "Well, he seems like a nice guy."

The next morning as I started the long climb to the top of the mountain, I was thinking about Brian and how it would be so nice to tell him I had a good race. I was propelled by this, and despite the broken wrist, felt strong as I worked my way past the midpoint and came upon Barr Camp and the huge aid station there. Spectators can drive to this point and hike a short way from the road to the trail, so it gets a lot of traffic.

It's also just about halfway on the ascent portion of the race. I got a burst of energy from the crowd and continued as the trail got even steeper. The next big checkpoint, called A-Frame, comes at 10,000 feet. If you don't make it to this point by a certain time, the race organizers make you turn around. The last three miles are above tree line and include tons of switchbacks.

I could hear the yelling from the spectators waiting at the top starting at about 11,000 feet. This always played with my head because it seems like you're close to the top, but with two miles to go and 3,000 more feet of elevation, this is the hardest section of the whole race.

I kept a steady pace, and when I reached the turn-around, I got my wind back and started flying down the trail. As I passed runner after runner, I was feeling more and more confident. With four miles to go, the switchbacks felt like a roller coaster as I swiftly took each turn gliding across the finish line in fifth place. I was ecstatic and couldn't wait to tell Brian.

Next on the competition calendar for Brian was the Canada Ironman. I wasn't going, but by this point, he was practically living at my house. He had to leave at 7 a.m. but was still packing at 3 a.m., and my living room was littered with his gear and clothes. I ignored the nagging voice in my head that kept warning, *something about this isn't right.*

As he struggled to organize his gear, I made excuses for Brian instead. He was a design engineer for Sweetwater Filtration, inventing filtration devices for camping, which was already impressive. Then throw in all the races and triathlons he trained for and participated in on top of 40- to 50-hour workweeks, I kept returning to the fact that he was the first guy I'd ever dated who had a similar approach to life and play as me.

However, Brian's sobriety also separated him from the other men I had dated. At first, I didn't think it was important. I loved that he could have fun without drinking, and I soon cut way back on my own. I was more of a social drinker anyway, only imbibing if I was with other people. I enjoyed being with Brian more and it wasn't a sacrifice not to drink.

Brian was open with me about his issues with alcohol and told me that he started stealing liquor from his parents and grandparents when he was 9. By high school, he was heavily into drugs and alcohol. Amazingly enough, he continued to play sports and was on the baseball and football teams. Such a gifted athlete, he was still able to excel at both despite his vices.

But at 18, he was arrested for dealing cocaine and spent three months in jail. His mom said she would bail him out only if he promised to go to Alcoholics Anonymous. When he got out, he moved in with his maternal grandfather who assisted in helping him find a job in car design. He did attend AA meetings and there he met several other guys in recovery who were getting into triathlon. This started his transition from substance abuse to extreme exercise.

Knowing all of this didn't deter me from wanting to be with him. Brian and I had started dating in July and in early September, I invited him to a friend's birthday celebration on the lawn in front of Chautauqua Mountain Park. Everyone had a beer in hand, yet Brian was totally at ease. He was a few feet away from me so I couldn't hear what he said to Paul that made him laugh, but it wasn't easy to sway Paul. I knew at that moment I could spend the rest of my life with Brian.

That fall, we went to visit his family in Michigan for a long weekend. We were staying with his mom and stepfather and decided to do a track workout one day at his old high school. We did our quarter-mile repeats and then started the run back to his folks' house.

"That's where I drove a moped through the window of the school," he said as he pointed toward one of the entrances. "My friends and I stole a moped and I was driving it on school grounds. I lost control because it didn't have brakes and slid into a window."

"What happened to you?" I asked.

"I was pretty banged up, but I knew they'd be looking for me, so I didn't go to the hospital. I just ran away and went to a friend's house. I ended up getting suspended anyway."

"Wow," I said. "You were a mess, weren't you?"

So, what happens when the man you fall in love with is so full of energy that he borders on manic? My once organized and controlled life became messy. This was enticing, as Brian was always up for adventure, and we trained, raced, and played together nonstop those first few months. I had often traveled out of state to race on my own, but the first time Brian and I did this together was in September 1996 when we went to upstate Minnesota for the Superior Trail 50-mile race. We had been together since mid-July, and I was feeling good about the relationship, even though Brian was still married to Tammy. In fact, Brian and Tammy had run this same race the year before, and I felt her presence right away—or should I say her absence?

When we went to the pre-race dinner to pick up our race packets, I got strange looks from some of the women who knew Brian from the previous year. Clearly, I was not Tammy, and although no one said anything to me directly, I felt the awkwardness of being the new woman who was not the wife.

The race began before dawn and we needed headlamps at the start. We stood in a dark parking lot at a trailhead. When the race director yelled,

"Go!" all of us streamed through a small opening that led to the single-track trail we would follow to the finish line. Point-to-point races are rare at that distance, and I was looking forward to the adventure of it. I had no familiarity with the course though, so I was content to stay in the mix with a group of runners who seemed to know the route.

The year before, Tammy had finished second to a woman who was in the race and I wondered how I would fare. I ran with this woman the first few miles, and the pace felt ridiculously easy. By the second aid station at eight miles, I had gotten in front of her. At one point, running by myself in the woods along the shoreline of Lake Superior, I wondered if I was off course. I wished that some of those runners from early on were still with me, but I pushed the doubts from my mind and kept running. After 9 hours, I crossed the line in first place. I expected Brian to be at the finish line, but he was nowhere to be seen. I found him, at the food table, chatting with someone.

"I thought you'd be at the finish when I came through," I said.

"I planned on it, but then I got hungry," he said. He must have read the disappointment I was feeling, the remnants of the wound of my mother's lack of interest in my running as he added, "I thought I'd have enough time to grab some food and be back to see you finish. I'm sorry, I meant to be there." It seemed silly to stay mad, especially since we'd both won.

The awards ceremony took place in a converted barn and we hung out until we each received a beautiful wood plaque and clock award. Even though I didn't know anyone, I was accepted by these runners. We sat on wood benches and ate burgers and macaroni salad on paper plates. A few people commented on the fact that Brian and I were the "couple who won," but no one made too big a deal of it. After a few hours, we drove back to the place we'd stayed the night before.

On the way, Brian said he needed to make a stop. I sat in the car in a parking lot while he went to use a payphone. I knew he was calling Tammy, and I was trying to figure out how to feel about it as the letdown of him not being at the finish line resurfaced. Their separation was new, and my insecurities rose knowing Brian needed to check in with her. On the other hand, I was happy that he could tell her we both won the race. But I also felt petty even thinking this.

When Brian got back in the car, before he had the chance to turn the key in the ignition, I told him how I was feeling, "It's weird to me that you had to call Tammy." Then I took a deep breath and asked the question I was really scared to ask: "Are you missing her?"

"No," he responded. "She asked me to call her after the race. It doesn't mean anything."

I asked him about it many years later, and he had no recollection of calling Tammy that day.

CHAPTER 11
A Three-Hour Tour

That fall was like a honeymoon.

We spent all our free time together, which meant most nights he stayed at my house since it was closer to work for both of us. A typical morning had us heading to the pool for a swim workout, a run, or sometimes both. We often headed west toward Mount Sanitas, a small peak in central Boulder just a few miles from where I lived. It has single-track trails that snake their way up, a thousand feet from the base, and I loved it because I could vary my route each time.

It was named for the Boulder-Colorado Sanitarium which opened in 1896 as a resort and health spa with claims to cure both body and soul. When I first found this playground, after a couple of years living in Boulder, I didn't think twice about running up and down the steep trails. Families would come to hike, and professional runners used it as training for mountain competitions. I'd often see one gentleman in his 80s hiking, and I'd always be in awe that he was still out there at his age.

Brian and I would start out on the quiet streets of Boulder before dawn, reaching the trailhead after a couple of miles and then proceed to race to the top. We loved pushing each other, and although he was faster than me, he'd let me set the pace. Once at the top, we'd take a moment to hold hands and look out over Boulder as the town slowly came to life before racing down the other side.

One day during our first winter together, Brian asked if I wanted to go snowshoeing. It was already mid-morning and I worried about starting out so late, but Brian assured me. "I know a route that will take us about three hours," he said.

We packed up a few supplies and drove to Rollinsville, a small mountain town above Boulder. Brian had asked a few of his buddies to join us. As we got higher, the clouds started rolling in, but we didn't think too much about it until we reached an open area at about 10,000-feet elevation. Suddenly, the sky seemed to close in on us and the conditions turned precarious. The wind howled and the snow blew sideways into our faces. My first thought was for our dogs Norman and Remy.

One of the guys decided this was the perfect moment to have a sandwich.

"Forget about the sandwich, dude," Brian said, echoing my thoughts. "We need to keep moving."

I felt like I had weights attached to each leg as we made our way across the wide expanse of open meadow. Snowshoeing in the best of conditions is a lot of work, but with the wind pushing me in all directions, it seemed I was making no forward progress.

By now we had been out for several hours, and we finally found some relief as we entered the woods. The trees provided some shelter, and the weather calmed. We realized we were above the local ski area. Soon, the sky cleared, and the sun peeked out behind the clouds. We all let out a sigh of relief. I didn't realize how scared I'd been until I felt safe again. Three of the guys decided to bail and head down the quickest way while Brian, Pete and I were lulled into continuing by the clear blue sky that had emerged after the storm.

We were having a nice time chatting about running and upcoming events like the Mount Taylor Quadrathlon, which all three of us were planning on doing. After an hour or so, the light started to fade and darker shadows formed in front of us. I glanced at my watch. It was now late afternoon.

"How close are we to the trailhead?" I asked Brian.

"Not far," he said. "It's just up ahead."

We kept trudging through the snow, but Norman was struggling. Brian needed to carry him every so often because his paws were raw from the cold. Remy was better off but I couldn't help feeling like a horrible dog parent.

Before we knew it, the light was gone, and we hadn't thought to bring headlamps. There wasn't much of a moon, but gradually our eyes adjusted to the pitch black above, and the whiteness of the snow provided some contrast to the dark sky so we could at least see the trail in front of us.

We'd brought very little in the way of food. Pete had one peanut butter and jelly sandwich that he offered to share. We turned him down. "I know where we are," Brian kept telling us, but then he'd move ahead to ostensibly check trail conditions. Each time he did this, Pete and I became more and more doubtful he actually knew where we were as minutes turned to hours.

Around 7 p.m. we passed by an old abandoned mine shaft. As I stared at the dilapidated wood structure punctuating the white snow, Brian said with great confidence, "Oh, I know where we are. We'll be down in no time."

An hour later, at the same time, Pete and I both asked, "Haven't we been here before?"

We all paused to look at the same mine we'd been by before, and I thought of all the horror stories of people getting lost in the mountains. Would we get frostbite, die from exposure, would the dogs be OK? But Brian with his typical optimism rallied and said, "For sure, it's this way, I promise."

Sure enough, nine hours from when we started, we made it back to the town of Nederland, miles from where we had started. But at least it was civilization. Fortunately, we had left Pete's vehicle in the parking lot of the grocery store to carpool to the trailhead, so we were able to go back to get our car.

Before driving back, we went inside the store and devoured pre-made turkey and cheese sandwiches, the only thing available that time of night. Once we retrieved the car and were driving down Boulder Canyon, Brian started singing the theme song from Gilligan's Island, and ever since if we're going out to do something new, he sings the song and I still laugh.

Next on our agenda was the Mount Taylor Quadrathlon, an event where you bike, run, ski, and snowshoe to the top of a 13,000-foot mountain in Grants, New Mexico. Then you do it all in reverse on the way down. The race always falls on or near Valentine's Day, so it felt like a romantic adventure designed just for the two of us. My belief in the relationship was growing stronger with each passing day, especially since Brian's divorce had been finalized.

I had done some skiing in my life but considered myself an advanced beginner at best. I decided I would do the race anyway, mostly because I wanted to be with Brian. I knew I could bike, run, and snowshoe and hoped that would carry me through.

The four events meant we needed a lot of equipment, and the day we were packing to leave, my front yard looked like a garage sale featuring bikes, skis, snowshoes, running shoes, bags to pack it all in, and clothes for every kind of weather. It was a mess, but I was looking forward to the race and the getaway, so I dismissed the chaos once again. It caused me some inner turmoil, though, as I'm a planner by nature, and leaving things to the last minute always ties me up in knots. I eventually came to realize this is how Brian operates—basically by the seat of his pants with no organization whatsoever.

When we got to Grants, we spent all our time readying our stuff for the transition areas. Neither of us had ever done the race so we didn't know what we were doing. As I put my bags together inside the tiny room we shared in a one-level motel off Main Street, Brian was waxing our skis in the parking lot. I got bored waiting for him, so I went for a walk thinking that by the time I got back he'd surely be done. Nope, he was so intent on making the skis perfect that we almost missed the pre-race dinner. When we did turn our equipment in, it was just minutes before the midnight deadline.

I was terrified of the downhill ski. This is one instance where ignorance was a blessing because had I known how steep this section was, I never would have agreed to go. For the uphill portion of the race, I was in my element. The racers start together in the center of town and head up the mountain on bicycles for 13 miles to the base of Mount Taylor, where the road turns to dirt. I was not much of a cyclist, so I just used my base fitness to get up the road. Brian was way up front, and I lost sight of him in minutes. When I arrived at the transition area, I was overwhelmed by the number of people helping the racers. I quickly changed into running shoes, grabbed my water bottle and was out on the run course in a matter of minutes.

The five miles uphill was my natural habitat, and as it got steeper, I passed more and more people, getting stronger as I climbed. Toward the end of the run, there was more snow in the trees and as soon as I crossed into the transition area, snow covered the ground. I found my gear in the midst of the rows of skis lined up on racks. I switched to ski boots, clicked into my skis and started up the hill with snowshoes on my back. I don't know how I made it up the hill on the short skis Brian had me use, but I did. Then at the top, I switched to snowshoes for the steep one-mile climb to the summit. I passed people as I made my way to the top of the mountain.

On the almost vertical downhill snowshoe, my feet were going under me so fast that I worried I might fall head over heels at any moment. Once I switched to my skis to go back down, I knew I was in trouble.

I had no control whatsoever, and the bumpy, narrow road was full of twists and turns. Faster skiers passed me continually, yelling as they came by, "Watch out!" and "Get out of the way." It was terrifying. At one point, I was completely alone, almost in tears, but I kept going. I fell eight times in four miles, cursing Brian the whole way for waxing my skis to make them go faster.

After about three miles of steep downhill, the course leveled out and momentum ceased to help. It became about putting one ski in front of the other. Although it was slow going, I preferred this portion of the course to the screaming downhill. There was still a ton of snow, and the trail meandered through the forest before emerging at the transition area where suddenly, there were a ton of volunteers, spectators, and racers.

Once I was off the skis and running again, I was back in my comfort zone. The rest of the race was an adrenaline rush as I passed people on the downhill run and bike portions. Coming back onto town, winding through back streets to the finish line, I pumped my pedals, willing myself to go faster. When I crossed the finish line, I knew I'd be back.

The next morning, on our drive home, we stopped in Santa Fe. Brian had suggested we stop at the local ski resort for some downhill skiing. Still smarting from my downhill ski the day before I reluctantly agreed. Before skiing, we made time for pancakes and coffee at a small café. We sat at a table for two against a wall decorated with framed photos of the nearby mountains.

As we went over the details of the race and how we could do better, I managed to tell Brian, "Next year, you don't need to wax my skis." He laughed and I did too, but I also made sure he knew I wasn't kidding. This became a ritual for us, talking about an event or training day, and working out what went right and what we could improve. The thrill of the race was still pumping us both up and despite my disastrous ski portion, we made plans to do it again.

"So," I said, "this was so much fun and I'm hoping we have many more races in our future. I'm wondering where you see our relationship going."

He looked at me with soft eyes and replied, "I never thought I'd be this happy in a relationship. I'm in it for the long haul."

"Okay," I said, "just so I'm clear what that means, are we going to get married? Because I seriously want children and at 36, I don't have time to wait."

"Yes!" he smiled back, "I'm ready."

We decided then and there that two children would be perfect.

As we headed to the ski area before driving back to Boulder, I wondered if the conversation had really taken place. *Were we engaged?* I asked myself because it seemed so random. But, after skiing, on the drive home, we started talking about dates and how we wanted to get married. I started thinking it was real.

I had never wanted a fancy wedding and we spoke about eloping, but that didn't feel right either, so we decided to pick a day to marry ourselves and just tell friends and family our plans.

When Brian and I got engaged we started looking for the perfect house. Tammy had gotten their Nederland house in the divorce settlement, and Brian wanted to keep living in the mountains. This sounded romantic to me, so I agreed. We made countless trips to the canyons surrounding Boulder, and as soon as we saw the house on County Road 68, we knew we'd found home.

Everything from the green gate at the top of the driveway to the 33 forested acres surrounding the property was magic. From our living room window, we could see the top of Forsythe Mountain, which became the destination for many of our day hikes. No more driving to a trailhead, we could just open our front door. The fact that it was just a few miles from Magnolia Road, a place where elite runners come to train, was one more reason to become enamored with the house and the neighborhood. Besides, several good friends lived nearby, so we had a built-in community before we even moved in.

We married on April 5, 1997. Even though we didn't officially own the property yet, no one was living there, so we decided to hike up Forsythe to say our vows. The ground was covered with snow from a recent spring storm. I wore Sorels and a white parka, Brian paired jeans with a heavy winter jacket.

As we made our way through the woods to the base of the mountain, Norman and Remy ran back and forth playing in the snow. The trees looked frosted, snow dangling from the branches, and the sun starting to peek through the clouds gave them an extra look of sparkle. It was already warm, and we shed our coats as we hiked higher up the hill. There's a slight grade from the house to the base of the mountain and although there's no actual trail, you can follow a gully as you head up. This pathway narrows as you go higher, and it seemed as though we were rising toward a sanctuary.

Once we reached the base of Forsythe, with the rock formation hovering over us, it truly felt like we were in an outdoor cathedral. We found a relatively level spot for the ceremony. We each had written our own vows but at the end, together we read a Native American prayer that included:

Now for you there is no rain / For one is shelter to the other

Now there is no loneliness / Now, forever, forever, there is no loneliness

The dogs were our only witnesses because you're legally allowed to marry yourselves in Colorado. That evening we had dinner with close friends at the Full Moon restaurant, at the time one of our favorite restaurants in Boulder. Afterward, we stayed at a B&B downtown that one of my oldest friends from childhood, Beth, treated us to as a wedding gift.

That very day I went off birth control. As soon as we got to our room, we were off to the races. Obviously, this wasn't our first time, but the idea that we could be making a baby changed the intensity. It was intoxicating and driven by a mutual desire to become parents as soon as possible.

The day before we moved into our new home, there was a massive spring storm. Brian's mom, Loretta, and stepfather, Bob, had come to Boulder to help us. As we drove the steep and windy road up to the house, we could see the snow increasing exponentially with each passing degree of elevation. As we got closer, his parents were visibly getting more nervous. "Are we going the right way?" Loretta tentatively asked from where she sat in the back of Brian's Astro Van, Bob sitting next to her, wide-eyed and speechless, holding on to the front of his seat.

"Uh, yeah," Brian said, "we bought the house. I think we know where it is."

I just looked at him sideways and then kept my eye on the road. I knew he could get us there, but I hadn't seen the road this bad. I was just hoping we wouldn't get stuck because I didn't want Bob and Loretta more worried than they already were.

Once we made the final turn onto our private road, the snow got even deeper. By the time we got to the green gate, the road was impassable and Loretta screamed when Brian slammed into a wall of snow. He and I burst out laughing. Bob, who was still gripping the seat, asked where the house was. Brian and I grinned at each other and said, "It's a quarter-mile down that driveway."

Brian grew up in the suburbs of Detroit. They had snow there, but nothing like this. Loretta and Bob were clearly shell-shocked. We all grabbed a box or a suitcase from the van and started toward the house. Once we got to the front door, Brian and I realized we didn't have the keys. Bob nearly lost it when I climbed through an opening that was meant for passing firewood into the house. When we all got inside, Bob asked if there was a phone. Brian responded, "Yes, you should call 911 and tell them your stepson is trying to kill you!" Again, he and I burst out laughing.

We gave them a tour of the classic mountain house, built of wood with an open floor plan. The downstairs was one big open space with the kitchen marked off by counters that separated it from the dining and living room. The deep red sink caught everyone's eye.

In the center of the living space was a wood-burning stove. There were very few walls except for the guest bedroom tucked away in the corner and the downstairs bathroom with another beautiful sink, this one made of classic Mexican tile in a Southwestern mosaic design. The stairs led to the master bedroom which had its own fireplace.

The master bath had Mediterranean royal blue tiles that always made me feel like I was near the ocean. The shower stall seemed like the builder must have meant to put in a sauna because the walls were made of deep wood and the glass door went up to the ceiling. It seemed unfinished and Brian talked about completing it, but never got around to it.

There was another bathroom in the loft area on the second floor and the sink was bright yellow. The guy who built the house must have liked primary colors given his tile choices for the bathrooms and kitchen. I always appreciated his attention to detail in the tile and woodwork throughout the house. I especially loved the built-in closet in the master bedroom. Its beautiful oak doors opened into my own private space a few feet above the actual floor of the room. It was like the magic wardrobe from *The Chronicles of Narnia*.

We delayed our honeymoon until early July to time it with a trip to the German Ironman so Brian and his friend, Tom, could compete. Because we went with Tom and his wife, Karen, it didn't feel like a honeymoon, but I wasn't much on traditions anyway, so it didn't bother me. I loved the idea of going to Europe, and I knew it would be an adventure.

The guys had managed to arrange homestays with families in Roth where the race would be held. Our host family's kids were 3, 5, and 7. Brian and I had babies on the brain, so we enjoyed being around them. We also loved the parents who seemed to have a great marriage. The husband called his wife "*schatzie*," a German word of endearment that translates to "little treasure," and Brian started using this as a nickname for me while we were there.

In fact, everything about this family made me want children even more. I even thought there might be a chance I was pregnant, but when I spotted our first day there I knew we'd have to keep trying. I was disappointed but decided to be as active as possible while on the trip to keep my mind off my fertility.

The day before the guys raced, Karen and I rode part of the bike course. I was exhausted when we got back. My limbs were heavy and I just wanted to lie down. "I don't know why I'm so tired," I told her. "I can usually ride much farther than that."

"It's probably the travel," she said.

I went to our room, laid down on the bed, and instantly fell asleep. Brian woke me up around 7 p.m. to tell me everyone was going out to eat.

"There's no way I can go," I told him. Brian frowned and asked me to rally, but my body felt so heavy, like I had a weighted blanket on top of me. His shoulders drooped as he closed the door behind him, but in my heart, I knew I couldn't face being in a smoky German restaurant.

The day of the race, Karen and I followed Brian and Tom's progress which meant being on our feet most of the day. Again, by the end of the day, I fell into bed.

We traveled around Germany and Italy afterward. A couple of days after the race all four of us went on a mountain bike ride. What was supposed to be a short ride to town for coffee turned into an eight-hour adventure when Brian and Tom said they knew a different way to get back. We found ourselves on the back side of a mountain going through private farmland trying to get back to the inn. I was pushing my bike through the thick grass, just trying to stay upright. My body felt like a bowl of droopy, wet noodles.

When we did finally make it back, the kitchen had already closed, but the inn owner was kind and gave us leftovers—roast beef, potatoes, and strudel for dessert. The food looked great, but I had no appetite. While I picked at my plate, Brian sang, "Just sit back and I'll tell you a tale," and he didn't stop until he reached the line, "three-hour tour." As he and I laughed, Karen and Tom looked at each other and just shook their heads.

Upon returning to the States, I suffered from what I thought was jet lag. But on the third day home, I got very light-headed walking the dogs back to the house. As I got to our green gate, I paused a moment, realizing this was home. The possibility of raising children in this enchanted place once again dawned on me as my main goal. As soon as I got up to the master bathroom with its blue tile and wood cabinets, I pulled out a pregnancy test. Despite the spotting in Germany, at that moment, I held out hope. When two pink lines emerged, I thought I was hallucinating. My fatigue in Europe and extreme aversion to cigarette smoke made sense.

Brian was at work, and although I wanted to tell him in person, there was no way I could wait, so I called him.

"Are you sure?" he practically shouted.

Hanging up, my whole body buzzing with joy, I stood there gazing at the pink lines. I wandered downstairs and felt the warmth of the late July sun streaming into our living room and called my mom. "I have news," I said when she picked up.

"No." she answered, "You're not pregnant, are you?"

"Yes." And then I heard her scream in delight.

We had moved into our dream house and everything seemed on track. We commenced getting all the baby equipment we'd need. A crib (although I knew the baby was going to sleep in our bed at first), a changing table, and a rocking chair were the first items on my list. I certainly wasn't going to leave anything to the last minute.

I continued to run, bike, and swim my way through the first trimester, and still taught my classes at the university. Everything was perfect.

CHAPTER 12
Twelve-Hour Amnesia

Everything was perfect—until the accident on Sept. 11, 1997, when I was pregnant with Jade.

It turns out that an epidural left in for 10 days can have unintended consequences. At first, it helped with pain management, but the resulting infection caused horrific burning and heat internally. My heart rate spiked to above 160 while just lying in bed, and I literally wanted to die. If Brian hadn't been there to get the doctors to do something, I'm convinced I might have continued toward the white light.

Once they took out the epidural, the pain still needed to be managed, which meant inserting another epidural. But because I was already in such extreme pain, this proved to be challenging. I'm a small person, so the space between my discs is slight. The attendant trying to insert it had a very difficult time. It took them more than half a day to get my pain under control.

It was a good thing Brian was by my side the whole time for other reasons as well. He recalls that the nurses kept coming in wanting to take X-rays, forgetting that I was pregnant. He had to keep reminding them to at least put a shield over the baby when they did take one. This still causes him dismay when he thinks about it.

He also serves as my memory for the time in the hospital. Between the brain injury and the pain, my recall of events remains fuzzy. He talked to the doctors and got information about my prognosis. The doctors hoped for a full recovery from the brain injury, for example, based on where my skull was broken. The three fractures were at the base of my occiput, on the back of my skull. If it had been on the opposite side, in my frontal lobe, the outcome would have been quite different.

They also told him it was most likely my marathon-trained lungs that kept me and the baby alive since I was relying on one lung to do all the work of breathing for us both.

One week after the accident, I ventured out of my room in the ICU at

St. Anthony's Hospital in Denver for another daily walk as prescribed by my physical therapist. I held onto my IV stand for support, and with each step, it rolled forward. The fluorescent lights overhead twitched as the hallway loomed. The distance around the nurse's station had seemed impossible, but that day I made the full loop. No finish line tape to cross, but it felt like a huge accomplishment while simultaneously laughable because it was less than 100 feet total.

Watching from the entryway of my room, Brian was my cheerleader. When I made the full circle, he smiled and gently helped me back to bed. Wiped out by the short journey, I fell asleep instantly.

That afternoon, a neuropsychologist came to do testing. Balding with a beer belly, he wore a white coat and spectacles. "We're going to play a game," he said to me like I was in kindergarten. Then he pulled out cards like the memory game from my childhood. There were pictures of animals and shapes—rabbits and horses, squares and triangles—simple images I had to match after turning the cards back over. But I couldn't do it. Angry and frustrated, I was unable to distinguish whether it was the brain injury or the drugs that made me so incapable. I just wanted to scream and make the doctor with his smug attitude leave.

Based on the nature of the head injury, the doctor told Brian I should recover fully, but there were no guarantees. I ached for Brian, going from having a wife with a Ph.D. who taught at a university to one who couldn't do anything on her own. Despite my fuzzy thinking, I still had a general sense of what was going on around me, and I knew that Brian was suffering, too, even if he never lost his optimistic attitude. He had a constant smile on his face, was upbeat and laughing most of the time, and to this day, I am amazed at how he managed to do that.

The hospital walls, the color of dirty dishwater, started to close in on me. My room was small with only a lounge chair for one person to sit on, a small television mounted to the wall, and a tiny bathroom in the corner. My bed had pull-up gates on each side. It felt like a prison every time I was lying there, which was most of the time.

Brian stayed by my side every minute for two weeks, but friends finally convinced him to go out for a run. It felt like he was gone forever. I had gotten used to him being there, and it made me sad, but I knew he needed to get out for his own well-being.

When he got back his smile was all I needed. That and the Slurpee he brought me from 7-Eleven—one of the few things I craved. As committed to physical activity as I am, it was beyond imaginable that Brian would go two full weeks without any exercise. I have thought about this many times since, as I am certain I couldn't go that long. If our positions were reversed, I would have figured out some way to get out for a run. I'm not proud of this, but it's the truth.

Brian and I didn't talk much about the baby growing inside me during the time I was in the hospital. There was an unspoken vow between us that if we just dealt with my recovery, Miracle Baby, because that was the name we used post-accident, would be fine. To monitor the health of the baby I had several ultrasounds and during one, the nurse asked if we wanted to know the sex. "Yes," we both said simultaneously, looking at each other nervously.

"It looks like a girl," the nurse said.

Brian smiled and said, "Best news ever." I was happy, but couldn't bear the thought that she might have suffered due to the crash. So I directed my energy toward getting better. I told myself that it would be OK if I never ran again, if only the baby were healthy. At the time, I needed to give everything over to healing with the hope that the pregnancy would go well.

After what seemed like an eternity, the doctors gave me permission to go outside. Brian wheeled me to the elevator and then down to the lobby. As we went through the front door, I was so happy to be in the fresh air that I didn't even notice Tom and Karen standing outside with Norman and Remy. I had no idea they would be there and then the dogs were jumping up and down beside me, and Brian was trying to calm them down so they wouldn't knock me over. Being wheeled around Sloan's Lake with the dogs by my side was the closest to normal I had felt since the accident. It was still difficult to be dependent on others for basic needs, but the sun on my body was like a warm blanket, and as I savored the blue sky above, I found some joy in the moment.

Later in the day, I heard Brian talking to the doctors outside the door of my room. I only caught part of the conversation, but I could tell they were talking about sending me somewhere other than the Mapleton Center in

Boulder—the place that had the warm water therapy pool I'd used when I was dating Joe. I might not have been thinking clearly, but I knew in my gut the only way I was going to heal was in that water.

When Brian came back in, he told me the doctors wanted to send me to a place near St. Anthony's, I got so angry I started yelling. Brian tried to calm me down, and then one of the doctors came in, and I insisted that I *had* to go to Mapleton. He shrank away from me as if I were going to bite him, yet he did say he would see what he could do. Exhausted from the energy I used to make my voice heard, I sank into my bed. I felt fearful of what might happen and frustrated by my own inability to articulate what I needed in a calm way. The brain injury made it difficult to form complete sentences and being angry didn't help.

That evening we got the news that I would be going to the Mapleton Center upon my release in a couple of days. Again, I cried, but this time from relief.

The last few days at St. Anthony's, I had this nagging feeling I might never fully recover my faculties, never teach again, never run again. The sensation manifested at the back of my head, right at the base of my skull. Months later, I realized this was occurring precisely at the spot where my skull was fractured. The ache stayed with me for years.

Moving day was not easy. I was still in a lot of pain and unable to walk on my own. They put me in an ambulance and drove me north toward Boulder and the therapy hospital, my home for the next three and a half weeks. Despite the sunny warmth of the fall day, knowing I was about to enter another hospital made the air feel heavy.

As I was being transported toward the front door of the Mapleton Center, I glanced at the far end of the parking lot and saw the trail I had run to the summit of Mount Sanitas countless times. I recalled each run up and down the technical trails of this hallowed ground, back to the days when Brian and I would race each other to the top without a care in the world. I remembered the view from the top overlooking the whole town of Boulder and I wondered if I'd ever get up there again on my own two legs.

I felt a twinge of regret and anger thinking, *How is it possible that a few weeks ago I was hiking up this mountain and now I'm in a wheelchair?* But then, I told myself to shake it off. I was there to heal, to use the warm water pool, and that the sacred ground the hospital was built on would give me the energy I needed to get better.

During my first day at the rehab facility, I went off pain meds. No weaning. I simply stopped. The drugs were keeping me in a fog and not relieving the pain that much. In fact, after a few days off the morphine, it was as if a veil had lifted and the real me re-emerged. It turned out that Advil helped with the pain even more than the morphine, and I could see with more clarity and feel with more accuracy so that when I tried to move, yes it hurt, but the pain was sharper, more real. That sensation lit a fire under me to make a clear plan about how I was going to tackle the beast of recovery.

For the next three days, doctors and therapists poked and prodded me. No one mentioned the pool, and I was getting anxious to get started with what I considered the only real therapy. One of the reassuring moments happened when both of my OB doctors, Dr. Mako Shimado and Dr. Lisa Jamroz, came to visit. These two amazing women had their own obstetrics practice, and I was one of the lucky ones to be their patient. Brian was in the room with me when they stuck their heads in the doorway. I was delighted to see them. Their calm demeanor was all I needed to have confidence the pregnancy would go well. "You're going to be fine," Mako said.

"We are here for you all the way," Lisa chimed in. They didn't examine me that day, their only intent was to let me know they were aware of the accident and would do everything in their power to assure things went smoothly. It wasn't until years later during a routine exam that Mako told me how worried they both were—not so much about the baby, but more about me since I was very broken when they first saw me.

Nights continued to be difficult, and it was no better at Mapleton than at St. Anthony's. Sleep was simply elusive, and late-night television continued to be my friend. Reading was impossible due to my blurry vision, so I'm not kidding when I say *I Love Lucy* reruns saved my sanity. Watching Lucy and Ethel in the candy factory eating chocolate after chocolate made me smile; I tried not to laugh because of my broken ribs, but I laughed on the inside, and that was enough.

On the fourth morning, the nurse told me I had a pool session scheduled at noon, and for the first time in days, I felt hopeful. I couldn't move

without pain, so the idea of being weightless was so enticing that I smiled
in anticipation. Brian made sure he was there to take me to my first session.
He showed up early and helped me put on my suit which would have been
impossible for me to do alone. He wheeled me to the pool and let Diane, my
therapist, get me into the water while I was still in the chair. As she pushed me
down the ramp, I thought, *Never take anything for granted again.*

Diane gently held my body, so I was floating on the surface of the
warm water with no effort on my part. I became mesmerized by the
ripples as she slowly rotated me in a circle. Then she moved my limbs and
torso to help my muscles start to activate again. The treatment is called
Watsu. That day, even the slightest movement scared me because my
bones were so sensitive, but Diane told me it would get better with time. I
believed her because being weightless had already delivered my first pain-
free moments since the accident.

Brian came to have dinner with me, and afterward, he took me to the
whirlpool room—basically a closet with a medical whirlpool inside. It was
private so, for the very first time since the accident he and I were truly alone
without the watchful eye of nurses or visitors popping in unannounced. Brian
carefully helped me get into the tub, then got in with me even though it was
just about big enough for one person. He held me on his lap and stroked my
body. Within 15 minutes of this intimacy we got out, albeit awkwardly, and
had sex in the small space next to the tub. I was still in a ton of pain, but we
managed, and this after-dinner whirlpool room experience became a ritual
for us the rest of the time I was at Mapleton. I was feeling the weight of guilt,
of putting Brian through this ordeal, of the effect on the baby. Having sex,
giving Brian pleasure, took some of that heaviness off my shoulders. I needed
it as well, to feel close to my husband again.

Two days later I had my next Watsu session at 11 a.m. I told Brian
I would get ready on my own which meant an hour before I started the
process of putting on my suit. Getting out of bed took a full 10 minutes as I
braced myself to stand. The roundtrip of going to the bathroom and peeing
took another 15 minutes; 10 to 15 minutes just undressing, and 15 minutes
more to put the damn suit on. Pulling the straps over my shoulders was
almost impossible.

Once at the pool, Diane wheeled me into the water, and then she told
me she wanted me to try to walk on the bottom of the pool. I managed a

few steps before I needed to stop and hold on to the side. Then I tried again and made it across the shallow end of the pool holding onto the railing along the ramp. Diane applauded and said I had made huge progress in a short time. I appreciated her enthusiasm and support, and it carried me through the tougher days.

The next day, my friend Kelly was getting married in Boulder and I'd been given permission to go, but it was a bad pain day, so I told Brian there was no way. He called Kelly to tell her, and I cried from the physical pain as well as the emotional pain of not being able to go. Then I curled into my bed while Brian tried to cheer me up by telling me silly stories about him and his brother, Bill.

Later that afternoon, as the sun started dropping behind the mountain outside my window, I heard a commotion in the hallway, and in walked Kelly in her beautiful, white gown and flowing veil of lace. She was with her new husband and several friends. Looking like she'd been cut out of a bridal magazine, Kelly said, "We tried to party without you, but it just wasn't working so we decided to bring the party to you."

When a tear rolled down her cheek, I started crying all over again, but this time it wasn't from self-pity.

Like most things in life, my recovery from the accident didn't follow a linear process. The very nature of healing and recovery can often mean the body will relapse after pushing past a boundary. It's how improvement happens, but the body can react negatively at first. It's always about finding the balance between work and recovery.

While sitting in a chair getting prepared to go to the dining room for breakfast, I tried to stand to move to the wheelchair when a sensation like someone stabbing a knife into my pubic bone erupted. I screamed an ear-piercing scream. Brian had stopped by before work and wasn't sure what to do. He called for the nurse. She tried to help me by telling me to lie down, but that only made me panic when I thought about having to get up again. Any change in position was simply unbearable.

Up until then, my ribs had caused the most pain; lying in bed at night was excruciating, making sleep impossible. But once I began moving more, my broken sacrum and fractured pubic symphysis (where the pelvis and hips join at the bottom of the sacrum) made standing up from any position a prison of pain.

My pregnancy furthered the complications because even a normal pregnancy can result in dysfunction of the pubic symphysis when the release of hormones loosens a woman's ligaments. The pubic symphysis serves as a pivot point for almost all motion, but with fractures at both the front and back of my pelvis, it's no wonder such position changes had become so painful. This meant I lived in fear of the pain in the interim periods. If I were sitting, I'd get anxious knowing that sooner or later I'd have to get up to pee. If I was lying down, I knew at some point I'd need to get up to go to therapy. It amounted to psychological and physical torture.

Later that day, the head nurse came and told me they were stopping my pool sessions until I felt better. I got so mad that I, once again, resorted to a verbal outburst insisting that I needed my pool sessions. Brian had stayed with me instead of going to work, and he defused the situation by taking the nurse out in the hallway where he convinced her I'd be better off if I went to the pool. She agreed but said they would be closely monitoring me and wouldn't hesitate to cancel my water therapy. After Brian told me this, I started calling her Nurse Ratched. But, from that point on, no matter how much it hurt, I stifled any urge to scream.

I was 36 years old, 19 weeks pregnant, and surrounded by people twice my age who were mostly dealing with the effects of aging. More than once, I asked myself, *What am I doing here?* Gradually, I started to accept where I was, to recognize that pain comes in many forms, and recovery is not limited to just one age bracket. This wasn't easy, and I can't say I was good at it. But being at the rehab facility affected me for years to come, and is one reason why later in my life, I chose to focus on helping people with injuries.

A different neuropsychologist came in to do more testing. We played the memory game again, and lo and behold, I was able to see the matches right away. I surprised myself. It was like getting that gold star in elementary school as the doctor congratulated me on my progress.

The next few days, I found myself delighting in my time in the pool, looking out the massive windows that overlooked the forest between the hospital and the trails of Sanitas. The leaves were turning colors, and time was slipping by and standing still all at once. Each day was bringing with it more progress, but also a sameness that seemed to drag on and on.

One morning, waiting for Brian to arrive for breakfast, my doctor came in and said, "I think it's time for you to go home." My mind was racing, and I couldn't wait to tell Brian. But in the few minutes before he arrived, I started to feel even more nauseous than normal. W*as I ready to go home? Maybe I should stay a few more days? After all, I'm only a hallway away from the pool. If I go back up to the mountain house, how will I get here?*

Every possible scenario wove its way through my mind. When Brian finally arrived, I was almost unable to tell him the news. He assured me it would be OK and that he would take care of everything. But that didn't make sense with him working full-time.

I knew he had to work and I also knew how lucky we were. Our insurance covered all my expenses. Between my health insurance from the university and our car insurance, we had no debt. I didn't give this much thought at the time, and I guess took it for granted. I know that not having to worry about expenses was a huge advantage. I could get the therapy I needed without stress over money which allowed me to focus on healing.

Through my experience, I've come to realize the inequity that exists in our healthcare system. It's why I am a proponent of universal healthcare. No one should have to worry about paying for treatment if they're in a catastrophic accident or have a disease.

CHAPTER 13
Homecoming

After 40 minutes in the car, we came to the green gate at the top of our driveway, still a quarter-mile from the front door. A warm feeling formed in my belly just seeing it because that green gate is the signal after every run, hike, or bike ride that I'm finally home.

Brian had built a ramp at the front of our house for my wheelchair. I couldn't walk upstairs, so he'd acquired a hospital bed for the guest room on the main floor. I also had one of those seats that go over the toilet and a hospital chair to use in the shower. But it felt so good to be back, I tried not to think about what I couldn't do and focused instead on being back in the mountains and getting to be with Remy and Norman again.

The drive had exhausted me. I laid down on the bed with the dogs lying on either side of me. Brian worried they would be too rough, but I wanted them near me. When I woke up, the light was just beginning to dim outside. Brian helped me get to the living room where I could look out the windows and see the forest that surrounded our house. In the meadow, I saw our neighbors' horses running free and derived a sense of peace and hope.

I placed my palms on my belly and infused the baby growing inside with the tranquility of coming home and the optimism this view had given me.

I got out of bed the next morning with less discomfort than ever. I used the walker to get to the toilet as the dogs followed my every move. There wasn't enough room in our small downstairs bathroom, so the dogs hovered by the door. I was now 21 weeks pregnant and having to pee more than ever. I started to have my normal feeling of terror at the thought of standing up, but that morning it didn't cause the usual sharp cutting sensation. Instead, I could stand without wanting to cry in pain. Just being in my own home gave me a sense of calm that I'd sorely missed at the hospital.

Within a week, I was able to give up the walker while inside the house. It was as satisfying as winning a race. When my friend Wendy came to visit, I was determined to walk the full quarter-mile to the end of our driveway with her. Wendy was someone I knew from the athletic world, so sitting around and just talking was not going to be enough for me—I needed to make it to the green gate. Wendy was the epitome of health with her lean body, long blond hair, and sun-kissed face. She exuded energy and optimism. She tried to encourage me and not show how shocked she was to see me so weak. I wanted to show her and myself that I could do this.

I thought back to the days when she and I would run and compete without a care in the world and used that as fuel to propel me. The driveway starts at the green gate and descends into our property through a nest of trees on either side. Reaching the gate meant walking uphill. It's a gradual ascent, but on this first venture, it felt like a mountain.

The dogs frolicked alongside us, crisscrossing the driveway about a hundred times as I slowly made my way. "I bet the dogs are wondering why this is taking so long!" I said, and Wendy grinned at me. The sun was shining, and the air had a crispness to it, on the verge of being cold. When I reached the gate, there wasn't confetti falling from the sky, but there may as well have been.

Two days later, I walked the dogs a full mile. This progress became a drug for me as I kept trying to increase my physical stamina. I came up with a schedule that included cardio and exercises I could do at home alternating with days in town at the pool. This involved a team of friends who would take turns driving me to town and back. The fears I had about it working out floated away.

I was so glad we'd bought a treadmill when we moved to the mountains. Initially, I wanted it for days when it was too snowy to run outside, but now it was critical to my recovery. I could walk on it at a steady pace without worrying about road conditions. Each day I got a little stronger. By mid-November, I was up to walking an hour and covering three miles, which translated to 10 in my mind.

The pool continued to be a huge part of my process, too, and soon I was able to swim a lap of backstroke. Although it should be noted that the length of this pool was only about 15 yards. As I alternated my arms back and over my head, I marveled at how my body had healed. When I finished that one lap of the pool, I held onto the edge, basking in the knowledge I had done something that just recently had seemed impossible.

After I finished my swim, I had a Watsu session with Diane, and the combination harkened back to the days I used to do two sessions of exercise back-to-back like a run/swim, and the sense of satisfaction filled the gaping hole that had formed since the accident.

Being pregnant during my recovery brought a lot of stress and additional complications. We'd head to the doctor's office for ultrasounds every few weeks, which I thought was part of all prenatal care. As Brian and I looked at the fuzzy picture, the tech pointed out her head and torso. But then the doctor came in and said there was a slight issue.

"I don't want you to worry," she said, "but, we see a small concern with the baby's left foot." It was unclear how severe, but they soon determined it was a club foot.

I learned that clubfoot can be a sign of serious problems such as cerebral palsy, yet there were no other troubling markers the doctors mentioned. I still felt anxious. A conversation in my mind went like this:

Worried me: *If the accident hadn't happened, you wouldn't be dealing with this now.*

Practical me: *But the doctors say club feet are congenital and have nothing to do with anything that happens during the pregnancy.*

Worried me: *But how do you know for sure?*

Practical me: *You need to stop thinking like this. There isn't anything you can do except be prepared.*

So I tried to find all the information on club feet available and learned that Dr. Robert Eilert was not only considered the nation's expert on the condition but that he just so happened to work at Children's Hospital in Denver, only a 30-minute drive from Boulder. I called him right away.

On the phone, he sounded reassuring and also intrigued that we knew about the condition while the baby was in-utero. He agreed to see her as soon as she was born.

Besides spending my time researching club feet, I was also reading every book I could find on parenting. *The Girlfriend's Guide to Surviving the First Year of Motherhood* by Vicki Iovine became my bedside companion.

One night in mid-November, I finished it and read the author's bio at the back. One of her daughters was named Jade, and I turned to Brian half-asleep next to me, and asked "What about Jade for a name?" He mumbled back that it sounded fine to him.

I loved how unusual the name was, but I also needed to know more before I named my firstborn. In Chinese tradition, jade symbolizes "protection from accident." That clinched the deal for me. Later when Brian was coherent, he totally agreed. We both knew there was no other option.

November 19, my birthday arrived, and I was six months pregnant and happy to be alive. But in 37 years on the planet, it'd never been my preference to have a party or celebrate with anything lavish, so I made sure Brian kept it low-key. We met our friends, Rob and Lynn, whom we knew from masters swimming, at an Italian restaurant at the base of Boulder Canyon.

Walking in from the cold, dark evening to the intimate, warm atmosphere was a welcome treat. The lights were dim, and candles at each table cast a glow on the walls. The waiter brought us the customary garlic rolls—big, crusty knots of bread that are soft on the inside. I nibbled on one as Rob and Lynn spoke lovingly about their 1-year-old daughter, Ali. The biggest gift they gave me that night was not to bring up my accident and injuries. We simply talked about the joys and trials of parenting. It was the first time since the accident I wasn't consumed by the trauma narrative.

More snow arrived in the mountains that month, and Brian started cross-country skiing. I was jealous—I'd normally be going with him. But there was no sense dwelling on it. Instead, I focused on my goal of going to full term with the pregnancy.

When he left to ski, I got on the treadmill to work out my emotions. Although I was feeling stronger every day, there were still no guarantees about the health of the baby or how my body would hold up as the weeks went by. Moving allowed me to put those thoughts aside. Brian and I had an unspoken understanding between us that we would assume everything would go well, and we never discussed the alternative.

The following week at physical therapy, I was given the green light to lift weights. My sessions until then had mostly consisted of work in the pool.

Adding some resistance training was the next step toward getting strong enough to deliver this baby. Before my Watsu session, I went to the physical therapy room and did resistance work with bands and some light weights. Before the accident, I would have taken this for granted. Even though I couldn't handle much load, this session was a breakthrough.

With less and less pain each day, the main sensation that lingered was in my upper back where the scapula intersects the ribs. By the end of each day, this area ached to the point where I had a hard time sleeping. Swimming alleviated some of the pain and helped with the constant nausea. I knew morning sickness was a side effect of pregnancy, but I hadn't expected it to last the whole time.

Floating in the warm water of the therapy pool, gazing through the huge windows at the surrounding forest and Mount Sanitas, provided solace. Colorado gets so many sunny days that usually during my sessions the blue sky would reflect off the water in the pool, and the sun would literally sparkle through the trees.

In early January 1998, when I was 30 weeks pregnant, I was given permission by my doctors to travel. I decided to go visit my father and his wife in Scottsdale, Arizona, enticed by the idea of warm weather. I also wanted to spend time with my dad. I went by myself, which was scary, as I was still feeling vulnerable and weak. The effects of the brain injury had mostly lifted, but my thinking was still fuzzy, and I tired quickly during conversations. That said, I hoped a change of scenery would do me good, so on a Friday afternoon, Brian drove me to the airport. My flight was at 2 p.m., and I made sure we left Boulder by noon. This was before 9/11 and the security lines we've all come to know and hate. But my temperament demanded that I always get to the airport with time to spare.

But Brian is the kind of person who is forever late because he thinks he can cram 20 tasks into the time it would take to finish 10. I tried to focus on my breathing and not the clock when Brian pulled into some sort of warehouse. I had no idea what he was doing, but it turned out he thought he could manage a work errand on the way to the airport. "Brian," I said, "are you kidding me? Do you really need to do this right now?"

"It'll only take a minute," he said, as he continued around the back of the building looking for the guy he was supposed to meet. I paced by the side of the car. It was approaching 1 p.m., and I was getting more and more nervous as the minutes ticked by.

Finally, we got back on the highway and Brian was going faster than the speed limit, trying to make up time. You'd think after the car accident, I'd be terrified, but having no memory of the accident meant I had no associated fear.

Then I saw the flashing lights as we got pulled over. I was beyond annoyed and wanted to yell at Brian, but realized it wouldn't change anything. I tried to remain calm while seething. The cop saw my protruding belly, and when we told him we were headed to the airport, he let us go. Brian drove the speed limit the rest of the way, but this made me even more anxious as I thought I might miss my flight.

When I arrived at the gate, they had already started boarding. Once on the plane, I sank into my seat thankful to be headed somewhere warm where I'd see my father.

Dad was at the airport waiting for me, and when he saw me, his eyes crinkled the way they always did when he smiled. "Vicki!" he exclaimed and then he hugged me and gazed at my huge belly. "Wow!" he said, as if he had forgotten I was pregnant. Once outside in the desert climate, I finally relaxed. We drove to the condo he and his wife, Jane, were renting at Gainey Ranch Golf Club in Scottsdale. The entire place was white, from the walls to the furniture, and reeked of newness. I was almost afraid to sit on the couch.

We did sit for a few minutes in their well-appointed living room before going out to dinner. Jane, impeccably dressed, her blond hair pulled back in a neat ponytail, asked how I was.

"Well, I can move without too much pain," I started to answer, but then I noticed both she and my father squirming in their seats. I think my reality was just too much for them to listen to, as it was so far removed from their perfect world.

It was strange to be with them at this point in my recovery. Sure, I was no longer in a wheelchair and could do almost everything I had done before, but they were so nonchalant about my condition—they were oblivious to how hard I had worked to even be there. Jane didn't have grandchildren yet and this wasn't going to be her biological grandchild, making for an even greater disconnect. But I was happy to be on a vacation so let it go and allowed Dad to spoil me.

Wherever Dad lived, he'd find the best places to go out to eat and would get to know the owners. Dad loved restaurants and good food. In my youth, when he took Wendi and me out on Tuesday nights, he never ate with us since we would only go to McDonald's. Afterward, he would go to a small tavern called Switchville where he would order a steak and a glass of wine.

There could be a line out the door but Dad was always able to get seated right away, even without a reservation. On my first night in Scottsdale, we went to an upscale Italian restaurant and the owner came over to our table throughout the evening as we enjoyed the homemade pasta.

The next day, I swam a mile in one of the several outdoor pools at the club. It was the ultimate luxury and remarkable to me given that a few months prior I couldn't swim a full lap. Dad sat in a lounge chair reading while I was in the pool. I told him I'd be fine if he wanted to leave, but I think he was nervous to leave me alone. I wasn't sure if it was because he was worried about me or because I was an unregistered guest. My dad was concerned about stuff like that, and I also suspected he didn't want to pay the guest fee if he officially signed me in.

On the fourth day, he drove me back to the airport, and I realized it was four months to the day since the accident. I was huge and looked like a cartoon character with stick legs and arms and a huge belly. "I think your belly grew while you were away," Brian said when he picked me up. "You look like you might burst."

Back home, I returned to my routine of physical therapy, swimming, Watsu, and weightlifting. On the days I stayed on the mountain, I'd walk on the treadmill or take the dogs outside, weather permitting. Besides my aching upper back at night, the constant nausea, and general fatigue, I was pleased to be able to move as much as I could, since only three months prior, I had been in a wheelchair.

One Saturday in early February, I told Brian I wanted to go snowshoeing. He questioned me at first but then knew better than to argue because if I said I wanted to go snowshoeing, I meant it. We headed to the local ski area. Eldora is super hilly, and no matter which way you go from the Nordic Center, it's up. Brian might have been concerned that snowshoeing was too much for me, but he let me go on my own while he skied. I headed out under sunny skies, bundled in a parka that ended up being way too warm.

With poles, I trudged up the side of the bunny hill. The snow wasn't too deep, but it took effort to lift each snowshoe and get to the top. My muscles ached from the effort. It wasn't painful except for the ever-present ache under my right scapula that, by this point, I assumed I would live with forever. I reached the trailhead for Jenny Creek, always a favorite because it's in the woods and civilization seems miles away even as skiers whiz by on the downhill section yards from the trail.

"Jade," I said, looking around and then at the slope that was my belly, "just wait, you and I will be skiing down this mountain in no time."

Surprisingly, the doctors cleared me to drive, and a month before my due date, I drove myself to physical therapy. Brian accompanied me just to make sure I was OK. He was clearly more worried about my driving than my snowshoeing on my own in the woods! But I had no fear, in this case, thanks to the twelve-hour amnesia. He, on the other hand, clutched the seat and was visibly tense, especially as we descended the steep curves of Magnolia Road.

My dad and Jane arrived in Boulder a few days before I was due to await the arrival of the baby. They stayed at the downtown Boulder Marriott, and because he was worried about me being in the mountains if I went into labor, Dad got a room at the hotel for Brian and me as well. I was happy to see my dad, but also so physically uncomfortable I wanted to crawl out of my skin. My heartburn was out of control, I had to pee every other minute, my belly itched and hurt at the same time, and to top it off, I started having contractions shortly after we got to the hotel. They weren't coming with any frequency, but I called my OB's office because I was increasingly uncomfortable. Dr. Shimado told me to relax and give it some more time.

But the contractions were painful, like someone was taking my insides and wringing them with their hands. I felt all twisted up, and even when I tried different positions, I found no relief. I'd try lying on the floor, curling up in a ball, squatting, but nothing helped.

Dad and Jane took us out to dinner for Chinese food that night, and I ordered a dish called "jade delight" thinking it might bring her out sooner. Of course, my belly was so uncomfortable I could only eat about three bites of the mild chicken and spinach dish. As much as I wanted more, my stomach had no room—the baby was literally occupying my entire being. Brian made up for it by eating everything I left on my plate.

I didn't sleep at all that night.

The next morning, Brian drove me to the therapy pool where I did a short session of aqua walking. He brought me back to the hotel and then left to go to work for a couple of hours. But almost as soon as he left, I started getting stronger contractions.

I tried to lie down on the bed, but that only emphasized the weight of the baby on my sacrum. Less than an hour after he left, I called Brian and told him he needed to come back. I was curled up in a ball on the floor when he walked in. "This is unbearable," I told him. My water hadn't broken, but the contractions were painful, and my back was aching.

"OK, let's head to the hospital," he said, "I'll call Mako."

I wonder if the memories of pain from the accident triggered a sympathetic response in my nervous system because of how afraid I was of what was to come. Fear only heightens the panic. I tried to breathe through it and employ other techniques from the birthing books, but it was impossible for me to relax. All I knew was I couldn't handle more. I didn't even think to call my mom, who had also come to Denver to await Jade's arrival. I was just focused on wanting to get the baby out.

I was miserable, but Brian being Brian stopped at Moe's Bagels just across the street from Boulder Community Hospital so he could get food. "Really, Brian?" I pleaded, "Can't you wait?"

"It won't take long," came the old refrain. Once again, I found myself pacing outside the car while waiting for him. I wasn't having active contractions at that moment, but my belly felt as tight as a drum, accentuating the twisted sensation inside.

It seemed like forever, but we finally made it to the hospital and into a room. There was only one main hospital in Boulder at the time, old and outdated. My discomfort level rose by the minute. The mental anguish that followed caught me off-guard. Suddenly, I was back in the ICU at St. Anthony's with no control over my pain.

Confused by the onslaught of emotions washing over me, I just wanted it to end. I needed it to stop. But I also really wanted to try for a vaginal birth. Brian, ever upbeat, was trying to keep me distracted by talking a lot, asking me what he could do and trying to be funny. But it just became annoying.

Mako met us shortly after we arrived and determined I was only dilated about a centimeter, a number that was beyond disappointing to hear. *How could I only be one centimeter when the contractions were so intense?* I questioned to myself. *If I could barely handle this stage of labor, how would I be able to survive the rest?*

I think I was on high alert, and every pain sensation I'd had over the last six months came washing back over me. The beginning of labor was just a tick, but it pushed me over the edge.

Mako broke my water to progress labor. "You've been through enough," she said. "Let's get this going." I quickly dilated to five centimeters, but the pain intensified. I felt like I had a huge cement block sitting atop my sacrum, putting added pressure on the pain that already radiated there.

I had read about water births, so Brian filled up the tub in the bathroom and I got in, but it didn't help. I was momentarily annoyed. Everyone talked about the miracle of birthing underwater, but it did nothing to ease my labor, so I begged for an epidural. All I could remember about epidurals was the infection I ended up with after the accident. But this time, the pain subsided, and I sank into the bed praising modern medicine.

However, the painkiller slowed progress, and with labor stalled, I stayed at five centimeters for several hours. Even after they gave me oxytocin to try to ripen the cervix and resume labor, I was stuck. Around midnight, Dr. Shimado came into the room and announced, "Let's get that baby out." I didn't argue.

As they prepared me for surgery, Brian was smiling and charming the nurses with his goofy ways. He simply had to open his mouth and they would laugh. Brian later told me he was slightly worried about me going under the knife, but also relieved that we were moving on.

I, on the other hand, wasn't nervous at all. Part of me had known a vaginal birth was going to be challenging, and perhaps I'd known deep down that it'd be impossible. There was no real disappointment. After all, my pubic symphysis—the very center of my body—had fractured. It didn't surprise me that I couldn't bear the stress of a vaginal delivery. All I wanted was to have a healthy baby in my arms.

They didn't put me to sleep, and I was grateful to still get to witness and be a part of the birth. I'd feared being put under, like my mother had been for all five of her births. The drug back then called Twilight, a mixture of morphine and scopolamine, caused women to forget the entire experience. Instead, I received a simple local anesthetic combined with the epidural. All I felt was some tugging as they pulled her out of me.

As I lay on the operating table, Brian by my side, I could see the doctors working behind a sheet. I had a strange sensation that Jade wasn't ready. Maybe I should have let her gestate longer, but at the time, I needed my body back. Maybe that's at the root of Jade's personality. To this day, when she's ready to tackle something, she does so with brute force. But if she's not ready she'll resist like an oak tree rooted in the ground.

Nevertheless, at 2 a.m., Jade Lee Hunter came into the world. (Lee was my Nana's middle name.) Though being pregnant made my accident and injuries more serious, the hormones created by the pregnancy helped my body heal. The new life inside me made me want to go on with my own.

With Jade's birth, I became full in a way I'd never been before. At the same time, I was also hungry for actual food for the first time in nine months, an unanticipated gift. It was the middle of the night so there wasn't much available, but for breakfast the next morning I ate eggs, toast, and vanilla pudding from the hospital cafeteria—it tasted like it came from the Ritz Carlton.

Brian had called my mom and Linda as soon as he could to let them know all had gone well. They came to the hospital later that day after my dad and Jane had visited.

Just as he'd promised he would do, Dr. Eilert came to the hospital to examine Jade's clubfoot. Brian and I didn't even blink when we saw the foot that was curled up in and on itself, resembling a fist more than a foot, perhaps because we already knew. But everything else about her was fine, and our focus was the miracle of Jade, her 10 toes, her 10 fingers, her perfect nose, her porcelain skin. Dr. Eilert put a cast on her that very day, the earliest he had ever done so on a child.

She took to my breast right away and it was the most satisfying sensation I'd ever had. Because of the C-section, I stayed in the hospital for four days. Nurses and visitors pampered me. I was content to lie around and breastfeed Jade while eating macaroni and cheese from the cafeteria and brownies friends brought when they visited. Then the day came to go home, and I started feeling nervous about the prospect of taking care of this infant on my own.

I wasn't worried about the immediate future since Brian had taken two weeks' leave from work, and his mom and stepdad were coming to stay with us the second week. It was more about the unknown: *How would we know if something was wrong? What if she stopped breathing at night? What if she got sick?* But then my euphoria would surge forth again and I'd go back to marveling at all the gifts that accompanied Jade's arrival to the world.

As Brian and I strapped Jade into her car seat and then started the drive, my body tensed with anticipation. She fell asleep right away, and this would be her pattern in most car rides while she was an infant. Arriving at the top of Magnolia, we drove by the ponderosa pine, now even more crooked than before, and Brian said, "There's your tree." Admiring the strong trunk, I acknowledged that this tree likely stopped the car from rolling over and bursting into flames. When Jade was old enough to understand, we would tell her that it was our tree, and she too would express gratitude. "Thank you, tree," she'd say every time we drove by.

Brian made the last left-hand turn onto our private road, the sun shining through the bare aspens on the side of the road. When we reached the green gate, I let out the breath I didn't realize I'd even been holding. At the bottom of the driveway, the house appeared like an oasis away from the hustle and bustle of town. For the next two weeks, we had the luxury of being home, sharing parenting. There was nothing to do but make sure Jade was fed, dry, and warm.

Jade slept in our bed. I had read about attachment parenting and not only did it make sense to keep the baby close, I also didn't want to let her out of my sight. When she'd wake up in the middle of the night to feed, Brian would change her diaper and then bring her back to me singing, "going to the booby, going to the booby," and we'd both be giddy with laughter. I'd gaze at her round face and pug nose, wondering how such a beautiful being came out of me. Then we'd all fall blissfully back to sleep. Night after night, we repeated this family ceremony for months, the joy radiating throughout our home like a shield against the outside world.

CHAPTER 14

The Athlete and Competitor Resurfaces

A week after we got home from the hospital, we were back in the car driving to Denver for Jade's first official appointment with Dr. Eilert. My thoughts about whether the accident had contributed to Jade's clubfoot returned, and I wondered how the months of treatment that lay ahead for her would go.

We parked on the street, put Jade in the stroller, and as we went through the front doors, it was like walking into a sanctuary for parents of kids who needed help. The lobby was painted in vivid colors, and murals on the walls depicted rainbows and balloons. There were play areas scattered throughout the hospital, and I pictured an older Jade playing on one of the structures.

On this first visit, I was thinking about what Dr. Eilert would recommend and what it would mean for all of us. As we waited, I noticed older children with casts and crutches in the waiting room. After about 20 minutes, we were taken to an examination room and Dr. Eilert, all six-feet-three-inches of him, strode into the room and sat down with a big smile like a gentle giant. "Let's see how Jade's doing with that cast." He took the cast off and looked pleased with her progress. "I think this is going to work," he said. "We're going to do serial casting every two weeks for the next few months."

Part of me was happy that he saw progress and part of me was thinking about the drive. Every two weeks, three hours roundtrip, plus the appointment meant a five-hour expedition. I admit it, one of my first thoughts was: *What would it mean for my morning runs?* I quickly readjusted because I'd do anything if it meant it would help Jade.

By the time Jade was three weeks old, I was back on cross-country skis. And though I breastfed until she was 15 months old, it didn't take long to resume my old habits. A typical non-workday began with an hour-long run before Brian left for work. Brian always supported this because he knew if I didn't go, I'd be impossible to be around. Of course, despite being able to run most days, it usually wasn't enough for me and I'd need to swim, too. So, three to four days a week, after running, I'd get Jade ready and we'd drive the 45 minutes to Boulder.

When she was six months old, we joined RallySport, a centrally located health club, because daycare was included in the membership. Prior to having Jade, we used the city recreation centers, but childcare was first-come-first-served and wasn't guaranteed. I didn't want to drive down the mountain only to be turned away.

The post-accident injuries and pain had mostly resolved, but I still had many imbalances in my body caused by all the broken bones and subsequent misalignment. This didn't stop me from getting right back into running and swimming almost daily. I think this helped me get stronger, but it also prolonged some of the issues I was having, like a sore scapula, aching feet, and a chronically tight hamstring.

I also did therapeutic yoga and continued Watsu for a short time, but I was more concerned with Jade and made her appointments the priority. She was deemed hypotonic, meaning she had low muscle tone. She had occupational therapy twice a week for a couple of years to help her muscles develop as this is important for joint control. Often, after her sessions, I'd take her swimming in the warm water pool, and it became part of our routine. Along with the bi-weekly trips to Children's Hospital, our schedule was full, and my own therapy took a back seat. But because I could run, I wasn't that concerned about my own pain.

Jade was five months old when I ran my first post-accident trail race. I chose one that Brian and I had done before, an eight-mile loop through the woods outside of Idaho Springs. No surprise, I ran a slower time, but I was ecstatic to toe the line. Brian agreed to watch Jade while I raced. I expected they would be at the finish and as I neared the end, I was looking forward to seeing her. I also seriously needed to unload the milk collecting in my boobs. But as I crossed the line, they were nowhere to be seen. I looked everywhere and then thought to start hiking backward on the course. Sure enough, after about a mile, Brian was hiking down the trail with Jade in a carrier on his front. She was crying and I was furious. "Brian," I hissed, trying not to further agitate Jade, "Where have you been?"

"Just out hiking," he responded.

"You didn't think I'd want to see the baby at the finish line?" I asked.

"Well," he sputtered, "sure, but I wanted to take her for a walk."

"Oh," I said as I figured it out, "so you had to do the whole course?"

"Yeah, I guess," he admitted. Brian, of course, made light of the whole thing. As soon as I fed Jade and she calmed down, I forgave him, but part of me was still upset that he hadn't been at the finish.

But a fire had been lit, and I turned my thoughts to the next races I wanted to do, including Pikes Peak Marathon, the race I defined myself by prior to getting pregnant. I realized that it was going to take some time to get back to that level of fitness and strength, so I committed to doing shorter races for a while. Besides, Brian and I wanted to have a second child, and training for Pikes Peak could potentially disrupt those plans, so I waited.

Thankful I had a career that I could go back to, I eventually returned to work. My concerns about not ever being able to teach again seemed a distant memory. I had both my mind and my health back. I taught two days a week and could manage office hours and class time in a five-hour block in the afternoons. My niece, Jenny, Linda's youngest, was a freshman at CU, and she watched Jade those two afternoons.

Of course, I had to get my workout in, so Jade and I would go to Rally in the morning. I'd breastfeed, then swing by Jenny's dorm on my way to the office and pass off Jade to Jenny. Her friends would meet us out front and coo and ah at Jade, as Jenny took the baby and the stroller loaded down with baby gear. Jade became the dorm mascot for those few months that first semester I went back to work.

Most of the early trips down to Children's Hospital have faded in my memory, but I do remember the first time I took Jade alone, so Brian wouldn't miss half a day of work. It was in early fall and the weather was perfect. As I drove down Boulder Canyon and got on Highway 36, I hoped I wouldn't miss the Denver exit. When Brian drove, I didn't pay attention—I always focused on Jade in the back in her car seat. Relying on myself to get there made me tense. With no Google Maps to guide me, I was afraid to glance at my written directions while trying to keep my eyes on the road.

When I successfully made it and had parked the car, I sighed and gave myself a little pat on the back as I realized I was almost back to the old Vicki who wasn't afraid to do things on her own.

Brian and I waited until Jade was 18 months old before we started trying to get pregnant again. I was approaching 40 and we weren't sure how difficult it would be. I had never been pregnant before Jade and had a history of an irregular menstrual cycle my whole life, so we had some fears it wouldn't happen easily. I know how lucky we are that it took only four months.

The nine months with Jessi in my belly were so calm there isn't much to report, but her conception story is worth telling. Brian and I had left Jade in the care of a babysitter while we went cross-country skiing. It was a weekday morning and the ski area was relatively quiet. We found ourselves at the bottom of Dead Man's Gulch and with no one around we went off trail and had sex. I didn't even take off my skis. I was able to pinpoint this as the day we conceived once I found out I was pregnant.

I kept running and even did a sprint triathlon when I was seven months along. It was in Louisville, just outside Boulder, and Brian and Jade cheered me on as I swam in a pool, biked 12 miles, and ran three. I got some funny looks because my belly was huge, and at the time, it was not a common sight to see. But I loved every second of it.

I remember asking my doctor about having more ultrasounds after the first one and she said it wasn't necessary. I'd had so many with Jade, I assumed it was standard procedure, but obviously, they had been ultra-cautious monitoring her development because of the accident.

Finally, right after Thanksgiving in 2000, Jessi Rose (named after my great-grandmother) came into the world. She was a big baby, and with my pelvic trauma, we opted for a scheduled C-section.

Someone once told us that two children are not simply twice as many as one—it's more like four times. This bore out as incredibly true for me. I love order, so I felt challenged from day one.

Running kept me sane, but when Jessi was about six months old, I developed a foot injury that wouldn't heal. My friend Pam suggested I go to her craniosacral therapist, Rich Nuzzi, to help with this stubborn injury. The concept sounded really far out there; from what I understood, the practitioner merely held your head or sacrum, and this was supposed to make changes in your body. I had been seeing podiatrists and physical therapists with no luck, so I figured I might as well try it.

Rich instructed me to lie down on my back on the table in one of two small treatment rooms. Then he put his hands under my sacrum for at least 10 minutes before moving to my skull where he did the same thing. It was so relaxing I almost fell asleep, but it didn't seem like he was *doing* anything. He held my foot for a bit, and that was it. He told me to come back the following week. Despite my initial skepticism, and the expense not covered by insurance, I went back. After three sessions my foot was cured.

Fast forward to 2001, and the life of a harried mother whose main concern is getting in her workout. Jade was 4 and Jessi was 1. I remember a particular day with them both in the backseat of my Subaru. Jessi was crying, slobber dripping from her mouth, and Jade was shouting. We were venturing home from RallySport but still had to make the trek up Magnolia Road from Boulder.

I don't remember anything specific that caused them to be upset, but Jessi's crying agitated Jade, and Jade's shouting made Jessi cry more. It was like a seesaw, and we never seemed to be in balance, especially in the car. This was what we endured four days a week, so I could get my pool fix as well as some time with other adults. Otherwise, it was just me and the kids in the mountains for the entire day, and I just wasn't cut out for that.

I pulled over at the edge of the canyon on a side street, got out of the car, and screamed. There was no one around, thankfully, because if someone had seen me at that moment, they might have called the cops on the crazy lady losing her mind with her children trapped inside a station wagon. I tried to take some deep breaths. I didn't want to yell at them, but I was trembling with anger and frustration.

In fact, by that point, I was crying, too. I had dragged both kids into town so I could swim, even though it would have made more sense to just stay at home given how Jessi was teething and Jade didn't have preschool that day. But the idea of not getting in the pool was not a possibility. I needed the movement in the water for my body, but also for my emotional self. I worried more about missing my swim than how I'd react to their meltdowns.

But the effect of the swim hadn't lasted. Even outside the car, I could hear the girls in the back seat.

"I hate my life," I said out loud as guilt overwhelmed me in waves of cold shame.

I looked at them as if they existed in some other universe separate from me, but, of course, they were part of me, and their discomfort was mine as well. Faces wet with tears, I wanted to make them feel better. I did. Yet I also wanted to run away.

To assuage my guilt, I stopped the car halfway up the mountain and let the girls out to explore one of the many trails on the side of the road. This was just as much for me as them, and at least it broke up the drive.

I came to the full realization that afternoon just how much I resented the daily tedium of taking care of small children. The drive up the mountain and the isolation once home were making me miserable.

The post-accident, postpartum happiness of Jade's birth was a distant memory. As much as I'd longed for motherhood, my drive to perform, to move, to be an athlete was still an integral part of my being. I'd already completely lost the lesson of the accident—to slow down and savor the moment.

Any parent can relate to this: the early years of raising children are exhausting. Their physical needs are endless. One day after leaving RallySport we headed to Whole Foods, which was probably a mistake, given how tired and hungry the girls already were. But I wanted my daily shot of wheatgrass, so we went. I ordered a smoothie, thinking it would be my lunch, but both girls wanted it and my attempt to not make a scene could only happen if I gave it to them. But Jessi was only 1, and holding a full smoothie was not going to end well. Sure enough, it ended up on the floor, a giant mess of purple goop. Again, I wanted to cry.

My impatient personality coupled with my competitive drive pushed me right back into the "go, go, go" mentality even though young children can't and shouldn't have to put up with that. Looking back at those early years of my kids' lives, I see how I went from being pregnant to a full-time schedule that included a lot of endurance exercise, on top of the already full-time schedule of a stay-at-home mom who also worked outside the home.

It wasn't only me. Brian had the same need. Most of our dates involved physical activity because this brought us both a great deal of joy and helped us deal with negative emotions—the "I hate my life" moments. But it wasn't the same for Brian. He didn't share the same day-to-day monotony I experienced because he got to go to work every day. Though I was working two days a week, I was responsible for driving the kids down the mountain and picking Jade up from preschool. My only real breaks were those two hours of childcare I had at RallySport. My sanity depended on that time.

One day, I was getting the girls ready to leave for town when I noticed Jessi's eye looked a little red. I used a warm washcloth to wipe the crusted yellow stuck to the corner of her eye, convincing myself it was just leftover from sleep. She wasn't acting sick, I told myself. After dropping Jade at the Children's Center on the CU campus where she attended a preschool program, Jessi and I headed to Rally where I dropped her off at the childcare room. As I was about to start my swim, the head of the daycare came out to the pool to tell me I had to get Jessi because she had pinkeye. I started to cry.

"What's wrong?" Serena asked, "Are you OK?" I knew I couldn't tell her I was upset because I was going to miss my workout—she'd think I was absurd.

"Oh, nothing," I finally managed to answer in a quivering voice. "I'm just upset Jessi isn't feeling well."

My mind, I realize now, needed that physical exertion more than my body did.

And then came 9/11. The sun was coming up in the mountains, and I'd already run because Jade had an appointment at Children's at 9:30 a.m. Brian was getting ready to head off to work. Strangely enough, I had the television on, which was not usual, but I suppose I was trying to keep the girls occupied. Brian was in the kitchen, preparing Jessi's sippy cup, which she never went anywhere without. I was gathering toys and diapers for the trip to Denver when we saw a news flash, something about a plane crash. It was still early so the newscaster didn't say much else. Brian sensed something though and said, "I'm coming with you."

"OK," I said. "But I'm sure it's no big deal, this is all happening in New York."

By the time we had radio service in the car, reports were coming in that it might be a terrorist attack, but there was still nothing official. I called the doctor's office and was assured we'd still be seen, so we continued. Walking into the lobby, Brian and I noticed how quiet it was as those few patients and families that were there had their eyes glued to the small television on the wall.

We asked someone what was going on, but no one knew anything concrete. I still thought it was a far-off incident that would have no impact on us all the way out in Colorado. All I was thinking about was making sure Jade had her appointment so the next cast could be applied, with the hope that this was going to straighten out her foot. Then we could say we had fixed it. I wasn't sure casting was the right thing, but I wanted to believe it was, so I put all my energy into making sure we stayed on track.

The whole time in the doctor's office was like being in a bubble. No one had any information, so we just continued the same routine. In fact, when we left, I had Brian drop me and the girls off at RallySport, so I could go to a class while he went to work.

This is single-minded Vicki at work. I wasn't the only one there, either. About 10 of us gathered in the group fitness room for our usual bout of strength and flexibility, and although we acknowledged what had transpired at the Twin Towers, we convinced ourselves there wasn't anything we could do. We might as well work out.

What I've noticed about myself over the years is that when I have a plan, it almost physically hurts if I don't complete it. That day, I needed to get Jade to the doctor, and I needed to go to my regularly scheduled class, otherwise, I'd feel a sense of failure.

After realizing the magnitude of what had happened, I questioned those needs. But I was grateful at the end of the day for having gotten them done.

In the weeks to follow, as the world processed the events, I took the time to appreciate my life and even the solitude of the mountains. I made sure I took the time each day to get the girls outside to play with no agenda other than watching them enjoy being children.

But it didn't last long.

Peggy Solomon (Nana) on her wedding day to Benjamin Golder, a U.S. Congressman from Philadelphia in 1930. This photo captures the elegance that my grandmother exhibited her entire life.

For me, this is an iconic photo of Nana (right), her sisters, and their mother, Etta Mastbaum. Taken in 1928 aboard ship, I assume they were returning from Europe. This is like many images I have seen of women in the 1920s, so it's interesting to me to see my own family dressed in this classic style.

This photo brings back memories of visiting Nana and Charlie at Rittenhouse Square and spending time in the trophy room drinking Shirley Temples. The trophies were from their many bridge tournament wins. It's not hard to see where my competitive gene comes from!

This photo, taken in the living room of their apartment on Rittenhouse Square, exemplifies my grandmother's and Charlie's relationship. They were a powerhouse couple in the bridge world, and their mutual respect for each other was always apparent. In addition, the Rodin sculpture in the background reminds me of my family's legacy.

My mother is pictured here on her wedding day to Bud Isenberg with her grandmother, Etta. This was taken in Philadelphia in 1950. My mother looks so young – with good reason! She was barely 20.

This is a picture of my older siblings and my parents at the wedding of my mother and my father. Pictured from left are Linda, my mom, Jody, my dad, and Jeff. What I appreciate about this picture is they appear as one happy family.

This is my mom and me outside my bunk at Camp Danbee. This was my first summer there, and I was unaware of the real trouble my parents' marriage was in. I'm assuming my father took this photo. I love my mom's smile and also that we are physically close.

In 1985, Sandy Koufax came to visit me at my mother's home outside of Philadelphia. My mom was so thrilled to have Sandy in her house because he was a hero to many Jewish people for how he stood up for his beliefs when he refused to play baseball on the High Holidays. She also thought he was really handsome, and I remember her being absolutely bubbly that day.

This is one of my favorite photos of my father and me. I felt so connected to him at the time this picture was taken – it was before I was married, and he was still the most important man in my life.

This photo is from October 1997, taken in the Mapleton rehabilitation center parking lot. Mount Sanitas is behind us, beckoning me. I hardly ever went outside in the weeks after the accident, so I'll always remember this day when Brian brought Remi and Norman, and we enjoyed the sunshine.

The dogs guarded a newborn Jade on our bed at the Magnolia house. This was a blissful time in our lives despite the challenges, including Jade's club foot and my ongoing back pain. We were extremely happy.

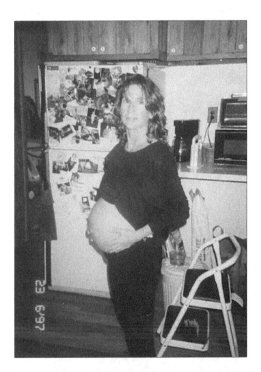

Shortly after this photo was taken in 2000, I stopped running until after Jessi was born. I was about 7½ months pregnant, and it was hard to run on land. While I'd been in the pool all along, I switched to only water running and swimming at this point.

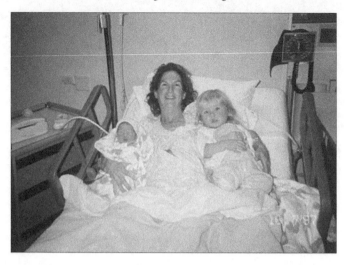

Here I am with both daughters in November 2000, shortly after Jessi was born. My mom had been taking care of Jade, and she brought her to the hospital. I love this photo because it captures the first time I had both girls in my arms. After a few days in the hospital recuperating from the C-section, we were packing for the drive home, and Jade looked up at me as I put Jessi in her car seat and said, "Wait, she's coming home with us?" Brian and I looked at each other and laughed, and I turned to Jade and said, "Yes, of course she is."

The girls loved to play dress-up, as this photo from the Magnolia house shows. This photo captures the essence of their big sister/little sister relationship when they were younger.

146

Happy times in the early years. This photo was taken on the front porch of the mountain house. We really were a unit in those days and spent many happy hours together.

This was taken at the mountain house and reminds me of the early years when we spent full days without ever getting in a car. The girls are wearing matching outfits that Brian's mom gave them. The girls call her Nana.

This is one of my favorite photos. It was taken when Jessi was in kindergarten, outside the school. It brings back the joy of those early years.

This was taken while we were in Florida visiting Mom a couple of years before she passed. We had been out at a restaurant, and she was still quite vibrant, so it was a good trip. From left: Jessi, me, Jade.

Brian took this photo of me finishing the Marquette 50-mile race in Michigan in summer 2015, and I love how strong I look. Plus, the girls were close by, cheering me on.

One of my favorite kinds of racing is cross-country, and here I am pictured with my teammates. From left: me, Stephanie, Lesia, Lisa, and Martha.

We tried to make the best of this trip to Cabo San Lucas. Although we look like a happy family, it was a tough trip, and the stress was getting to all of us.

This was taken in a shopping mall parking lot in late January 2016. Jade was staying at my sister Linda's house, and we met there while Linda facilitated a dog rescue. It's hard to believe how much Jade was struggling at this point.

150

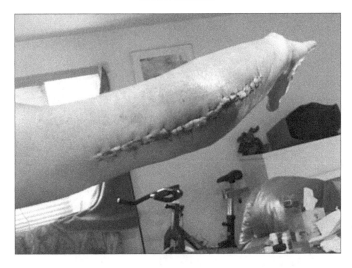

This picture was taken a couple of weeks after my second arm surgery which resulted in 20 screws and three plates. It looks bad and it was – this second surgery was hard to recover from. I like the photo, though, because it reminds me of what I went through and makes me appreciate being pain-free now.

Here I am on a trail run with my niece, Jenny, three years after I fell while running with her and broke my arm. I am so happy my prediction I would never run with her again did not come true.

We went on a family trip in the spring of 2017 to Kauai and had a fun time. The girls were in a good place, and Jade's recovery seemed on track. Through thick and thin, the girls are there for each other.

In the summer of 2017, we traveled to Kenya to visit my nephew Brian Ash, who was living there and doing nonprofit work. We stayed at the orphanage he was supporting and also went on safari and did some fun runs. This photo shows Brian and me doing a founder (the signature pose from Foundation Training) while out on a run. I love it because I am with my nephew and because of the ruggedness of the terrain.

Here I am on the start line of the half-marathon I did while in Kenya. It was an unusual race just outside the Maasai Mara National Park. At one point, I saw zebras crossing the road! I was the only woman to do the half-marathon, and each runner started individually. The men lined up behind me mostly finished in front of me.

I invited Jade to do a goat yoga class with me in Boulder. I was so happy she agreed to go, as this was still a period of time when she was quite withdrawn. The goats gave us both some joy that day.

Jade took this photo and was able to capture the goat standing on my back.

I had the great opportunity in 2019 to go to a retreat in Costa Rica with the Foundation Training team. Brian accompanied me. I am pictured here during one of the sessions that took place in this wonderful outdoor space.

Once again, Brian was there to support me while I ran with my friend Coco, who was training for the Leadville 100. I was one of her pacers, and this particular day we did a 30-mile adventure on some of the course. Brian drove me to Leadville, and while Coco and I ran, he went for a bike ride, meeting us in the quaint town of Twin Lakes, one of the major transition points in the race. He didn't blink when we said we were adding on to the run and would see him later.

I like to vary my training, and stand-up paddling is an enjoyable way to add balance work and mobility to a program. Adding Foundation Training to the mix makes it even more challenging, and here I am teaching a class.

This was taken in the summer of 2021 at our local running track. Jade wanted to join me for a workout, and nothing makes me happier than my girls wanting to run with me. I love this photo because we look so in sync with one another. Photo credit: Dave Albo.

Brian and I have found a new activity that we can share: pickleball. It has provided us with a fun pastime and also a great new group of friends.

Brian took this photo of Jade atop the Continental Divide. It shows her taking in the vastness of the wilderness and her connection to nature. She seems at one with her surroundings.

This is me on the way to the summit of Mount Audubon, one of my favorite peaks close to Boulder. It tops out at 13,000 feet, and it was one of my favorite training runs when getting ready for Pikes Peak. In this photo, I am hiking to the top, not running, but it still provided me with the same exhilarating feeling.

By the time Jessi was 2, I had decided I was going to run Pikes Peak again. I told myself it was because I wanted to see if I could be competitive, and that was part of it, but I also knew how much training time was necessary to run this race, and I saw that as an escape. Brian and I worked out the logistics of child care so we could train. And Pikes Peak became an annual event for our family.

The race takes place in Manitou Springs, an old mining town with a certain antiquated charm. When the girls were young, it was a fun family trip where we would stay in a cheap motel on the main strip in Manitou. The area at the base of Pikes Peak always reminded me of going to the boardwalk in Atlantic City as a kid with its penny arcade and amusement rides. The girls loved this part of the excursion, and we'd always take them there several times over the course of the weekend. Playing skeeball the night before the race was a ritual I'd started years earlier, and I considered it a good luck charm. Afterward, going to the arcade was the kids' prize for being so patient during the race.

In the early years, Brian also did the race and we'd get a sitter to come and watch the girls while we ran. Later, when it was only me racing because Brian's knees could no longer handle the impact, he would spend the day with the girls, and they'd all be at the finish line when I crossed.

I was usually in an almost delirious state at the finish. The effect of coming down from 14,000 feet and running hard was like a drug. During the race, I would focus on the sensation of putting one foot in front of the other, allowing me to let go of my day-to-day anxiety, one step at a time. The angst that first showed up at Camp Danbee my first summer in the form of severe stomach aches morphed into a sensation of tightness that would grip my whole body. I can only liken it to the sensation of holding on for dear life. I am sure the feeling of being out of control is what triggered this in my 10-year-old self. Being so far from home and having no idea what was going on with my family must have been frightening, but I never acknowledged feeling scared. Instead, I made myself sick to get the attention I craved.

As an adult, the physical release that occurred from running hard up and down Pikes Peak is what kept me coming back for more each year. That and placing well in the standings. The entire process was what held me in its clutches for so long. From training to thinking about strategy to race day, I was consumed by it for almost nine months out of the year. I'd start thinking about it the moment registration opened.

There were times during the race when my mind would wander, and I'd find myself going from flying down the trail to suddenly being on the ground. One year, at about the 18-mile mark where the terrain is rough with rocks everywhere, my toe caught a root, and I went flying like an out-of-control Superman. I slid for what felt like an eternity but managed to pop back up and continue down the steep trail. The fall had knocked the wind out of me, but it had the effect of a rocket booster being lit under my feet as they lightly hit the ground for the remainder of the race.

As I sat in the finish line medical tent getting cleaned up, the girls who had just been screaming, "Yay, Mommy," when I crossed the line were begging to go to the arcade. I was still high enough from the run that I said, "Of course!" Even though I was exhausted, my palms and elbows raw and bloody, and would have rather gone to the park to lay in the grass before the awards ceremony. In that moment, I was still able to tap into the feeling of freedom the race gave me.

During those hours I was running the race, I wouldn't think about anything else. Knowing that Brian was with the girls was enough to allow me to let go of my worries. But this feeling was always temporary. In fact, the high of a race for me is often followed by a complete letdown a few days later. The initial euphoria gives way to fatigue, and since I back off from training while recovering, the endorphins aren't accessible, making it a double whammy. It's as if the race never happened. Then I need to do it all over again to duplicate that high.

When registration for the 2012 race opened, I turned all my energy toward training, spending as much time running at altitude as I could. Three weeks prior to race day, Brian and I headed to the Indian Peaks to do one of our favorite 15-mile loops that traverses the Continental Divide. One of Brian's friends came along, and I was feeling amped that I could keep up until we got to the last few miles when they pulled away, racing each other on the steep, rocky terrain. I was pissed Brian had taken off and left me behind. With my anger fueling me to run faster, I decided I could catch them. But then in a split second, I turned my right ankle and heard the pop.

At first, I refused to believe it was that bad, but in minutes the ankle grew to the size of a grapefruit. I tried hobbling down the trail but couldn't put any weight on my right foot. I didn't make it 25 yards before I saw Brian coming back up the hill.

"Why did you take off and leave me?" I demanded but he didn't really have an answer. Even though I knew it wasn't his fault, at that moment I needed to blame him, otherwise, I would have had to take responsibility for my own competitive drive and the price I paid for it.

Over the next three weeks, I tried every therapy possible to speed the recovery of my ankle. Unwilling to let go of the idea of doing the race, I spent each waking moment trying to get my ankle to cooperate. I tried acupuncture, massage, and craniosacral therapy. I thought I had tried every method in the book, but then a chiropractor friend suggested dry needling. I trusted Lauren—this tall, Amazon of a woman with long brown hair, who was a great athlete herself—to make me better. As I sat on her table, watching her pull these long-ass needles out of her kit, I cringed. But then I gritted my teeth and told her to go for it.

"Oh my god, that hurts," I practically screamed, but holding out hope that something that hurt this much could be the answer, I swallowed the pain and let her continue. I had never experienced that kind of pain in a therapeutic setting before. Acupuncture needles are applied very differently—they're meant to stimulate meridians. But dry needling goes directly into the injured area to relieve inflammation and promote healing. I tried this a few more times in the weeks leading up to the race, despite the pain.

I water ran, and even though I didn't believe a higher power was going to intervene, I prayed my ankle would magically heal.

I also thought of every possible race scenario: I could run the ascent, which would avoid the impact of the downhill section. Or I could run the uphill portion of the marathon and then drop out at the top. I even contacted the race organizers to ask about switching to the ascent, but they said no. I was relentless, and I know Brian was beside himself because it was all I could talk or think about.

Finally, on the day before we'd have to drive down to Manitou if I were going to race, I came to the realization I had to let go. That it was OK to not do it. I was in such inner turmoil before that moment, but once I made the decision, a sense of relief filled my whole body, and it was as if I could breathe for the first time since I had sprained my ankle.

It was one of the hardest decisions I have had to make, and yet it was obvious to everyone but me that it had been my only choice. This would end up being a turning point in my competitive life as I never returned to Pikes Peak after that year. Once I made the decision, I never looked back, and the freedom to not train for that race in subsequent summers gave me a new lease on life.

Boulder has an open system of enrollment for primary and secondary schools which means children don't have to attend their neighborhood schools, rather families can apply to other schools based on focus or location. University Elementary was right across from the university, and they had an experiential track, making it perfect for Jade. That it was close to my work was a bonus, so we enrolled her there for kindergarten. She loved it and her teacher, Jimmy, who happened to be the brother of a good friend of mine.

But the drive up and down Magnolia Road was making me lose my mind. Brian loved the mountains. For him, being up there all day, every day was heaven. But for me, it was hell. Even though I had thought living in the mountains was my dream, it turned out I wasn't cut out for it. I hated the inaccessibility of daily necessities. I hated the drive. I hated the isolation.

In Jade's first year of kindergarten, I knew I needed a change, so we started renting a condo in Boulder where we stayed during the week. Then on weekends, we'd head back to the mountain house.

The day we signed the lease, the girls and I stopped at Target to pick up some cleaning supplies and then went straight to the condo. We walked in the door, and though there was no furniture, and it was a quarter of the size of our Magnolia house, I literally cried with joy. Jade and Jessi ran from room to room, and I was in total bliss knowing I didn't have a 40-minute drive ahead of me with them squirming in the back seat.

The hard part was my father.

"Hey, Dad," I said on the phone shortly after we had signed the lease. "We're living in town part-time to make weekdays easier getting to school for the girls and work for Brian and me."

"I don't understand," he replied. "Did you buy another house?"

"No, Dad, we're just renting for now."

He went on to say that it was fine, but advised against buying anything and that he would never think of owning two houses. He suggested that we just move, but I told him that wasn't what we wanted right now.

My mom, on the other hand, was ecstatic. She loved the idea of not having to even think about going to the mountain house and hoped we'd sell it as soon as possible and move into a real house in town.

For the next few years, we'd spend weekdays in town and weekends in the mountains. It was the perfect balance. I loved to play in the mountains, and two days up there to run and hike was ideal. The girls got to play in the woods, and all was well.

But I came to dread Thursdays because it meant I needed to start shopping for food for the entire weekend and pack items that we might not have at the mountain house. *Did the girls have their winter coats up there?* I'd ask myself. *Will I have enough food to last the weekend?* This drill started to wear on me and soon I was making excuses to Brian about why we could go for only one night.

"The girls have soccer on Saturday morning," I'd say to him. "It doesn't make any sense to drive up Friday, just to turn around and come back the next morning." He wouldn't argue even though all he wanted was to get up there.

When Jade finished kindergarten, we found out that her elementary school was changing, and the experiential program was being phased out. I was assured by the principal that Jade's class would continue as planned. But when I got the class list and there were only three girls, including Jade, out of 18 children, I was concerned. I thought I'd wait and see what transpired. The first day of school fell on a Friday, so I decided to go early to pick her up knowing we'd be heading up the hill anyway.

As I entered the classroom with Jessi in tow, there were little boys playing everywhere, literally throwing blocks across the room. I couldn't even see Jade, but then, in the back of the room on a couch in the corner, I found her curled up, asleep. I was horrified. I went and gently woke her up and said, "Get your things, Honey, we're leaving."

The teacher was busy trying to control some of the boys, and I saw one other girl on our way out. She appeared older than Jade and this made sense since they had combined grades to keep the experiential program afloat.

I marched straight to the principal's office and demanded to see her. While Jade and Jessi sat in the outer office, I confronted the woman who had promised me that the classroom would have more girls. "Unfortunately, enrollment just didn't go as planned."

"But you told me a week ago that there were more girls enrolled," I replied.

"Some parents pulled their kids," she said.

"I'm not leaving Jade in a classroom with 16 boys and only one other girl," I replied. "What are my options?"

She told me I could petition for a change of school, but I'd have to go to the superintendent. I demanded she call first to explain the situation. I told her that the only school I would accept was Boulder School for Integrated Studies, which was in our neighborhood. But it was a focus school, so you had to apply. Parents drove their kids from all over town to go there because of its experiential and arts focus. I could see the school from the front door of our condo, and I had often wished Jade went there instead of Uni Hill. I got the girls in the car and drove right over to the administrative building and filled out some paperwork. I asked how long it would be before I got an answer and was given an indefinite answer.

An hour later, driving up Magnolia, my phone rang. I was in the one place on the switchbacks where there was cell coverage, so I pulled over and answered. It was the school district telling me the petition had been approved. It was as if I had just won the jackpot. I screamed, "Yes!"

"What happened, Mommy?" Jade asked.

"You get to go to BCSIS," I told her, and because I seemed happy, she was too, but starting a new school is always scary.

On Monday when I took her, she held my hand tight. At the front office, the secretary told us to go down the hall to the farthest classroom where teacher Jen would greet us. And sure enough, a vibrant woman with shoulder-length brown hair and an infectious smile let us in. She held Jade around the shoulders and guided her into the room. Jade didn't even notice me leaving as the other children welcomed her into the space. I left the school with a huge weight lifted from my shoulders.

After a few years, the condo started feeling too small, so we looked for a house in the same neighborhood and found a nice four-bedroom home just minutes from the condo complex and still close to BCSIS. The house, a classic, bi-level 1970's red brick and wood-paneled home, had a beautiful cherry-blossom tree in the front yard. The girls were thrilled to each have their own rooms. The horrible yellow cabinets in the kitchen desperately needed updating and the tile was even worse. But I truly didn't care. The idea of having more space and remaining close to their school was key.

Until we lived in the mountains, I didn't realize how important being within walking distance to school was in my parenting philosophy. I remembered the independence I felt walking to elementary school, and I wanted that for my girls.

I ignored Dad's voice in my head saying, "Don't ever own two houses." Brian only wanted to make me happy, so he was going to do whatever it took to make this work financially and otherwise.

An older couple, Ron and Cathy, lived across the street and they were delighted that a family had moved in since their kids were grown and gone. There were a few other families with kids the same age as Jade and Jessi and they all went to BCSIS. Jessi found her best friend, Jack, who lived one street over, the first year we lived there. They were inseparable and it was commonplace for Jack to be at our house or Jessi to be at his.

That first fall, we even invited most of the block up to the Magnolia house so they could see where we escaped to every weekend. When they arrived, we all gathered in our dining area where I'd laid out brunch. It was a chilly but sunny day, and everyone was content to look out the windows at the open space.

Eventually, we all walked out to the horseshoe pit in a clearing a few hundred yards in front of the house. The kids ran around, and we all took turns playing the game. Looking back at the rustic but sizable house, Cathy said, "I can see why you like to come up here every weekend." I couldn't help but feel a surge of pride. This helped keep me hooked on dividing our time between the two houses. But Boulder was becoming more and more the place I wanted to be.

During the week, I had my same routine of running before Brian left for work. I reserved one day to hire a babysitter, who would come to the house at 6 a.m., so Brian and I could run together before he left for work. One winter day when the sitter was scheduled to come, there was a huge storm. Liza called to say she wasn't going to be able to get to our house. I told Liza that Brian would get her and bring her home afterward. Brian looked at me like I had two horns coming out of my head. Still, he did go pick her up and we got to do our run.

Being in town during the week and in the mountains on the weekends, even if it was just one day, was the perfect life, but I started noticing small changes in Brian. He was always working, always on the phone, always distracted. I wrote it off: "That's just Brian." It wasn't that he was a workaholic, more that he always had a million things going on at once, so it didn't faze me.

But my mother noticed, too, and she wasn't willing to just let it go. On one family trip to Mexico, we were heading back from dinner in Playa Del Carmen, strolling the promenade in front of the hotel. I was walking next to Mom, and Jade and Jessi were up ahead with their cousins. Jody and Linda were laughing about something while Jeff and his wife, Vivian, supervised the kids. Brian was about 30 yards in front of us closer to the entrance of our hotel, frantically talking on the phone. I could see him waving one arm but couldn't hear what he was saying.

"Why is Brian always on the phone?" Mom asked. "Can't he relax and be with the family?"

"Mom, he has a lot going on at work," I replied. But the truth is, I was also annoyed. His distraction seemed out of proportion to what I knew of his job responsibilities. Later, I confronted him.

"I just needed to take care of some things at home," he said, his shoulders hunched, and forehead creased. "It's nothing for you to worry about."

One of the reasons I married Brian, besides falling in love with him, was I knew he'd be a good dad. But, he was also my playmate, and his distant behavior was concerning. I was fortunate that he loved being with the girls and always made time for them, from coaching their softball teams to taking them sledding at midnight on Christmas Eve. I convinced myself this was just temporary, reminding myself how lucky I was that he was such a devoted husband and father.

What mattered is that he and I were both on the same page with parenting. We were open with the girls concerning Brian's drug and alcohol history. From the time they were in elementary school, we were clear with both Jade and Jessi that because of Brian's past addictions, they were predisposed to having the same issues. Brian and I thought if we talked to them about it, we could keep them from going down that path. So even though I saw some signs that Brian was struggling, I continued with my busy schedule.

For a couple of years, Brian had been asking me to sign documents. He'd show up at the breakfast table while I was getting the girls ready for school and place a document in front of me. "Here," he'd say, "I need you to sign this." I really had no interest in the details because all I was concerned with was getting the girls off to school, so I could get my workout in before I had to go to campus to teach.

One day, in September of 2009, I went to a yoga class at RallySport. As always, I left before *savasana*, the resting pose at the end of class because I couldn't stand the idea of lying down for three minutes when I had a to-do list as long as my arm. There was no school due to a teacher in-service day, so the girls were with me when we went to the grocery store. While the girls were entertaining themselves at the front of the store, I waited in line to check out. The total came to $54.33. I handed my credit card to the clerk.

After swiping it, the clerk looked at me expectantly and said, "Your card has been declined."

"It must be a mistake," I anxiously replied, "let me try again." But it didn't work the second time either, and I started to panic, the line of other shoppers getting longer behind me. I felt people's eyes on me. I asked the cashier if I could call my husband because something must be wrong with the card. I hit the call button when she sighed but nodded. When he answered, I asked if something was wrong with the card.

"We need to talk," was all Brian said.

I paid for what I could with cash, leaving cereal, juice, and bread at the register. It seemed like everyone behind me was looking at me with pity. I felt naked. The knife in my back was already sinking into my scapula going toward my heart.

When we got home, I tried to stay calm until Brian arrived, but it wasn't easy. I took the girls to the park with the dogs and then started preparing dinner, making the girl's favorites, spaghetti with homemade meat sauce and steamed broccoli drizzled with Bragg's amino acids. Cooking was never something I loved, but I did get satisfaction when the girls liked what I made.

After dinner, the girls were playing downstairs when I confronted Brian in the kitchen. He was sitting at the table, shoulders hunched, as I stood over him. There was a hole in the pit of my stomach thinking of the possible implications. I recalled how often he was away from home telling me he had to meet with his bookkeeper. I hadn't given it much thought, but now I couldn't help but wonder.

"Brian, tell me what the hell is going on."

He looked down as he started to tell me the truth. I had no idea that each time I signed one of those documents, we were buying a new property. He had accumulated 13 in Michigan and Colorado. When the market started tumbling in 2008, they lost most of their value. He was defaulting on the loans, and we were facing bankruptcy. Thinking he could somehow fix it, he had kept it all from me.

"How could you not tell me?" I asked. He said he was trying to protect the kids and me.

I couldn't look at him. In my mind, this was all his fault. I went downstairs to get the girls ready for bed. Reading them a story as I did every night, sitting on the floor in the hallway between their rooms, while they lay in their beds, I tried to keep my mind on Harry Potter playing quidditch, instead of the nightmare I was tumbling into.

My biggest fear was telling my father because he was always very conservative with money, and I knew when he found out, he'd be furious with both Brian and me. My grandfather had worked so hard to build his business and left the family with an inheritance that my father was benefitting from. When he passed away, I would too. If we went bankrupt, much of that would be lost.

Later that week, I finally told my father. I could hear his exasperation on the phone as he sighed and said, "I knew this could happen if Brian followed through with some of his ideas about real estate." He insisted we talk to a bankruptcy lawyer. I will never forget the day we drove down to Denver and met with the lawyer. Both of us hated going to the city, so neither of us looked forward to the drive or sitting in a law office for half a day. But we were in deep trouble. Even though Brian insisted he could manage it, I wasn't convinced, and I was afraid of disappointing my father.

As we sat in chairs across from the lawyer behind his expansive desk in his well-appointed office, Brian and I listened as he laid out what he saw as the only option: declaring bankruptcy. Brian tried to argue with him, saying he could do short sales and negotiate with our creditors, but I was so defeated by this point, I just assumed filing was unavoidable.

For the next few months, Brian and I lived in a constant state of turmoil. We had countless meetings with the lawyer on top of countless arguments afterward. I found myself unable to pay for items I normally took for granted, like manicures and buying lunch at Whole Foods. Now, I would always pack food when I left the house or wait until I got home to eat instead of spending money. I sold some of my jewelry to get a little extra cash.

When I went to my hairdresser, who I'd been seeing for over 20 years, I told her to "just cut my hair and forget the highlights."

"Why?" Debi asked, "You always get highlights."

"Brian and I are having money problems," I said, starting to tear up. "I don't have the money to pay you right now.

"You can pay me later," she insisted with kindness in her voice. "This will make you feel better." Sitting in the chair while she washed my hair and massaged my scalp was heavenly. The act of getting my hair done released me into a state of gratitude.

It was a similar situation at RallySport. Even though I worked there, we spent money too. I had a personal trainer, and the kids were constantly buying food from the café. They allowed me to forgo paying my bill after I confessed to the general manager the trouble we were in. Ditto with Rich and the craniosacral work I relied on to keep me whole.

I thought about trying to hide it and go without these self-care practices, but that wasn't my way. The act of telling was like a cleansing. When all these people offered to continue the relationship I had with them and let me pay down the road, I believed everything would work out. But it did nothing to stem the resentment I had toward Brian. I had never been late on a bill in my life, and to be faced with this now was forcing me into an identity shift I didn't like. I hated it, and I hated Brian for putting me in that position.

My father called me almost every day. He didn't call to commiserate. He called to make sure I was on top of Brian and the whole mess. He wanted me to fix it and fix it fast, but there wasn't anything I could do to make it right. It was so deep that I didn't even know how to make sense of it all.

"Vicki," he scolded, "you need to take back overseeing the bills and watch everything that Brian does from now on. Promise me you'll do that?"

"I will, Dad."

But the thought was overwhelming. Taking care of the girls, the house, and my job had made it so much easier to let Brian take care of the money.

Running as much as I could was my only refuge. One Sunday, Jade had a softball game. Since Brian was coaching the team, he took her to the field. Sundays were my day to do a long run. I left the house early to be back in time for the game. I told Jessi when I got back, we'd go to the ballfield.

I ran to the trailhead, only planning to do my favorite three-hour loop, which seemed like a compromise to me because if I had more time, I would have run longer. I headed west toward Chautauqua, a renowned mountain park full of trails that attract runners, climbers, and hikers from all over the world. It's at the base of the Flatirons and unmatched in beauty. As I made my way through some of the wealthier neighborhoods in Boulder toward the mountainside and then onto the trail leading to the Enchanted Mesa, where you can see Denver on a clear day, my mind was already spinning stories.

I was mad at Brian but also hurt that he didn't share what was going on. My whole understanding of relationships was based on honest, open communication. I insisted this was one of my core values and yet, here I was, amid total deceit. As I was bemoaning my situation, I tripped and fell, literally falling off the trail and down the slope that went to another trail below. I only went a few feet but could have continued had I not caught myself. I was a bit shaken, but dusted myself off, got up, and it was then I noticed my wrist was bent at a weird angle. I knew it wasn't right, and I took a moment to contemplate what to do. I had a conversation in my head.

Practical Vicki: *It might be broken; I should go home.*

Addict Vicki: *I came out to do the whole loop and I am not going home until I do it. I won't feel good unless I finish what I set out to do.*

The idea of not covering those miles, of not completing my sacred loop was more terrifying to me than the possibility I had a broken bone. I continued south on the Mesa Trail over familiar terrain, but the effect of the injury was making me light-headed, so instead of a clear view, it was more like running through a child's finger painting where one shape overlapped with the next. I'm not sure how I made it down the rocky, uneven trail without falling again. My arm started throbbing, but I ignored it, believing that if I could run, it couldn't be that bad.

By the time I got home, I was delirious. Jessi, only 10, helped me get changed. She took me to my room and helped me pick out clothes. Then she pulled off my running clothes. "Mom," she said, "are you sure you're okay?"

"Yes, Honey," I assured her, "I'm fine. I just need something to drink and then we can go to the game." She got me some water and juice and the dizziness went away. Still holding out hope it wasn't broken, I drove us to the game, which might not have been the smartest move, but at least it was only two miles away. Brian was on the field throwing balls to the girls, and I went over to tell him I'd fallen during the run.

"I might have broken my arm," I said, holding it up for him to see, but he'd already turned away—distracted by warm-ups, or pretending to be as a coping mechanism for the difficulty in communication we'd been facing. He was most likely expecting me to criticize him so, to avoid that, he chose to basically ignore me.

"I doubt it," he said, tossing another practice pop-up for one of the girls to catch.

I can't remember whether they won or lost or how I even made it through the game. I do remember I was very uncomfortable and knew I needed to get an X-ray. Brian said he had to go to work. The girls and I went home as I attempted to maintain my composure, but Jade could see how much pain I was in and said she'd go to the emergency room with me. Jessi went to Jack's while we went to the hospital.

Sure enough, it was broken. My anger at Brian had been building. I was furious that we were in financial trouble. It was causing a serious rift between me and my father, and I had lost all trust in Brian's ability to handle our finances. When he dismissed me at the game, it was as if a referee blew the final whistle and said, "Game over."

By fall, I insisted Brian and I go to counseling and that we start family therapy, too. The strain on all of us was taking its toll. Jade seemed especially despondent and was struggling in school. I fully blamed Brian for the mess we were in and did not want to take any responsibility. He was the one who bought all the properties and didn't stop even when things got out of control. The fact he didn't tell me made me feel belittled and angry. I was humiliated that we were in a position of having everything we had worked so hard for taken away. It was true I didn't want to live in the mountains full-time, but my understanding of our life was that we could afford to have a weekend getaway. I had no idea how much trouble we were in, and I was afraid. My ego was bruised as well. I remembered my father's words. His belief that no one should own two homes came crashing down on me.

I had worked my whole life before marrying Brian, and I'd never had any credit card debt. His excuse of trying to protect me and the girls wasn't enough to make me forgive him. I was having a difficult time even talking to Brian without anger, so I focused on the girls, work, and running. But I couldn't totally avoid him. One day he asked me to meet him at his office, and as I got there a woman was leaving. She seemed to be in her early 30s, tall with long dark hair. Brian introduced her as Kate, the woman doing his books. We said hello and then she left.

I felt like I'd just been kicked in the stomach. A feeling of complete despair overcame me, thinking Brian was having an affair. All those lies weren't just about the houses. I confronted him. "Are you fucking her?" I spat out at him.

He looked at me like I was crazy. "Absolutely not," he said, standing taller and looking at me with wide eyes, like a child being accused of something he would never do.

"Well, I don't believe you." I choked back tears. He was adamant he wasn't, but my lack of trust in him went so deep at this point, it felt like he was having an affair even if there wasn't an actual physical or emotionally intimate relationship happening.

I was done with him and with the marriage. That evening I asked him to leave.

"I think you should go stay at the Magnolia house for a while," I said. "At least until we get through this."

"No way," he responded. "As soon as we take that step, it's over and I'm not going down that road. We will get through this."

I'm not sure what kept me from making him leave. Perhaps it was my 10-year-old self reminding me of the promise I'd made to never get a divorce. I could see young Vicki in her room, making sure not to disturb her sleeping mother across the hall, vowing not to make the same mistakes. How could I go back on that promise I'd made to myself? I also couldn't ignore Brian's commitment to me when I was rehabbing from the car accident. He had stuck with me when I was near death's door, so how could I turn on him now?

We went weekly for couples counseling. We found a therapist, named Del, referred by a mutual friend. The first time we saw him, we pulled up to a compact house in North Boulder. I led the way down a rock slab path to a small office around back, with Brian lagging behind. Del met us at the door, and we sat down in his cozy office.

As I started to explain why we were there, Del expressed sympathy for my viewpoint that Brian was mostly responsible for the mess we were in. His validation of my feelings of betrayal was all I needed to know that I wasn't being unreasonable. I left walking tall and satisfied. But Brian seemed smaller and broken down.

"I think this is really going to help us," I said as we approached our car, "He seems to get us."

"Well, yeah, I guess so, but I'm trying here Vic," Brian replied, "and I feel like a punching bag."

The good thing is, although it took me a moment to realize it, therapy wasn't just about me being right. Del also understood Brian. He too had struggled with addiction and knew what that looked and felt like. And as our sessions continued, he didn't let me off the hook. I came to see that by checking out, I had subtly given my permission for Brian to go overboard with the house-buying.

I was still having a hard time accepting my role in the possible bankruptcy we were facing. Then, during one session, Brian said through tears, "I've been skipping lunch to save money." I can never make enough food to keep Brian satisfied, so hearing that made me break down and cry. It was at this moment I started having some compassion for him.

Family counseling was equally painful. The girls dreaded going, and I was the one forcing the issue. It was up to me to make sure we all got to the sessions. We didn't have to pay because we went to the CU counseling center covered by my benefits. As we loaded into the car for the first meeting, Jessi said, "Where are we going again?"

"We're meeting a therapist who's going to help us talk about some of the stuff we are dealing with as a family," I explained.

"I don't want to talk about anything," she said.

"Me either," Jade groaned.

"Too bad," I said. "We all need this, whether you realize it or not, and we're going." I turned to Brian for some support, but he just shrugged his shoulders.

When we got to the building on the east side of campus, I realized there was no parking available in front. I told Brian to go around the corner and just park in front of a business office. Running late, we didn't notice the tow-away signs as I hurried everyone along. When we arrived, we found a tiny waiting room with one small couch and one chair. The girls and I sat on the couch while Brian paced and scrolled through his phone.

The counselor, a trim woman in her mid-30s with dirty blond hair that hung to her shoulders, came out after a few minutes and called us into her office. I had done an intake with her on the phone, but other than that had no previous contact with her. Janet turned out to be warm and welcoming and seemed to connect with the kids.

When she asked why we were there, the three of them just looked at me. I explained that we were struggling as a family given some financial issues and Brian's emotional absence from the family. I cried, the girls cried, and Brian sank lower and lower in his seat. There was also some yelling, mostly Brian and me, but also Jade. She was angrier than I realized. She was almost 13, and I assumed it was teenage angst. Jessi said very little and sat close to me.

At the end, Janet suggested we split up for the next session. The girls would come in first, and then Brian and me, and then we'd all have time at the end together. I thought this was a great idea and told her so.

As we walked back to the car, I was thrilled. "Doesn't everybody feel better?" I said. "We released all of that anger and tension."

"Sure," Jade said, "If you say so, Mom."

"I'm hungry," Jessi added.

"Me, too," Jade agreed. Brian didn't say anything. Everyone was arguing about where we should go for food, when we reached the car and saw the boot.

"Are you kidding me?" I screeched.

"I'll take care of it," Brian said. Then we saw the signs and I realized we would have to pay $180 to get our car back. We had no choice but to call the number listed. It took another hour to get the car freed. Brian waited while I walked the girls over to the nearby Taco Bell. It was as if the universe was saying, you might want to try to fix this, but it isn't going to be that easy.

One of the biggest divides Brian and I had during this time was deciding where we would live. He wanted to move back to the Magnolia house full-time and rent out the Boulder house. I was adamantly against that, even though it was where we got married and had many wonderful memories. The romance of that was not enough to outweigh the load of owning a house in the mountains. It represented fear for me. Maybe the accident was tied up in that, but it also had to do with the lack of control I'd feel every time there was a snowstorm in winter or a wildfire scare in the summer. Those feelings of dread were just too much for me. For Brian, those events created excitement.

Sitting on opposite sides of the couch in Del's office, we had several heated discussions about this issue. "The idea of driving up and down that road every day makes me cringe and sick to my stomach," I bluntly stated.

"But we'd save a lot of money and the girls could grow up in the mountains," Brian countered.

"And what about when they're in high school and only want to be with their friends in town?" I asked.

"We'll bring their friends with us," he responded.

"Like that's going to happen," I said. "What teenager is going to want to spend time up in the woods when they can be at a party in town with all their friends?"

Del let us spar over this for several weeks. I was happy to not have to be in a car for hours a day. Dragging the girls up and down the mountain was my idea of hell. This was hard for Brian to accept; he loved the space we had in the mountains. He loved chopping wood and getting away from town.

But I liked that I could ride my bike to work from the Boulder house and the girls could walk to school. After several months of going back and forth, we agreed to rent out the mountain property, even though if I had my way, we would have simply sold it. Brian had a vision that someday we'd move back there. For the time being, we'd live in Boulder full-time.

At around the same time that Brian gave in on where we'd live I started to accept my role in the whole debacle. I had never taken the time to ask Brian what I was signing or even read the documents myself. I knew, at some level, he was investing and that his goal was to make us financially secure, but to take the time to question it meant I would have had to take time away from what I really wanted to do, which mostly was to run.

Yoga had been a part of my life since the accident, but I never had much patience for it. One day, about a year prior to Brian's disclosure of our money situation, I decided to give Kundalini yoga a try. The name sounded weird, but my friend Becky and I thought, *What the heck?* and went into the yoga room.

The class opened with chanting and words that sounded like gibberish. When the teacher told us to face each other and play patty cake, Becky and I rolled our eyes at each other and tried to keep from laughing. When the class was over, we both agreed it was the strangest yoga we'd ever done. "I'll never go again," I told her.

Later that day though, I felt this odd sensation inside my body; it was a release, a complete letting go of any tension and expectations, and it was familiar and unfamiliar at the same time. I wanted more of that feeling so I went back later in the week. I continued going on a regular basis. It was during this time that I found myself looking forward to *savasana*, relishing the time to relax and let go. This transformation was gradual, my body was craving downtime, even though my mind wanted to fight it. I ultimately had to let go, and corpse pose gave me that opportunity.

A year later after that first class with Becky and a day after a counseling session with Del, I went to a Kundalini class. During the meditation, while we chanted *sat nam* and simultaneously clapped our hands overhead, I suddenly broke down in tears. *Sat nam* means "truth is my identity," and this struck me like a dagger right in the center of my heart. I was carrying all this shame and guilt around money and loss, and I felt so exposed. While I was humiliated by other people seeing me cry, it was cleansing. I needed to shed the layers that were preventing me from getting deeper to my soul. Running away was not working to keep me from feeling pain. I needed to feel that pain to move through it.

I asked Brian to start coming to class with me. He had always been reluctant to do anything inside because he believed real exercise only happened outside. I told him this wasn't about exercise. Knowing how vulnerable our marriage was, he agreed to come. The first time we went, I was worried about how he would react. After all, I almost didn't go back myself. He had no experience with any yoga except doing the occasional family yoga I dragged us all to when the kids were young. He knew what a downward dog was, but that's about it. How would he feel about the chanting, long meditations, and sitting?

To my surprise, he loved it. Class always starts with the same chant, *ong namo guru dev namo*, and it means to call on our highest consciousness to receive. As soon as he heard the first verse, he jumped in, and his voice was one of the loudest in the room. I was amazed because I was so reluctant for anyone to hear my singing voice, I didn't raise my voice above a whisper. But Brian belted it out. He felt challenged and for him that's everything. Every class is different, but the main intent is to do physical movements (asanas) to prepare for sitting meditation.

Neither Brian nor I have ever been very good at sitting, but there was something about this format that helped us get to a point where we could do a sitting meditation for 30 minutes. For a while, we were going to class at least twice a week and when it came time for corpse pose, Brian was the first to lie down and often the last to get up. Sometimes he'd fall asleep and the whole class could hear him snoring. No one gave him a hard time about it, but there was some laughter from the class. Brian would laugh right alongside them. It was medicine for both of us.

We occasionally brought the girls to some of the classes. Jade connected with it right away and continued to practice as she got older. Jessi never enjoyed it, requiring bribes of ice cream after class just to come. Sometimes, I'd worry about her as she sat trying to get comfortable on her mat, but I believed our family needed what Kundalini offered. The chanting and the postures are meant to help move us from darkness to light. Sitting in class with my whole family around me, chanting with others, was like being wrapped in a cocoon of protectiveness from the turmoil going on outside the room.

Jade later shared with me that at the time she thought we were going to get a divorce. I knew she and Jessi were affected by what was going on, but this shocked me as I thought Brian and I did a fairly good job of keeping the appearance, at least, of a stable front. I have since learned that you can't really hide the truth from your kids because they are watching all the time, even if it doesn't seem like it.

I don't know how he did it, but Brian managed to personally negotiate with every creditor, and, in the end, we avoided having to file for bankruptcy. It involved cutting back on our expenses. We rented out the Magnolia house. We stopped going out to restaurants except to occasionally take the kids to Noodles after their sporting events. Our credit was so damaged that it wasn't until 2019 that I was able to qualify for a credit card again. I realize how fortunate we are that we came out of this with our home and cars and no debt.

One of the reasons I married Brian is his positive attitude. I think he was able to fix this huge mess because he never doubted that he could. Sometimes his upbeat attitude in the face of incredible adversity drives me nuts as I want to scream, "Don't you see how bad things are?" But I remain thankful that he refuses to give up on me or any obstacle he faces.

CHAPTER 16
Grand Influences

Running can seem selfish to the non-runner or to the family member that gets left at home but, once you've experienced the physical and emotional release that can happen during or after a run, there are few replacements. Nothing melts away anxiety like finishing a good long run or a race. The constriction I felt from my mother every time I was near her would dissipate during my runs. Problem was, it always came back. This is both the benefit and the potential source of tension. If I can't run, and there's no other source for finding peace, internal conflict, as well as relational conflict, can arise.

Going for a run has been my drug since I was a teenager. It continues to bring me peace. I still crave the ego pump that comes from doing well in a race, and most people with that experience will want more of it. I like the way it feels when I excel. I like to push myself and see how I do against others.

As per usual, I was registered to run a team-format race on November 15, 2014. But on November 7, 2014, my father died suddenly. I found out on a Wednesday that he was in the hospital with stomach pain, and two days later he was dead from a bleeding ulcer. The doctors couldn't stem the bleeding because of the blood thinners he'd been taking. We flew to Phoenix Saturday morning for his funeral on Sunday. I wasn't sure if I would or could compete at the race I had looming, but it was something I thought about while away.

When we got home, I made the decision to race because I didn't want to let my team down. I had mixed feelings from the past weekend at his funeral and I was prepared to feel like crap. I was incredibly sad, but I also had anger and the combination was either going to bring me down or light a fire.

The gun went off and it was as if my father was underneath me lifting me over the course. I floated the entire race and ended up finishing as the second-highest scorer on our team. We won our division. The whole experience was surreal and further convinced me to always go for it because you never know how you will feel on a certain day.

In the summer of 2015, knowing Brian wanted to visit his family in the Detroit area and that his mother wanted to see our girls, I came up with a plan so that I could get my race fix while fulfilling the need to go visit his family. My idea was that we travel to upstate Michigan in his mom and stepdad's RV, so I could do the Marquette 50-mile trail race.

When I told Loretta, she readily agreed and proceeded to make all the arrangements; she booked all the campgrounds, planned the itinerary, and made sure we'd see all the sights on the way. I have always been thankful to have Loretta as my mother-in-law. She has been nothing but loving and supportive since the day I met her.

Upstate Michigan has so much to offer, and we stopped at all the tourist attractions. Sleeping Bear Sand Dunes was first on the schedule. Brian, the girls, and I hiked up to the top of one of the main dunes and then ran down, laughing the whole way as the sand swirled around us. Then the girls and Brian jumped into Lake Michigan at the bottom of one of the dunes. I didn't join because the water was freezing and I, of course, was thinking about my race and didn't want to expend the extra energy going up and down that steep drop. The girls loved it, though, and it was fun to watch them practically fall down the hill and then work their way back up, passing people on their way and beaming with pride.

We went to Traverse City next where we stayed at a campground that had little one-room cabins. Loretta had booked one for us while she and Bob stayed in the RV. I was thankful for a bed and some space. The RV was very nice, but with all six of us on top of each other, it could get very cramped.

Before dinner, Brian and I took a short run to check out the area. I was pleasantly surprised to find a whole trail system that went beyond the confines of the campground. We approached an intersection and I turned to Brian and said, "I think we should turn around before we get lost."

"We won't get lost," he replied as if he knew these trails. But he'd never been on them before. I realized then why he wanted to keep going—as we went a little further we found a deserted spot in the woods to have sex. Afterward, Brian agreed to turn back. I was relieved because I knew he might have easily gotten us lost if we had gone any farther.

While we prepared dinner, Brian and Jessi went for a bike ride—she was going to be on the mountain bike team at Boulder High that fall. It was getting dark and when there was still no sign of them, Loretta asked if we should be worried. At first, I said "No, it's just typical Brian," but then it got dark, and I was starting to question myself.

Suddenly, the two of them skidded into the campsite, their bikes nearly hitting the ground as they swerved to avoid us, both gasping for breath. "Where were you guys?" I exclaimed. "You had us worried!"

"I thought I knew where we were, but then we went down a road that took us miles out of the way," he said. I just shook my head, knowing that Brian will always take the turn that takes him farther away from wherever he should be.

"Dad just wanted to torture me!" Jessi added, hanging over her bike handles, relieved to be back at the camp. We all laughed.

Race day arrived and I placed second overall female. The girls and Brian were at the finish, and Jade and Jessi ran the last stretch with me. I was pleased with how I had done coming from out of town, not knowing the course. I hadn't even known to bring a headlamp for the start which meant I had to keep pace with a few guys on technical single-track trails the first few miles.

"Mom, what do you need?" Jade asked.

"Just water for now," I said, and she ran and got me a bottle. After a few minutes, I walked around with Jade and Jessi. When we saw the fresh-cut watermelon, we all took some and continued to wander around the campsite-like setting. The finish line was crowded with spectators and volunteers, creating a party-like atmosphere. I was soaking it all in, but 14-year-old Jessi was getting impatient; we needed to get rolling soon. She never liked being in one place too long. The race director found me to give me my award, a mug that said *Second Place Overall*, a hat, a T-shirt, and a neck gaiter, which meant we didn't have to wait around for an awards ceremony.

We got back to the RV where my in-laws were waiting. They asked how it went and I told them.

"That's nice," they said.

It didn't matter to them how I fared in the race; I knew that they were proud of me. In the great scheme of my life, it was another temporary fix for my constant itch. The kids and Brian had gone cliff jumping into Lake Michigan while I was racing. His parents hung out all day at the campsite. They couldn't relate to the idea of someone running for 11 hours through the woods.

All that was left to do was pack and move on to the next stop.

CHAPTER 17
Ego-Driven Vicki

In late July 2016, I planned to meet my accomplished ultrarunner niece Jenny in Aspen to run the 27-mile Four Pass Loop. The intense course crests 12,000 feet four times. Though it's not an organized race, many ultrarunners consider it a classic training run. I'd done it several times, but keeping up with Jenny, 20 years my junior, provided a real sense of pride.

We started out before dawn on an ideal morning for a mountain run—a bit chilly with clear skies. We got to the trailhead as the sky was just starting to lighten. Even so, the parking lot was already filling up with SUVs loaded with bikes and camping gear. Jenny had mentioned that a few people she knew from Steamboat Springs were planning on doing the same run that day, and sure enough, we bumped into them at the trailhead. I knew at least one of them well and dread crept into my skin at the thought of running with a bigger group. Jenny and I had been doing a long trail run together at least once a year for a while, and I always treasured my time with her. I didn't want to share her with anyone. I tried to ignore the surge in my belly as we started up the trail together.

Besides my desire to just run with Jenny, I knew that each person added to a run changes the dynamic, and, for better or worse, I have always been sensitive to this. I attribute it to my natural impatience. If there are two people and one person needs to stop and pee behind a bush, it results in a 30-second pitstop; add four more people to the mix and the time adds up. If I had been prepared for a group run, I might have been fine, but it threw me off as we started out together, and my nervous system took a hit.

Plus, the temptation to run the loop faster than Jenny's friends became my unstated mission and fueled me in those first hours. My legs burned with each stride as we made our way to the top of the first pass.

Describing the sensations that occur while running is an elusive endeavor because it's so singular in its nature. The very reason I love to run so much is that it's my experience and mine alone. I have no idea what Jenny was feeling as we made our way up that first pass. My internal conversation went something like this:

Ego-driven Vicki: *I want to get ahead of those guys and stay ahead.*

Worried Vicki: *My legs are already talking to me. I can barely stay with Jenny, and we are only on the first pass. This is going to be a long day.*

Ego-driven Vicki: *It's fine, once you start going downhill, you'll recover.*

My guess is that Jenny wasn't having this same conversation; she wasn't pushing the pace. She was just doing what felt natural. I, on the other hand, was working hard to stay with her, and that early in the run, I shouldn't have been exerting so much energy. I was determined to do the loop in a fast time, so I ignored the warning signs: heavy legs, high heart rate, and a general sense of fatigue.

The sound of talking and laughter from Jenny's friends below eerily floated up and surrounded us as Jenny and I silently made our way up Buckskin. The entire day, Jenny beat me to the top of each pass, and when I would get there, I didn't want her to have to wait another minute, so we'd just start up again. The single track was covered with rocks and roots, and I was mindful to keep lifting my feet, but my legs felt heavier and heavier as the day wore on. It was a beautiful day with the sun shining and little wind, so we could have spent time at the top of each pass taking it all in, but we just kept moving. When we did stop, it was just to pee or get food from our packs.

I typically can get by on a low number of calories compared to other runners. I attribute this to my marathon training days when I did long runs with nothing but water. I also think my small stature helps. I have never been one for scientific methods to determine calorie intake. I've always gone by feel. I seem to have an intuitive sense of what I need.

However, on this day, I was so intent on a fast time and not making Jenny wait an extra second, that I didn't do what I needed to properly fuel. I certainly had enough with me—Justin's almond butter packets are a staple for me, along with some gels and energy bars. I just didn't consume enough. I take complete ownership of this. Ego-driven Vicki won one battle that day, but she was also about to lose big-time.

At the top of West Maroon Pass, the fourth and final one on our route, I knew I needed to rest. The effect of the fast early pace was catching up with me. I struggled on the last pitch. My legs, weighted sandbags, made each step a burden. Jenny was at the top sitting on a rock waiting for me where at least 50 people were milling about. Maroon Pass is a popular day hike and so I wasn't surprised, but I was annoyed. Despite needing a break, I didn't want to be around that many people, so I said to Jenny, "Let's just get going." Ignoring the fatigue, I told myself I'd be fine once we started going downhill. Jenny got up and started heading down the trail and I followed.

At first, I did feel better, and my mind wandered to the pool run Jenny and I had planned for afterward, along with where we might go for dinner. I fantasized about a juicy burger.

After a couple of miles, we came to a stream, and I knew I should take the time to fill up my water using my filtration device, but I just wanted to keep our pace going. In hindsight, the three minutes it might have taken to fill up my water was negligible in terms of a whole day out on the trails, but ego-driven Vicki said, *Keep moving*. Her tone was determined, so I did what she instructed.

Jenny seemed to be floating along the trail in front of me, and I only wanted to keep up with her. I looked at my watch and gleefully realized we were on track to finish in under nine hours, the unstated goal I had for us at the start.

I was thinking about the time and all the crazy people we passed going the other direction. It was getting late in the day, and heading toward the pass is not smart because of the possibility of storms coming in. One guy was smoking a cigarette while leading a bunch of boys, which made my body tighten with anger. Less than 30 seconds later, I tripped over a small stone and landed hard, the right side of my body making impact with a huge boulder. One second I was running, the next I was on the ground. I yelped.

I popped right back up and was standing when Jenny turned around and ran the few feet back toward me. "I think I just broke my arm," I told her as I looked down. My right forearm hung like a wet noodle; my elbow was so crooked it didn't look like it was part of my body. It made me woozy, and I sat back down. The color drained from Jenny's face when she saw my arm. Her eyes wide, she asked, "Are you OK? What should we do? Should I run ahead and try to get help?"

We were still three miles from the trailhead and by the time she got down I'd be worse off. "We're just going to have to walk out," I finally admitted. I was more upset that I'd ruined her day than about my arm. When I apologized, she brushed it off saying, "Don't worry about it." I know she meant it, but all I could think about was how we missed running a solid time on the loop. Ego-driven Vicki was not ready to take responsibility. Instead, anxious Vicki felt guilty about ruining the day.

I shook myself off and we pushed on, down the rocky, technical trail. The arm didn't hurt much, not yet. It was as if I was in a dream; the outline of the trees and rocks were fuzzy, and the dirt under my feet felt like quicksand as I struggled to stay balanced.

I used my left arm to cradle my right arm, and with each step the bones moved under my grasp. Blood trickled from my right ear, which seemed minor compared to the arm so I didn't even mention it to Jenny. We'd gone from a run to barely moving at all. I needed to stop often to rest and take short breaks from the constant holding. Jenny had a long-sleeved shirt we used as a sling which helped a bit, but I could still feel the bones shift with every step, a sensation that made me nauseous. Finally, we got to the parking lot and headed straight to the hospital at the base of the road.

A nurse greeted us at the door of the emergency room. "This looks like it might just be a dislocated elbow," he said, and I prayed he was right.

"That would be awesome," Jenny said, standing by my side.

But soon enough the X-rays revealed otherwise. As I lay on a gurney, the other nurses looked at the results and visibly shook their heads. Even though they didn't say anything out loud, I could almost hear the collective, "Oh my!"

They asked if I wanted pain medication, and when I refused, one of them responded, "Are you sure?"

"Yes," I said, "I'm sure. It doesn't even hurt that much."

They gave me a bed in the corner of the crowded emergency room crammed full of machines, beds, and various staff members. As I looked around at the other injured people coming and going, I wished that the doctor would come soon and say it wasn't a serious break, and I'd be out of there quickly. But as the hours ticked by, I started to lose hope. I was dirty and cold. At one point, I turned to Jenny, "That was the last trail run I'll ever do with you."

Shaking her head, she replied, "No way." But I had serious doubts I would ever trail run again. I kept seeing myself fall over into that boulder, wondering if there was some way I could have avoided it.

The nurses asked me multiple times if I wanted anything for the pain, and I repeatedly said no.

"You're the toughest person we've seen in here in a while," one of them said. "Usually everyone says yes to the drugs."

Jenny and I just looked at each other.

I was trying to get comfortable on the stretcher-type bed, shifting side to side, but it was impossible. I couldn't even sleep. It was taking forever for the surgeon to come to examine me, but the nurses told me she was dealing with another emergency and was the only one on duty. They had moved me to another section of the emergency room, behind some makeshift curtains on moveable rods. Jenny was next to me when the surgeon finally arrived and apologized for how long it had taken.

"You've broken your humerus," she said, glancing at her clipboard. "The bone above your elbow. The good news is I may be able to reduce the fracture so you can avoid surgical repair." I clung to this statement hoping she was right.

After her initial words, she started moving my arm more and the ensuing pain caused me to wince and squirm. Jenny stood there helpless as she saw tears start to roll down my face. It felt like the bones were moving independently from the rest of me, my nerve endings lighting up like fireflies.

Seeing the effect the movements had on me, the doctor stopped and called the anesthesiologist over to talk to me about options for pain management. I told them I only wanted a local anesthetic as I was planning on driving back to Boulder the next day. The doctor and anesthesiologist looked at each other, rolled their eyes, shook their heads, and at the same time said, "That's a bad idea."

"You definitely shouldn't plan on driving tomorrow," the doctor said.

"This is not going to be fun for you if you don't have a good amount of anesthesia," the anesthesiologist added.

"Well, I don't want to be put under, so what is the least invasive technique you can use?"

Jenny had moved off to the side as I spoke to the doctors and didn't offer her opinion. I think she knew me well enough to know I wasn't going to change my mind unless I was forced.

As I think about this now, I can't believe I was contemplating driving home by myself. Boulder is more than a three-hour drive from Aspen, and that's if you go over Independence Pass, which is narrow and steep. I wanted to prevent Jenny from having to drive me home and Brian from needing to come and get me. If I could be independent and get myself home, the break wouldn't be so demeaning. Most runners I know have the same stubbornness bordering on a maniacal desire to do everything on their own. The doctors and I ended up compromising.

We agreed on a low dose of anesthesia along with a local numbing agent while the doctor tried to line the bones up to set the arm in its original position. I was awake the entire time as the surgery played out on a video screen. It was like seeing someone else's body as I observed the doctor moving my bones. The anesthesiologist and his assistant were bantering back and forth, and I was half-listening until one of them said, "I wish I hadn't forgotten my glasses," and the other responded, "Well, this is just an experiment, right?" and I laughed for the first time since the fall.

It was after 9 p.m. when Jenny and I returned to the Airbnb. Our hosts greeted me to say how sorry they were, yet they also kept their distance as if I might be contagious. This was probably because I was gritty with dirt and mud. When Jenny helped me shower, it was an ordeal. She helped me undress, but my arm was in a sling and couldn't get wet, so we covered it with a plastic bag. I got into the shower and told her I'd be fine. She left and said to yell when I needed her. I washed with one arm, hardly making a dent in getting myself clean. I still had streaks of mud on my calves when she came back to help me towel off.

I hadn't eaten much in hours, so Jenny made me try, but all I could manage was some almond butter on crackers. That night, I hardly slept knowing Brian had decided to leave Boulder at 5 a.m. with a friend to come get me. Knowing he was driving all that way to just turn around and go back made me sad, but also grateful.

Looking back now, I am amazed by how my ego has ruled my life and so many of the decisions I've made. I wish I could go back in time and say to my ego-driven self, "Just let go, enjoy the day in the mountains, and don't worry about how long it takes to finish. Just be."

Hindsight is helpful now, but at the time I was just beginning the real saga of healing. It was 2016, nearly 19 years after my car accident, and while my arm was the most recent injury, the body remembers trauma. It knows when you're ready to confront it.

The events leading up to my broken arm, including my mother's passing earlier that year, revealed how much I still had to learn about thinking through my actions. Often, and especially when things seem to be going well and I'm flying over mountain passes like a fit 30-year-old, I ignore crucial signals my body is sending my brain. When we hit the top of the last pass, I was almost dizzy from fatigue but decided to keep going to meet some arbitrary goal. We weren't even in an actual race. Why would I put that kind of pressure on myself except that's what I'd always done in the past?

But it's essential in both training and healing to listen when our bodies tell us to back off. This is the flip side of another truth: We need to sometimes push into discomfort to make gains. This is how it is training for a race: Train too hard and injury or illness strikes, but if you don't push hard enough, improvement doesn't occur. Finding the balance is the art of both training and healing. It comes down to a deep internal listening, and I have long been a master at turning to another channel where I apparently do everything other than hear myself. The ego can be a driving force that helps us excel, but on the flip side, it can bring us to our knees. Ego-driven Vicki is the queen of this ongoing drama that is my life.

One important difference between my recovery after the car accident and this injury was where I was in life. I wasn't working full-time at a demanding job or pregnant. As a result, I had time—lots and lots of it—to contemplate the meaning of the injury and how I wanted to proceed.

My mother's passing had come and gone, and I had failed to truly grieve and process it. Sure, I had cried some tears, but I went right back into my busy life with little time to contemplate the loss as well as where I was headed. It wasn't until much later, after recovering from the arm, and the writing of this book, that I dreamed of my mom. She was in a sunny location, with lots of animals around her, and flowers everywhere. It was very green, and she was calling me on the phone. "Vicki," she said, "you need to bring the girls here, it's so lovely." The dream was so vivid. I woke up and didn't feel sad, just happy that she had made the effort to call me.

The broken arm was as if someone had noticed and said, "Whoa, Vicki, you need to slow down and think about this year and how you want to spend your remaining ones on this planet."

As soon as Brian delivered me back to Boulder, I was eager to get on with it. I went to Rich for craniosacral work that same day. Though he usually doesn't work on Saturdays, he graciously agreed to see me.

The following day I had hoped to see my orthopedic surgeon. I waited anxiously by the phone for his call back, but he was away on vacation. He put us in touch with the doctor on call, but he was unwilling to come to the office on a Sunday. I couldn't sit still and tried to make Brian persuade this doctor to see me, but he had no luck.

I knew each day that passed without seeing an orthopedic surgeon was one day added to my recovery; the very thought made me quiver with uncertainty.

The pain was escalating and even though I didn't want to take medication I finally succumbed Sunday afternoon and took some of the Oxycodone the emergency room doctor had prescribed.

I had retired from the university only weeks before and was thankful I had prepared for a second career that included teaching Foundation Training.

Monday morning, I went to teach my class at RallySport. At the time, I needed to teach to feel like my old self. Foundation Training, developed by Dr. Eric Goodman, is about correcting the collapse that happens in our bodies if we don't do movement to prevent it. After my car accident, my whole body collapsed in on itself. Now my arm was broken in half, and once again I was confronted with a body that was not holding up against gravity. Foundation Training proved to be one of the things that put me back together.

Brian and I usually went to Kundalini yoga after Foundations on Mondays, so I attended class that first day back. The yoga room was across from the childcare center, so it tended to be chaotic in the hallway outside the door. This day was no different than any other as parents tried to corral their kids into the nursery, and the yoginis gathered their mats and props for class.

When Karuna, our teacher, saw me and my arm, she gave me a compassionate wink and a hug. "Just let the sound current immerse you and the energy from the group heal you," she counseled.

The theory behind Kundalini holds that sound current can produce healing effects. I have had teachers tell me that if you can't do a posture, imagine yourself doing it, and it will have the same effect. So that's what I tried to do.

Cool and dark, the room felt like a cocoon where I could hide. As I sat on my mat and watched the others do frog pose—basically moving in and out of a deep squat continuously for several minutes and a pose I'd always struggled with—I expected to feel sorry for myself. On the contrary, the chanting and meditative atmosphere lifted my spirits, like I was getting a big hug from everyone there. Then Karuna hit the gong and we lay in *savasana*. A wave of peacefulness washed over me, and I let myself melt into the mat. For a few moments, I forgot that I had a broken arm that would probably require surgical repair.

After yoga, Brian drove me to the doctor. The Boulder Orthopedic Center occupied a brand-new building that housed almost every orthopedic specialist in Boulder. The nurse ushered us into an examining room and Dr. Master, a small, wiry man, came in shortly afterward. He was younger than I expected and handsome in a boyish way.

"The surgeon in Aspen told me I might not need surgery if we try splinting it," I said before he even had a chance to introduce himself.

He looked at Brian, and then at me. "There's no way the arm can heal without surgery," he said, and proceeded to show us the X-rays as he explained why.

But I had already shut down, overtaken by the looming fear of going under a knife. I'd heard of too many people going in for routine surgery and not coming out of it.

Even with the extent of my injuries from my car accident, I didn't need surgery, so this was monumental. The only operations I'd had were the emergency appendectomy when I was 29 and my C-sections with both girls.

Those were necessary, but somehow this seemed different. I kept hoping it could be avoided. *Why can't we just let it heal on its own?* I wondered. Later, Brian told me this was the best and only option. I argued with him for a bit, but he managed to convince me that there was no other way.

The day of the surgery, August 4, 2016, was a typical warm summer day in Boulder. Brian and I walked to the appointment near the original Boulder Community Hospital where I had both girls. Even though it was four miles, I never thought about having Brian drive me there. I needed to walk to try to satisfy that never-ending tic of mine.

The surgery center at the new orthopedic practice wasn't up and running yet, so all operations were happening at their old location. Brian had knee surgery at this place years before, so I was familiar with the layout. It was all on the ground floor and quite small. I was grateful for the lack of people in the waiting room.

When I woke up in the recovery area three hours later, I was euphoric to have come through. Maybe it was the pain meds, but I was so happy to just be alive that for a little while I forgot about the arm. About 20 minutes later, I started to feel some discomfort from the six screws and one plate now lodged in my arm, which resulted in tissue damage and inflammation. But within an hour, I felt well enough to be released.

Brian took me home and set me up on the couch with pillows, a glass of water, and my pain medicine nearby. Feeling optimistic, I thought to myself, *This recovery is going to be a piece of cake.*

I felt well enough the next day to teach water running from the pool deck at RallySport. My class was glad to see me, but I also think they wondered why I didn't just stay home. I was able to relax the rest of the day knowing I had done something with my time. The nagging in my mind of having to be productive was still there and wasn't going anywhere just because I was recovering from surgery.

A few days later, I attended a Foundation Training workshop that took place in a historic building at Chautauqua near the famous auditorium where concerts are held. Years prior, Linda and I had seen John Hiatt play there. Garage-like doors on the sides of the building open during summer concerts, allowing passers-by to listen in. Sometimes we'd take the girls to picnic outside the hall to catch a performance.

This was a Level I Certification, like the one I had taken earlier that year, and I knew most of the instructors. I had been told I could observe any of the sessions, even though I wasn't formally enrolled. This was one of the things I loved about Foundation Training and the teachers, their willingness to share their knowledge and expertise.

I had already taken myself off pain medication, so I could have driven but decided to walk to the park. With my leg muscles contracting in that familiar way as I strode uphill, I felt a sense of power. But that sensation evaporated when I walked into the classroom full of young, healthy participants. I brushed off the concern of my former teachers because the last thing I wanted was pity. I observed the class and did what exercises I could.

During one of the sessions, I found myself in a pose with my arms in front of me. The bones in my right arm moved the way they did before the surgery. "This doesn't feel right," I thought, but knowing a plate and screws were holding it together, I continued with the workshop. Later that day, as I walked home the bones felt even looser, and it was more difficult to ignore.

By the end of the weekend, I was beyond uncomfortable. My arm was itching, and I couldn't sleep at all. I called Dr. Master's nurse and asked if I could get in to see him before my scheduled appointment. She tried to dissuade me and told me to take Benadryl. That pissed me off. I told her that wasn't going to work as Benadryl hypes me up. "Plus," I said, "something seems to be wrong, it just doesn't feel right."

Reluctantly, she made an appointment. Brian, once again, took me. He didn't seem at all worried, so I tried to take on his positive attitude. I was just looking forward to getting the wrapping off so I could scratch my arm.

Dr. Master decided to order new X-rays. I liked Dr. Master; he seemed athletic, although when we spoke about all the endurance activities Brian and I did, he shook his head in dismay. The nurse set the X-ray up for him to review and he went behind the curtain to look at the film. He came out, frowning and with downcast eyes, and said, "A screw has come loose, and the plate isn't holding."

Tears rolled down my face.

"Do you know why it came loose?" Brian asked as he held me.

"It could be any number of reasons," he replied. "We can't know
for sure, but we have to go back in." I was crestfallen. The biggest
disappointment was the idea of having to go on pain meds again. I'd been so
confident this recovery was going to be swift and easy. Already being off the
meds was such an accomplishment, and now I was moving backward.

During the second surgery, which took place at the larger hospital in
town, Dr. Master reconstructed my arm and inserted three titanium plates
and 20 screws. When I woke up this time, there was no euphoria, just
excruciating pain—lightning bolts coursing through the length of my arm
into the center of me.

In the recovery room, less of a room and more of a waystation between
the operating room and the main floor of the hospital with curtains
separating beds, one of the nurses helping me happened to be a friend of
mine. That sense of familiarity helped Worried Vicki feel calmer, while Ego
Vicki wanted to be strong in front of her. But the pain was so much more
than I expected.

I felt helpless as I lay there unwilling and unable to move. She told me
it went well, and the team was impressed with how strong my bones were.
This was a big surprise to me as I had been diagnosed with osteopenia
years prior, and it made me wonder what was true. I went into a dark,
narrow tunnel with no end in sight. I had to ask the nurses for more pain
medication, and it took almost three hours before I was ready for Brian to
take me home. I think it was so much worse due to how much hardware
was now installed in my arm, and no one had prepared me for that.

The misery lasted for days. At first, I couldn't do anything with my
arm. Helpless and annoyed, I envied Brian who continued to live his life.
He checked on me during the day, but I hated asking him for anything.
Even though part of me wanted him to just stay by my side, the other part
of me didn't want anyone around. The girls were off doing their own thing

as well—Jessi was about to start her sophomore year and had pre-season basketball practice almost every day. Jade was 18, working part-time at a restaurant near the university.

I'd never taken so many pain pills in my life, but the pain was unbearable without them. After the car accident, I was on morphine, but it was administered intravenously; I wasn't aware of how much was going into my system. Taking the pills myself made it much more obvious. My arm throbbed and the Oxycodone with Tylenol every four hours plus Oxycontin every 12, didn't touch the surface. I tried supplementing with extra Tylenol, but it didn't seem to do anything, either.

I was angry. Part of my anger went toward Brian because he was the closest to me. Even the fact that he could sleep through the night while I was tossing and turning on the living room couch got my hackles up. I knew it wasn't his fault, but I had a pity party for a few days while coming to grips with my situation. I was also mad at Dr. Master. *Why didn't he do the surgery right the first time? Why did I have to go through two recoveries?* Of course, later I realized how unreasonable I was being. But in those first few days, I stewed.

I hated the fuzziness in my brain that came with painkillers. Ghostly memories of my car accident visited me, echoes of that pain level. As I lay on the couch in our living room watching *I Love Lucy* reruns at 3 a.m., it felt like my body was back in the ICU at St. Anthony's. The feeling of déjà vu was so powerful it was scary; it seemed like my body was possessed by the shadow of my injured self from 18 years earlier. But this time my mother wasn't there to sit with me during the day or even offer words of comfort over the phone. She was only ashes in a box sitting in my study. This time, I didn't have a life inside of me needing me to fight.

Being in that much pain made me question who I was. All my self-doubts rose to the surface. The demons left over from my car accident appeared in my head saying, *You aren't strong, Vicki. Who are you kidding? Here you are brutally injured again. You deserve this. Suck it up.*

Despite this internal dialogue, I knew I had no choice. Just like 18 years prior, I needed to take ownership of my recovery. No one else was going to do it for me, so after two days of extreme pain and very little ability to do anything, I decided to get on with it. Each night was a challenge, but during the day I put my game face on and started to do what I could to get better. In some ways, this meant putting on a show, acting strong, not just to convince others, but to convince myself.

My goal became to do as much as physically possible each day. In the first 10 days after the second surgery, this meant very little. I was taking so much pain medication that even swallowing my vitamin supplements was a major undertaking and frustrating. The fact I had nothing else pressing exaggerated the void of time stretching out into what seemed a hellish eternity.

At the same time, my friend Benji Durden, a former world-class marathoner, was in treatment for colon cancer. He was trying to get out to walk every day. It was late August and that meant warm, sunny days in Boulder, so I started meeting him. Our walks became one of the highlights of my recovery. The first day we met, I walked almost 12 miles and was ecstatic.

When I got home and told Brian, his reaction was not quite the same. "Isn't that a bit too much?" he asked. I ignored his comment and even the idea of it being too much because it had made me feel so good; I was finally tired in that physical way I craved.

Benji and I walked on bike paths to minimize the danger of falling and we didn't move fast at first. I was still treating the arm gingerly, and he was tired from chemo. Still, this time of moving and talking was so critical to my emotional well-being. We talked about everything from training to politics. He was a wealth of information, and I loved hearing his thoughts. We were both worried about the upcoming presidential election and spent many hours bemoaning the state of politics in the U.S. Crazy to think this was just a few short months before Trump would be elected, a possibility neither Benji nor I believed could ever be. Daily, it seemed something in the news revealed his lack of integrity and morals. "How can people support him?" I asked Benji one morning.

"I know," he responded. "Like the time he mocked that reporter with the disability?"

"Or what about how he talks about women?" I questioned. "It doesn't make sense to me."

"Me either," Benji replied. "I'll be so glad when this election is over."

We were convinced there was no way anyone would vote for him. Equally disturbing were all the sexual harassment and rape accusations made against Trump that seemed to slide off him like water. It gave us a lot to discuss, but we both wished we didn't even have to tolerate him as a candidate.

Benji and I spoke about the frustrations of being injured, but also the luxury of time and being forced to be in the moment. For people who are always thinking about and planning for the next thing, this was a different way of existing. Benji and I had always been doers, so having to let go was a work in progress for both of us. He was married, and although his wife, Amie, was picking up the slack in their business and home life, he didn't have the added responsibility of children. I couldn't do laundry, clean, read, work, take the kids anywhere, or grocery shop. If the pain weren't so bad it would've almost been like a vacation.

The act of recovery can be lonely, so these walks gave Benji and me the support we needed to fight through the doubts we'd ever get back to where we wanted to be with our running. Neither of us had illusions of being as fast as we once were. It was more about getting back to our potential at our respective ages. There was also the understanding once we started running that it wouldn't happen magically. We had to put in the time and effort to get there. When you come back from an injury and people see you doing your regular activities, they don't necessarily understand what it took to get there. Having a partner to go through it with made a huge difference.

One of the strangest sensations during my recovery was the arm no longer felt like part of my body. The limb seemed to have a separate existence and moved in its own field of gravity. This was accompanied by the swelling sense of time, as if I were in a vacuum. Each moment took on a life of its own.

I had never been someone who derived my feeling of self-worth from being a mother and/or wife, so that wasn't the hard part. It was more that Brian, Jade, and Jessi really had no idea how much pain I was in. I wasn't going to show them and this meant the experience was truly mine alone.

I started walking everywhere I could. I was still on drugs, I hated relying on anyone for rides, and walking opened a whole new world. My route varied, but often I found myself coming home from RallySport on 30th Street, one of the busier roads in town. Seeing people rushing around, running red lights, and honking at other cars, made me grateful to have no schedule.

Walking became my mode of transportation, but also my meditation. It slowed me down and gave me time to contemplate and see my surroundings. I'd notice the Flatirons casting their shadow over Boulder in the late afternoon and simply take it in. I'd stop and see the cracks in the side of the mountain and wonder how many people were climbing routes up the face. Instead of being jealous, I felt a sense of awe.

Even though my recovery was much quicker than it was in 1997, it wasn't fast enough for me. Dr. Master had admonished me not to run or bike or swim. Two weeks after the surgery, Benji and I were out for a walk, and he told me he had started to add a little jogging into his walks. That day he had planned a one-minute jog, followed by three minutes of walking. If Benji could do it while on chemo, then why couldn't I? Screw the doctor and his warnings.

It's well-known that human beings learn from seeing others. Before Roger Bannister ran under four minutes for the mile, it seemed impossible. But now that's no longer a barrier in the running world.

When you see someone do something you don't think is possible, it opens a door. I was compelled to join Benji. As I took those first careful steps, I couldn't believe I was able to even do it—run. That moment when both feet were in the air was glorious. Plus, the bones in my arm weren't moving. I was confident for the first time that I would be back to running sooner than I expected.

I came home and told Brian, who said simply, "I don't think that's smart. Be sure you don't overdo it."

"I won't," I promised. But each time I met Benji, the ratio of running to walking increased. Benji had made the U.S. Olympic team in 1980 only to have his chance to compete dashed by the boycott. I can't imagine getting that close to a lifelong dream only to have it taken away by something out of your control. Benji, however, is a pragmatist at heart and didn't dwell on the past. Certainly, he was proud of his accomplishments, but what I loved about spending time with him was his focus on staying fit and moving in the present. No matter that he was a former Olympic athlete, he just wanted to beat cancer and move his body in the now.

Sometimes, we'd meet right after a particularly rough chemo session, but he never let it stop him. He'd say, "Today, it's five minutes running, one minute walking, times six." His motivation fueled me, and I wouldn't have started running again so soon if it weren't for him.

Staying out of the pool proved to be the hardest rule to follow. I didn't understand why Dr. Master had made four weeks the timeline until I could get in the water. At three and a half weeks, I said the hell with it and borrowed a waterproof sleeve and got in the pool with my water running class. Though my arm rested on the surface in an awkward plastic bubble, I was in the water, moving and happy.

Once I was off the painkillers, time resumed its usual pace. Enrolled in physical therapy and with a conscious focus on healing, I rapidly improved. Within a few months, I was back to running and doing almost everything I'd been doing before. My arm functioned again but looked like a completely different arm than what was there before the accident. The elbow bone stuck out to the side and a huge scar ran the length of my tricep. I told myself it now matched the rest of my crooked body, with my off-center pelvis and ribs that look like a bunch of Xs. This time, I refused to be self-conscious about the deformity, unlike after the car accident when the gaping hole where my scapula used to be made me so self-conscious that I wouldn't wear a sleeveless top for years.

I progressed to running on easier trails. I found unexpectedly that I had fear and hesitation when any obstacle was in my way. After my car accident, I hadn't been afraid to drive or get in a car, but in that accident, I had no memory of the crash. This time, I could recall every single moment leading up to the fall. Twelve-hour amnesia was not there to rescue me this time.

The first trail I ran on was the Bobolink, a flat, groomed dirt path that most trail runners wouldn't even call a trail because it more resembles a road. But even the small obstacles like twigs and roots would make me wary and nervous about falling. I wondered if I would ever get back to that carefree feeling I once had while skipping over rocks and branches. I started to use my favorite Kundalini mantra, *sa ta na ma* to calm my nervous system, matching one syllable to each step. Each time I muttered this healing mantra, I absorbed its intent to connect with my divine nature. I started to feel more comfortable and added more trails to my runs.

Nine months after breaking my arm, running a 25-mile trail loop seemed reasonable to me. Brian was concerned and asked if it was necessary to run that long. But he knew I needed it and let it go when he realized I wasn't going to listen. I refused to admit it to Brian, but I was a little on edge beforehand as I still didn't have my confidence back. But ego-driven Vicki pushed that aside. I had started to use hiking poles on my runs and I was far from the runner I had been before. My thoughts wandered to the days when I ran down the Barr Trail on the descent of the Pikes Peak Marathon with reckless abandon and wondered if I'd ever get close to that feeling again.

My friend Lisa picked me up and we drove to Gold Hill, a small mining town near Boulder situated 9.000 feet above sea level, the highest altitude I'd been at since falling in Aspen. A few months before my fall I had run a trail marathon here and wanted to run the course again to prove to myself I had it in me. Lisa, an easy-going blond beauty who everyone loves, was the perfect person to do this inaugural long trail run with, as I knew she'd let me determine the pace and would be fine no matter how long it took.

We parked in front of the Gold Hill Store and started heading west on the dirt road. The road led straight up, and I was amazed at how easy the running seemed. I started to enjoy myself and stopped worrying about falling. Even as we left the dirt road and the trail got rocky and uneven, I remained confident. I hadn't brought my poles that day, determined to complete this run without aid. Again, it was ego-driven Vicki calling the shots.

After meandering through the woods for about 13 miles, talking the entire time, we had failed to notice our water getting low. Just then, we came to a trailhead and saw a couple of guys dressed in running clothes filling their water bottles at their car. We asked if they had any water to spare.

They said sure and then one of them asked, "Are you doing laps?" Lisa and I looked at each other, both of us wondering what they meant.

"Um, no," I said, and then, "Are you?"

It turned out they were training for an upcoming 100-mile race and were doing the same loop we were, only twice. We thanked them for the water, and they said, "See you soon, we'll be right behind you."

After that, all I could think about was trying to not let them catch us. My urge to stay in front, do more, and run faster, was still there, lurking under the surface. Ego-driven Vicki had reawakened, and she was ready to go.

Lisa and I started down the trail, chatting away. The trail was quite rocky with no real clear path, and I was trying to avoid the bigger rocks while also pushing the pace a bit. Sure enough, only 10 minutes later I tripped and found myself on the ground. My foot caught a rock and down I went. I was mad. I had been feeling so good, and yet I still fell.

What's wrong with me? I asked myself. What happened that made me want to stay in front of those guys? Over and over this scenario has repeated itself in my life, and not just on the trail. Ego-driven Vicki took over, worried about those runners catching us, and prevented me from enjoying and staying in the moment.

Did it matter if they caught us? No, but that old drill sergeant in my head was saying, *Stay in front, do better, be the best.*

I'm not only competitive, I'm impatient. This impatience, I believe, stems from a sense of urgency that I always need to get somewhere. Is it that ancestral legacy haunting me, never letting go? Is it simply that my parents were both impatient? Neither would wait more than 10 minutes at any restaurant, regardless of how good the food was supposed to be. Whenever I was with either of them, it seemed like we were always talking about the next destination, the next meal, the next event, instead of enjoying the moment.

Too often, this has been my mindset: trying to get as much done in a day as I can because of a fear of not having enough—enough time, enough love, enough control. Did I learn this from them? Did they learn it from their parents? Perhaps? But, knowing this, I believe I still have time to choose another path.

I got another chance months later when I went on a weekend getaway with my girlfriends. Headed to Princeton Hot Springs to celebrate a birthday, we stopped at Staunton State Park for a group run. I hadn't run with this group of women since before I broke my arm, and ego-driven Vicki was poking her nose into my mind. *Vicki,* she pointed out, *you're usually in the front when you run with them. What are you going to do about that?*

I'm proud to say, I ignored the voice and chose to fall behind the group and stay in back for the whole run. I used my poles, took my time, and finished unscathed and happy. It was a victory for the new Vicki.

Standing at my desk on March 11, 2021, 23 years to the day when I went into the hospital to give birth to Jade, I think back to my fall on the Switzerland Trail in Gold Hill, Colorado, and try to come to terms with my need to be in front. It isn't straightforward, but I do know that running gives me a sense of control. But control is impermanent.

I'm a work in progress, as my little fall trying to stay ahead of the 100-mile runners showed me once again. I'm working on a new point of view, one that lets me ask, as I step out the door to run: *What can I learn about myself today?*

We used to joke when Jade was a little girl that despite having not yet been born, she had already ridden in a helicopter. She always laughed, but I think deep down she cried, too.

The doctors who treated me after the car accident promised that Jade couldn't feel anything. At the time, she was smaller than a finger protected by an ocean of amniotic fluid, but my gut tells me Jade felt something. When my only release from the pain was to scream, I knew she was either listening or screaming with me. By forcing myself to let go of the painful sensations, I tried my best to protect her. Knowing she was inside of me helped me move through those moments.

Those first weeks were challenging, in part due to the brain injury that was preventing me from thinking clearly, but also because I had no control over my body. When the pain hit, it was often so acute all I could do was yell. This was always followed by a pang of guilt that the baby deep inside could hear me. That I was scaring her.

Jade also got to go through rehab with me, and there is nothing more soothing than being in the warm water and experiencing Watsu. Two things strike me about Jade that were noticeable from an early age: her utter sensitivity and empathy for others and her love of water. The fact that she is a Pisces may explain some of her natural love for the water, but I maintain that spending so much time in the therapy pool also contributed.

When Jade was born, it was as if a light turned on in the world. She truly radiated. A happy baby, she was the joy of my life. For both Brian and me, it was absolute euphoria. Even waking up in the middle of the night for feedings was fun because of Brian's booby song.

But the struggles we had with her clubfoot also left an indelible mark on her and us as a family. Shoe shopping was always difficult when she was young because her left foot was quite a bit smaller than her right. By elementary school, she was much more conscious of how she looked, and that made shopping even more difficult.

We found out that Nordstrom would sell a pair of shoes in different sizes. While this helped, it was still an ordeal and brought back memories of my mom taking Wendi and me shopping at the end of the summer for new school shoes. I dreaded getting dressed up and going to the kids' shoe store. I just wanted to rip off my dress and go play outside. I simply didn't care about shoes at that age. But Jade cared about finding shoes she liked, probably because it wasn't easy, and so the pain cut in a different way.

When I was taking Jade to have her foot casted and for physical therapy, I tried not to make it seem out of the ordinary. It was just something we had to do, like going to the dentist. She never indicated that she was troubled by her foot, and so Brian and I assumed it wasn't an issue. We encouraged her to be as active as possible and to try every sport, including soccer, gymnastics, and swimming. But there was a point early in elementary school when she realized she was different. When she was in third grade, she came home and told me that some of the boys teased her and called her "clubby."

I tried to help her through this, but I think I may have done just what my mom did one day when I came home from elementary school and told her a boy had punched me on the way home from school. She said, "That's what boys do when they like you." And then told me to get over it. I hated that Jade was getting bullied, but I also didn't want to beleaguer the issue. I just encouraged her to move on.

Her ability to hide her true feelings is something I didn't fully realize until she was in high school. I don't know, and probably never will, whether I inadvertently caused this by always wanting everything to just be OK. I didn't want her club foot to be an issue, so we acted like it wasn't. She was active and happy—at least that's what I thought.

School was never easy for her, and she needed extra help starting in kindergarten. She was late to read compared to many kids her age, but I wasn't concerned at first. I knew that in some educational theories reading literacy is not expected or desired before ages 7-9. This is based on the idea that children can be more observant of their surroundings if their gross motor skills are developed first. In our educational system, this is considered drastically late, but I knew that you can't force a child's readiness to read, just as you can't force a child to walk who isn't ready.

But by first grade when she was still struggling, I didn't hesitate to do everything I could to bring her up to speed. I took it on like a mission assigned to a hired analyst. She worked with a reading specialist at school named Thea. I also took her for vision therapy after an ophthalmologist diagnosed her with tracking issues.

She was just a kid, and all she cared about was fitting in and having friends. Being pulled out of class for her sessions with Thea only added to her dwindling self-esteem. Little did I know how hard school was for Jade because she felt dumb. Later, I found this written in one of her journals, which she gave me permission to read and use in this book: "I struggled a lot in elementary school. I thought that there was something wrong with me."

It pained me to read those words. At the time she was getting the extra help, and I didn't think it affected her, especially not as much as it clearly did. All I wanted to do was be her advocate. Any support we could find, I was going to sign her up. But, for Jade, the extra attention simply highlighted the fact that she was different.

Yet, she was a well-adjusted kid. She had no problem making friends; she was invited to lots of birthday parties; and she always had playdates. I failed to see that her need to fit in was overwhelming. She was forming a barrier with the world and with me.

On the surface, Jade's childhood was unspectacular. When she was 18 months old, I enrolled her in a preschool run by the speech and language department at the University of Colorado. This school was unique at the time because they mixed children with special needs with kids who didn't have obvious limitations. There was one boy there with lymphatic filariasis (commonly referred to as elephantiasis) who Jade became good friends with. Connor and Jade were practically inseparable the entire time she attended the school.

One afternoon, in the early fall of 2000, my belly swelled with Jessi inside. I arrived to watch through the observation window, where parents could see their children unnoticed by them. Jade was hovering over Connor making sure he had all the art supplies he needed. She had built a small wall of pillows around them. Her blond hair looked almost white under the fluorescent lights, and Connor was gazing up at her as though he was looking at an angel. Connor's mom, Julie, was there with me and we shared the moment, each thankful our kids had found each other.

The flip side to this is how people can take advantage of such sensitivity. Jade's trusting nature has also led to great pain. In elementary school, she invited the popular girls to her birthday party—a sleepover at our mountain house. The girls had all been inside after breakfast, and then they were gone. Jade was left by herself, standing in our living room. I asked her where they all went.

"I don't know," she said, looking small and vulnerable. She wanted to be with them, but then the "mean girl" thing happened, and she was the one ostracized. I'm pretty sure most children experience this, but Jade's sensitivity set her especially at risk.

Later, in high school, I saw her repeatedly befriend girls who were not nearly as loyal to her as she was to them. Jade has a warmth and openness to her that can attract people who are either needy or cruel.

That spring day, up at our mountain sanctuary, I wanted to make those girls pay for hurting Jade. But instead, I found them playing outside and asked them if they were ready for a snack. They came running into the house and then, as if nothing had happened, surrounded Jade as they gathered at the table for lemonade and cookies. Jade joined in the chatter, and I moved toward the kitchen to start packing for the ride back down to town, glad in the moment that she was happy. I didn't allow myself to recognize how this was just another temporary fix.

Jade was social in middle school and had a core group of friends who lived differently than we did. Jade seemed to like that her friends lived in big houses. She became enamored of these families and their lifestyle of parties, dressing up, and drinking.

I'm not sure if this is when Jade started imbibing, but I know that the parents of these kids drank, and there was alcohol present. Our house was alcohol-free. During this period, Jade began lying and developed a life we knew nothing about.

One spring day in Jade's eighth-grade year, I bumped into a neighbor while walking the dogs. She told me she'd seen Jade get into a car around midnight a few nights prior.

As I stood there, dogs straining at their leashes, she continued. "I can't be certain," she said, "but the girl had blond hair, so I assumed it was Jade."

"That can't be right," I replied. "But I'll ask Jade about it. Thanks for telling me."

Jade and her friends were all around 14 and about to enter high school. She didn't have permission to be out past midnight and, as far as I knew, didn't have any friends who drove. Our rules were clear: tell us where you are, don't lie, don't steal, be kind. I still thought of Jade as my innocent daughter who would never go behind my back.

I prided myself on having good communication with both Jade and Jessi, but I hovered outside Jade's bedroom before knocking on the door. She invited me in, and as I looked around, I realized I hadn't been in her room in a while. I tended to do what my mom did, which was leave teenagers alone, especially if they were in their rooms.

She had moved her bed into the corner, draping it with Mardi Gras beads that dangled from the ceiling like a curtain. I could smell lingering incense that she must have lit earlier, despite our rule not to light matches. She was lying on her stomach on the floor, painting her nails, bits of pink polish dotting the carpet. I decided not to mention that or the smell and told her what the neighbor had said.

She sighed and told me it was another girl—one who had stayed the night at our house recently.

I thought to myself, *Of course, it was her*. She's so much more mature than Jade, and I could imagine her knowing a guy with a car. Plus, she had long blond hair like Jade, so I dismissed any concerns.

Eighth grade proved to be difficult for Jade, and the final few weeks were the worst. She attended an experiential school that was mostly project-based. Initially, we thought this was the best option for her since she struggled with traditional academics. But the lack of supervision and the expectation that kids would manage to do the work on their own didn't suit her.

When it came time for the graduating eighth graders to do their final projects, Jade was lost. I take some of the blame for not intervening, but I truly had no idea how far behind she was. I blamed the teachers for not calling us in sooner. It was too late when I finally found out.

Students ran their own parent-teacher conferences once per semester. The student would introduce the parents and then conduct the meeting by going over their portfolio. Jade's last conference of middle school was scheduled for a Wednesday afternoon. As Brian and I walked down the hallway toward the classroom, we saw Jade by her locker. She acted like she hadn't seen us.

In the classroom, the glare in the teacher's eyes suggested that something wasn't right. Jade sat at the end of the table, near me and as far away from the teacher as possible. As she started to go through the talking points laid out in front of her, it was clear she wasn't prepared, and a painful meeting commenced. The teacher grilled Jade about why she hadn't done the work.

"Jade," I asked, "why didn't you let us know you needed help?"

"I thought I could do it," she said, tears starting to well in her eyes.

Then I turned to the teacher. "Couldn't someone have tried to tell us she was falling this far behind?"

"That's not how we handle things here," he said with a shrug of his shoulders. "We expect students to be adults. After all, they're headed to high school next, and that isn't how it works there."

The conference ended with no clear set of instructions for how Jade was going to successfully complete eighth grade. When we got home, Jade revealed that this teacher had told her she'd never graduate high school. She was hurt and embarrassed but hid it by becoming even more attached to her friends, losing interest in school, and rebelling more.

Fortunately, the other teachers in the program weren't this callous and they helped Jade get through the remainder of the year. But the imprint was there, and it settled in her like mud at the edge of a river after a rainstorm.

Jade's first year of high school continued the pattern from eighth grade. Early in the first semester, a friend whose son was close with Jade, told me that Jade was falling asleep in class, and he was worried about her.

I appreciated her candor, but replied, "Oh, she's been staying up late and I'm sure that's what it is. Thanks for telling me, though." Once again, I spoke with Jade and she confirmed that she was just tired.

Turns out, Jade was hungover.

How could I not know? It's easy to see what you want to see. I believed Jade was being honest with me and that our relationship was a good one. After all, she never said, "I hate you" to me, as I had to my mom, so I was convinced our relationship was on solid ground.

Around this same time, I went hiking with the mothers of Jade's best friends from middle school. We were attempting to stay in touch as the girls navigated freshman year. We went to Chautauqua one afternoon, the air crisp with the smell of fall. As we hiked back down toward the Mesa Trail, I casually said to one of the mothers, "Hey, I think your daughter might be seeing an older guy. One of my neighbors thought she saw her getting into a car late one night at our house."

"Um," she replied with pursed lips, "I think you should pay closer attention to what Jade is doing rather than be so quick to point your finger at my kid." The other two moms stayed quiet and looked away.

I was taken aback and didn't know how to respond, so I cut the conversation short. After that, I didn't get together with those moms again.

Jessi was in sixth grade at this time. She was thriving in middle school—she got good grades and had a group of friends who lived nearby. One day after school she asked if she could talk to me.

"Of course," I said, thinking she wanted to talk about her sexuality, as I had an inkling that she was gay. It turns out, this is the case —she ended up coming out to us in about a year. On this day, though, she handed me an essay she had written for her English class.

I read her words: *I found empty bottles of beer in Jade's room, and I think she is doing other stuff. I am afraid to tell my parents, but I am also afraid not to tell them.* My heart broke.

"Jessi," I said trying to reassure her, "I am so glad you told me. I'll talk to Jade."

"But," she said, "she'll know I told you, and then she'll be mad at me."

"I won't tell her you told me," I responded. "I'll just say I was looking for something in her closet and found it."

"But Dad will be so mad at her, and he'll get angry," she almost cried.

"I won't tell him."

And this was a source of inner and outer conflict for me because I knew that Brian had zero tolerance for substance use by our girls. I was a realist and knew that teenagers are bound to experiment. I did when I was that age and expected that they would, too. But I was convinced it was just a phase that wouldn't lead to anything too serious. Brian thought any drug or alcohol use would lead to more, so I hid that information from him to avoid his anger.

Was this the best way to handle it? I have no idea. At the time, Brian's inflexibility around experimentation made me feel backed into a corner. I parented the way my mom did, leaving the kids to figure it out mostly on their own. The difference, I thought, was that my kids would come to me if anything were really wrong. Jessi bringing her paper to me was my proof.

It's difficult to admit how much you don't know about your child. I always thought that my experience with my children would be better than my own relationship with my mom. For one thing, I wasn't depressed. I tried not to be controlling or judgmental. I sincerely thought I was doing a good job.

Then they became teenagers, and I thought, *Who am I kidding?* Jade went from being a fun and easy child to someone I had a hard time being around. She was unpleasant, bossy, and arrogant. She'd roll her eyes when Brian or I spoke to her. If she and I were in the kitchen at the same time trying to make food, it became a battleground. She'd push her way in front of me to get to the refrigerator, then take up all the limited counter space to make a sandwich. I hated being in there at the same time as her and found myself avoiding the kitchen if she was using it. If I really wanted food at the same time, I'd find myself taking on the same stoic, rigid stance as her, two soldiers fighting for the same territory. We'd warily trade places as one of us opened the fridge door and the other took over the counter. If I even came close to her, she'd jump as if she got an electric shock.

Jade has an ability to change the dynamic of any situation she's in. If she's light and happy, everyone is. But if she's grouchy and moody, she drags everyone else down with her. This was always evident when she played softball. If she was up, the whole team was up. If she was down, so was the team.

During one game where the team was losing, Jade got angry. Fuming, she sat in the corner of the dugout in a storm of frustration while the team was at bat. The upbeat and cheery bench turned morose, and the 10 girls slouched side-by-side, not cheering. The team wasn't even rooting for the batter. Typically, Jade would lead the girls in cheers, but she just stopped talking. I encouraged her to snap out of it and get the team's spirits back up, and for some reason, she listened to me that day.

As I walked back to the bleachers to sit with one of the other moms I heard Jade yell, "We don't wear no miniskirts." This was followed by a chorus of confused and half-hearted echoes, "We don't wear no miniskirts." But Jade was undeterred and belted out the next phrase, "We just wear our softball shirts," grabbing the chain link fence that separated the dugout from the diamond. The other girls joined in just as loud, jumping to their feet and stomping their cleats in rhythm on the cement.

No matter what Jade did, I was able to make an excuse for her. There was the occasion I was away with some girlfriends at a running race, and Jade called me out of the blue. We were on our way to a restaurant for dinner when I answered the phone. Jade sounded scared.

"What's wrong, Honey?" I asked her.

"Mom, you might get a call from the police and I wanted you to know I didn't do anything."

"Why would I get a call from the police if you didn't do anything wrong?"

Apparently, a friend had stolen her parents' car, picked Jade up, and they'd gotten caught after curfew. Her explanation made sense to me at the time. I even bragged to my girlfriends after I hung up how proud I was that she called to tell me before anything came of it. They all agreed, congratulating me on doing such a good job of parenting. I never told Brian about this transgression as I assumed he would overreact. I was still convinced Jade was just being a typical teenager.

Later I found out that she was lying. She and another friend had stolen that dad's car and gone for a joyride. They got caught by the police, but they never called as the dad ended up not pressing charges.

There were other telltale signs: the countless calls from school reporting Jade missing class; her assurances that she was only late turned out to be more lies. I so wanted to believe her. But by the spring semester of ninth grade, it was clear Jade was falling further and further behind. We investigated switching schools, and she decided she wanted to move to New Vista, the main alternative school in Boulder. I had always wanted her to choose New Vista and had recommended it when she was in eighth grade, but she had insisted on one of the two mainstream schools where her friends were going.

When she told me she wanted to make the change, I was happy because I thought it was a better fit for her educationally—it was smaller and experientially based. Brian went along with it, but when it came to decisions around education, he deferred to me. I had always been the one to take charge and navigate the ins and outs of school for both girls. Brian came to some of the parent-teacher conferences throughout the years, but somewhere along the line, this became my domain, just like coaching their softball teams became his.

I was still grasping for anything that might alter Jade's trajectory. I had always put emphasis on education, believing that if she were in the right program, had the right help, and was in the best setting, she'd succeed. I was unwilling to admit that there were other issues, separate from what school she was at, contributing to the problematic behavior.

Shortly after school let out for the summer, right before we were headed out of town to go to Washington, D.C., for my work, we got a call at 1 a.m. from the Boulder police station telling us they had Jade in custody, and we needed to get her. Brian was the one to go, and when they got back to the house at 3 a.m., she came into my room where I had been waiting for them, unable to sleep.

She crept in, head hanging, to apologize. She and her friends had gotten into the house of someone they knew and taken some of the girl's clothing and jewelry. I was sitting up in my bed, arms crossed over my chest. I glared at her, trying my best to emulate my mother's look when she was angry. "It was Amanda's idea," Jade insisted. "I just went along with it."

I asked her what possessed her to steal from this girl. "Amanda knew where the house key was, and then it just kind of happened," she replied, as she sat on the edge of my bed, gazing down at her Doc Martens. I was in no mood to discuss it further and said her father and I needed to discuss what punishment would be doled out. She skulked down to her room.

Brian sat on the edge of our bed for a moment and looked at me with those "I told you so" eyes. "Now do you see, Vicki?" he scolded. "You've been too easy on her and it's not working."

"Well, what do you suggest we do?" I asked. "Lock her up in her room?"

She was just being a teenager, I insisted, remembering what one of my friends with three adult daughters once told me: "All teenage girls lie." But I agreed with Brian that we had to do something.

Amid the whirlwind of getting ready for the trip, we told Jade she'd be grounded for two weeks when we returned from D.C. She looked at us with her doe eyes and simply said, "OK."

The trip was a welcome escape for us all. As we did the typical sightseeing, it was just us being a family again, and I became confident she was only going through a phase, like I had at 15. Our biggest arguments during the trip centered around whether we were going to walk to the next museum or take the Metro. Both girls loved the train, but I preferred to walk as much as possible. It became a family joke when we walked that everyone needed to keep up with Mom. From that time on, anyone walking fast was noted to be doing "the mom walk."

Upon our return, we followed through with the grounding, but it did little to stem the tide.

One morning I woke up and went out to get the paper. "Brian," I said, "there must be a skunk nearby."

He took one look at me, rolled his shoulders, and said, "Really, Vic?"

I guess I was the last to know that weed smells like skunk. Sure enough, by this point, both girls were experimenting with it. Jessi was more subtle, and it never escalated with her. Jade used pot for a while, but once again

I remembered my usage at that age and excused the behavior. I never got used to that smell though, and for a couple of years, I thought I was smelling a skunk outside our door.

Brian continued to worry that Jade was on a dangerous path, convinced that she was exhibiting the behaviors of an addict—skipping school, having anger issues, and hanging out with questionable friends. We had many arguments about what to do about it. He thought I was way too lax, and I thought he was overreacting. Around this time, Brian started drug testing Jade, and a year later he was also testing Jessi. He didn't trust them, and I was at a loss for what to do.

Brian kept the tests on hand and if he had any sense the girls were high, he'd test them as soon as they walked in the door. Jade failed the first couple of times and Brian had a zero-tolerance policy, so she'd be grounded. But she figured out how to trick the test by getting sober friends to pee in a bottle for her. And she also spent less and less time at home so that when she was stoned, we didn't see it.

Then there was the time Jessi was in ninth grade, basketball season was in full swing, and she came home one Saturday night from a concert at the Boulder Theater and admitted to me she'd been smoking weed.

"Mom," she said, "my friends were all doing it, so I had some. I didn't even have that much, but if Dad finds out he'll be so mad." Brian was in the other room already pulling out the drug test.

She was right, and I didn't want to deal with his anger. I also didn't want her to miss any basketball—if she was grounded, I was uncertain Brian would even let her go to practice. I went into the bathroom with her and I peed in the cup.

Jade started 10th grade at New Vista and liked the smaller classes and more attention from her teachers. But soon, she struggled to complete assignments on time and fell further behind. While this school seemed to be a better fit for Jade, it was a mixed bag because the teachers gave her a lot of leeway and didn't hold her accountable. It was hard to fully understand what was going on because she maintained a semblance of functioning, even thriving, in certain areas, especially when it came to sports.

New Vista didn't have its own team, but she was allowed to continue playing basketball for Boulder High. This was a huge success because she had to get herself to practice. I interpreted this initiative as a sign that she was not too far down the rabbit hole of ugly behavior. How bad could things really be if she could continue playing sports and get herself to practice? We went to every game—she seemed to be having fun and got along with her teammates.

At the end of the season, Jade told us she didn't want to play basketball anymore. Just as my mom had done with me I told her she needed to do something, either play a sport or get a job. She decided to try out for the golf team. Both Brian and I were glad she chose another sport as it was firmly our belief that this could keep her on a better path.

In Colorado, golf season for girls starts in March, which can be challenging with the unpredictable weather. Many golf practices were at an indoor facility. When Jade's latest boyfriend started taking her and picking her up, I was happy because it saved me the trip.

At first, we rarely saw the boyfriend because he'd drop her off without coming in. But then I insisted we meet him. One evening after practice, he and Jade walked into the house and we all stood around in the kitchen for a few moments. He was tall, extremely thin, with dark hair and eyes. He never smiled, not even once to be polite as you'd expect a teenage boy to do when he's meeting his girlfriend's parents for the first time. He hovered around Jade and mumbled a few words to Brian and me and then left.

All googly-eyed over him, Jade claimed he was just really shy, so I ignored any misgivings I had. When she started spending more time at his house, I was relieved because, although she did seem to be doing better in school and sports, she was still difficult to be with at home.

I attributed it to normal teenage angst. This was a confusing time because there were many happy family moments, such as going to cut our Christmas tree on the Magnolia property and then decorating it together. Even after we started renting out the house, we continued to make the annual trek up the mountain. We had family game nights, and Jade would join us. But then, like a switch, she'd turn off and become sullen and angry. If I attempted to touch her, she'd shrink away from my hand like I had the plague.

Again, I chalked it up to hormones. I thought about all the times I told my mom I hated her when I was 15. I believed she'd grow out of it, like I had. This was around the same age I was when my mother and I reached a truce. It was after I got kicked out of camp and resolved to focus on school and sports. Even though Mom and I stopped fighting, there was that underlying tension that lasted far into my adulthood.

I convinced myself that my relationship with my daughters was different. After all, they communicated with me in loving ways, writing me letters on Mother's Day and birthdays because I always told them that a handwritten card meant much more to me than any gift. In her 15th year, Jade wrote me the following:

> *Momma,*
>
> *You know I love you to death. Well, ha, ha, I kinda have to, don't I? You have been an amazing mother to me. You have loved me through it all. Growing up is hard, as you know. Juice becomes alcohol. Candy becomes weed. Timeouts become detentions. Bikes become cars. Smiles become tears. Hearts get broken. Cooties become STD's. Everything becomes impossible. And yet we couldn't wait to grow up. Everything we all do is a decision that affects our futures. No matter how big or how small the decision is, it still does. And I have finally realized that 15 years into my life. Yes, school is very challenging for me and it always has been. But I also haven't made the best decisions. I'm learning though, I promise I am. And one thing that I've realized is that I have learned more from you than any high school or college is ever going to teach me. I love you and I look up to you more than anyone. You honestly are my idol. I love you so much Momma. Love, Jade*

> *"The more a daughter knows the details of her mother's life, the stronger the daughter will be."*

> —Anita Diamant, *The Red Tent*

Both of my girls regularly wrote such letters to me, although finding this one recently tucked away in my memory box was particularly poignant. It might help explain why I clung to the notion that Jade was just going through the trials and tribulations of the teenage years and was ultimately going to be fine.

Toward the end of 10th grade, Jade decided she wanted to switch schools again. She didn't think she could meet the requirements of New Vista and graduate on time and wanted another fresh start somewhere else. I was glad she was being proactive but also concerned she was still having trouble with school. I couldn't help but worry that she was running away rather than learning how to problem-solve. Even though I wasn't entirely sure a school change would be the answer, I was willing to let her try, so I arranged a visit to Boulder Prep, another alternative public school in Boulder County.

I was sold as soon as we walked in the door. There was a small reception area, but no security to go through like at the bigger high schools. Couches lined the entryway and off to the side, two boys played hacky sack while a girl with purple hair drew in a sketchbook. Other kids talked loudly and laughed in an adjacent area. Jade was not so easily impressed and had sunk into herself—she hardly seemed awake. Lili, the headmaster, met with us and asked Jade why she was interested.

"I don't like it where I'm at right now," she said, her hair hanging in her face as she looked downward, fidgeting with her fingers, chipped turquoise nail polish on the tips. Then we met with Andre, who'd been a lawyer before founding the school. During his career, he'd seen a need for alternative education for kids who didn't fit into what was being offered. He retired from law and devoted his life to providing a safe and effective learning environment for anyone who needed it. He wanted to change the perception of alternative schools, as well as the one regarding the kids who go to them, so he made the decision to have the school be college preparatory. To graduate, students must apply to five colleges and receive at least one acceptance. The school is small with about 100 students.

Andre sat with Jade on one of the couches and started looking through her transcript. Putting it aside, he turned to her and asked, "Jade, what do you want to learn?"

She looked at him like he had two heads.

"I don't know," she said.

He told her that at Boulder Prep she could take classes she was interested in, and possibly even bypass math, which he could see from her grades had been a problem area. He asked if she liked horses and told her about the horse therapy class they offered. Jade sat up a little straighter and almost looked directly in his eyes. She still didn't smile, but she was listening. I was embarrassed by her lack of interaction and even interjected at times, trying to cover up for what I perceived as her insolence. Andre didn't seem to notice or care and continued to speak to her like she was an adult.

The one issue that could have been a deal-breaker was Jade had enrolled in hairstyling at the tech school and was scheduled to start in the fall of 11th grade when she would enter Prep. The schedule at Prep was arduous. There were all-school meetings every student was expected to attend; Jade would have a hard time making those if she were attending the technical high school simultaneously. I brought this up, and Andre assured us they could make it work even though they didn't have many students attend tech precisely due to this reason. His assurances opened possibilities for Jade that we hadn't imagined.

As soon as we walked out the front door, I asked her what she thought.

"I love it," she admitted.

I realized her stance inside had been a protective cover, and I couldn't help but wonder, *Had we, perhaps, found the answer?*

Jade had always wanted to do volunteer work abroad, so that summer after her sophomore year we arranged for her to go on a service trip to Costa Rica for three weeks. She told everyone she encountered about the upcoming trip, which would include a homestay with a family, time in the rainforest, and learning to surf. But when it came time to leave, her devastation at the thought of leaving her boyfriend was something I wasn't prepared for.

As we stood in front of the house, waiting for her to get in the car, she clung to the boy and refused to let go. Brian made himself busy loading her bags and going in and out of the house while I stood nearby watching. She was in tears and almost inconsolable. I finally snapped. "Jade, you're only going to be gone three weeks. Get in the car."

As I look back now, I see that her feelings of longing for him were so overwhelming she would have done anything for him.

Jade came back from Costa Rica re-energized. Eleventh grade left the impression she had figured it all out. She was prospering in school, getting As in all her classes. At parent-teacher meetings, we got rave reviews. One of her teachers even had her doing some student-teaching.

In hairstyling, she won one of three awards given to students for a term project. The fact she had worked on it for months and stuck with it was an accomplishment in and of itself. Getting acknowledged was the jackpot after a series of what I already considered wins. We went to the awards ceremony, and when she was called on stage, her smile was as big as the auditorium, despite her boyfriend not showing up. She also made the varsity golf team and won "most improved golfer" for the season.

I was lulled into thinking she was back on track and everything would be fine.

The boyfriend was still in the picture, and at the end of summer 2015, they went on a road trip that Jade had planned. It was all she talked about for weeks. I had consented, despite any misgivings because, once again, I heard my mom's voice: "Let them explore, be independent, and make their own mistakes."

While they were on their trip, I was in Leadville, Colorado, at a running camp with the Boulder High cross-country team, where I was an assistant coach. I was in the car with the head coach as we pulled into our small roadside motel with its redwood cabins nestled into the woods when Jade called and confided things weren't going well.

"I'm going to break up with him," she told me.

Inside I was ecstatic, but I tried to stay calm. "Why?" I asked.

"He doesn't want to do anything," she responded. "Every time I suggest something to do like go explore a new town or try a restaurant, he says no."

I was sad for her that the trip wasn't meeting her expectations, but I couldn't have been happier that she was ending the relationship. As I hung up with her, I had a huge smile on my face.

At the time, I didn't make the connection, but now I realize I was relieved because I had lived this same scenario with Joe, picking a person who didn't match me in energy or spirit. Now Jade, years younger than I was when I broke up with Joe, was showing a self-awareness that took me a lot longer to develop.

The first two months of fall 2015 were uneventful.

But while things seemed calm in our lives, what this truly signifies is my failure to notice Jade's mood going from bad to worse. She was disconsolate about her break-up with her boyfriend. She holed up in her room when she was home and if she did come upstairs, it was just to get food before disappearing again. I told myself she would get over it.

One way she coped was to become extremely close with her ex-boyfriend's sister, Nora. At first, I was happy Jade had someone to be with, and Jade seemed genuinely fond of Nora and vice versa. But as time went on, the relationship led both girls down a dangerous road.

One day in mid-October, Jade came home from school and was animated for the first time in a while. "Mom," she blurted out, "can I go to Paris?"

"What?" I asked. "With whom and why?"

"Nora is going with her mom, and they invited me."

"When is this happening?"

"In three days."

"Are you kidding me? And they just invited you?" Incredulous, I wondered how on earth we could make it happen.

"Please, Mom!" she begged. How could I say no to such an opportunity? I always considered traveling the best way to learn. Nora's mom was a business owner and could position the trip as being ostensibly for work. I knew Jade would get to see the sights and sounds of Paris.

You might be asking how we arranged all the details in such a short time and how much it cost? Well, the truth is it wasn't that difficult. Both schools agreed to let Jade go and, in the true spirit of Boulder Prep, the teachers there were enthusiastic and thought it would be a great learning experience. Nora's mother said she would take care of the flight, lodging, and food. I was blown away by this generosity, but also realized I had done the same for both my kids at various times, paying expenses for a friend to join us on family trips. Still, I was touched by the offer.

There was a catch though. Nora's mom expected Jade to work off the cost of the trip at her business after they returned. Jade was excited about that opportunity as she was interested in the business and wanted to be part of the luxurious world Nora's mom lived in.

I had my doubts about how this would all pan out and how many hours she expected Jade to work. The ticket was expensive, and Jade was coming back not only to Boulder Prep but to the very demanding hairstyling program. I didn't see how she'd have the time to work off the ticket.

The next thing I knew, Jade was sending us pictures of herself and Nora standing on a spiral staircase. They were dressed to the nines in slinky dresses and high heels and smiling from ear to ear. I thought to myself, *How lucky we are that Jade gets to have this experience.*

In hindsight, there was something almost perverse about it, though. At the time I couldn't put my finger on it, but Jade later reminded me that her ex-boyfriend's mother and sister were treating her like a member of the family while he wasn't even invited on the trip.

Little did I know that Jade's drug use was escalating during this time and that she was getting deeper and deeper into a world that might have swallowed her forever. Jade told me that after Paris, she started using meth. Apparently, she had a whole other group of people she was hanging out with that were heavy into meth, and she went along for the journey.

When Jade returned from Paris, she was on cloud nine for a few days. Then reality set in. She was behind on schoolwork and struggling. About a week after returning, she told me her hairstyling teacher was being mean to her. "I'm trying really hard on the hair coloring project, but she keeps telling me I'm doing it wrong. She won't give me any extra time to finish."

"Should I talk to her?" I asked. "You know, you still qualify for special accommodations and should be given extra time to complete assignments."

"No," she replied. "I'll deal with it."

I couldn't help but wonder if Paris had been a mistake.

Not only that, but Nora's mom became a thorn in our side about Jade working to pay off the ticket. She would call me telling me I had to make Jade fulfill the bargain. My philosophy was if you invite someone on a trip and say you are going to pay for them, you don't then ask them to work it off. "You need to work this out with Jade," I said. "After all, neither one of you even bothered to tell me about this arrangement until after you bought the plane tickets."

But she continued to badger us. I struggled with what to do because while I knew the trip was expensive, she had asked Jade to go. Yes, Jade agreed to work for her, but there was never any concrete agreement about what that would look like. Of course Jade agreed—she was 17 and being offered a trip to Paris.

Little did I know that Jade was high most of the time after the trip, and she and Nora were inseparable. This partnership would culminate in one of the scariest moments of our lives.

Crisis

On the night of the last day of school for the fall semester, Jade and Jessi both had friends over to celebrate, including Nora. They were all hanging out downstairs laughing and having fun. Our family was scheduled to leave in a few days for a family vacation to Mexico, so this seemed like a good time to have a small going-away party. I ordered pizza. After dinner, the kids went downstairs to play pinball and hang out. Around 10 p.m. I went down to say good night.

Around 3 a.m., I woke up to red and blue lights blinking outside and strange noises in the house. Brian and I jumped out of bed and ran downstairs to find men in uniforms going toward Jade's room. "I called 911," one of the kids said to me, "because I think Jade ODed."

I was furious. "Why didn't you come wake us up?" I snapped at him, before turning my attention to the EMT who was already going into my oldest daughter's bedroom. Brian stayed in the hallway with the other two emergency personnel and the kids while I joined the EMT. There, in her 10x10-foot room, we found Jade curled up in the corner of her bed, huddled under the covers.

"Jade," the paramedic said in a soothing tone, "I'm going to examine you and see how you're doing. Can you tell me what you took?" She was moaning and crying, but she was awake and aware I was in the room. She didn't answer his question.

"Mommy," she cried, "I just want to go to Mexico." I went to her and lay next to her. I held her and told her everything would be alright.

"She's agitated, but her vitals are normal," the paramedic said to me. "At this point, it's entirely up to you whether you want us to take her to the emergency room."

Here was my 17-year-old, crying like I hadn't seen her since she was 7. My heart was breaking. I tried to calm her down and somewhat succeeded. Because the EMT didn't think she was in imminent danger, and she begged us to let her sleep it off, Brian and I agreed to keep her home.

I still didn't know what she was on, and really, I didn't want to know. She was able to talk to me, and I took that as a sign that nothing was truly wrong—that she'd be fine. When I heard it wasn't urgent that she receive medical care, I jumped on it as a reason to let her be. Although Jade's behavior was alarming, it was clear she had not overdosed.

When you want to believe something, especially about your kid, you can convince yourself. Plus, in Jade's own recent words to me, "Mom, I was lying to you all the time, and I knew what I was doing." It was easy for me to continue the game of charades.

What I came to find out about that evening is that Nora and a boy were flirting with each other and making out in front of Jade. At the time, Jade had a huge crush on the boy, but he liked Nora. Jade had been devastated seeing him with Nora, and her longing to be loved and her feelings of rejection led her to try to numb the pain with drugs, including oxycodone and alcohol.

When the emergency crew left, everyone tried to go back to sleep. But by 6 a.m., I was up and getting ready to do what I always do when I am backed against a corner—run.

I look back at that day and wonder if I should have skipped it and stayed home with her. But running has always been my way of coping, and going for that run allowed me to settle myself and come back and deal with the aftermath. It did help, but the truth is when I was up at 3 a.m. dealing with the crisis, one of my first thoughts was about my ruined workout the next morning.

This is the way addicts think. How different were Jade and I, really?

When I got home, mid-morning, Jade was still in bed. Some of the friends were awake and talking downstairs. "I need you to go home now," I said, "I'm still not sure what exactly happened last night, but it's time for you to leave."

The next few days before leaving for our trip to Cabo San Lucas remain a blur of survival. We had gone there a couple of years prior and had a great time, so I'd planned this trip months earlier knowing we'd all appreciate the break from winter. I was thankful this trip included only our immediate family, as I couldn't have handled the dynamics more people would have added.

As soon as we stepped off the plane into the sun and the tropical air enveloped us, I believed everything would be fine. A few days on the beach would make everyone feel better.

When we got to our hotel, La Blanca, white stucco buildings greeted us, and everything looked warm and inviting. Our room was a suite with a large kitchen and living room. We gave the girls the master bedroom so that Brian and I could get up early to work out without disturbing them. We had a beautiful view from the deck that overlooked the center courtyard of the hotel with brick pathways lined with flower beds. The entire hotel was white, so the contrast of the walls with the flowers made everything that much brighter.

We put on our bathing suits and headed toward the pools and beach. The hotel was all-inclusive—we didn't have to think about the cost or timing of getting food. We went right to the poolside café. Brian got fish tacos; the girls ordered burgers and fries; I asked for a fruit salad. Jade was antsy and couldn't sit still while waiting for our order. She kept getting up and walking to the edge of the restaurant where the beach and ocean were in clear view. Once the food came, she seemed to calm down.

But over the next few days, her manic behavior was bizarre and threw me off balance. We developed a routine that included my morning runs, then meeting for breakfast at the buffet, followed by beach time. There were activities on the beach, and we paid for the girls to use wave runners one day. Jade had her own while Jessi and Brian were on another. He let her drive as soon as they were far enough out. I was content to lie under an umbrella and read magazines.

There was always a sand volleyball game happening right in front of our hotel and while Brian and Jessi played some, Jade was obsessed and joined in whenever she could. When she was out on the court, her long blond hair flowing behind her as she dove for a ball, I had moments of convincing myself she was back to herself, and all she had needed was this getaway.

One night we had dinner plans that required reservations. Jade had specifically requested we eat at this restaurant, so I'd made the reservation even though I preferred just showing up whenever we were ready to eat.

It was about 5 p.m. when Jessi asked if I would go up to the room with her so she could shower. She had always hated having sand on her for any longer than necessary. Brian was paddleboarding, and Jade was playing volleyball, so I agreed but told her I was going to the gym for twenty minutes to lift some weights while we waited for Brian and Jade to come up and get ready for dinner. As I walked through the courtyard on my way to the gym, I was thinking about how happy I was to be in the warm weather, savoring the few minutes of alone time.

When I got back to the room, Brian was in the shower, but Jade was nowhere to be seen.

"Brian," I asked through the bathroom door, "did you remind Jade to come up when you left the beach?"

"No," he responded, "I didn't see her."

"She was right there on the volleyball court," I said, annoyed that he hadn't taken the time to stop.

I went down to the beach to remind Jade we had a 6:30 reservation. There she was in the middle of the court, surrounded by other players, male and female, all laughing and waiting for the next serve. "Jade," I shouted to her, "we have a reservation."

"I know, Mom," she said, waving me away. It looked like she was practically swaying on the court and I wished I could see her eyes, but the truth is I just thought she was being difficult for the sake of it.

"Alright," I said, "but you probably need to come up soon if you want to shower." I went back up to the room. Brian was out of the shower and getting dressed and Jessi was waiting for me. At 6:15 we went back down, and Jade was still playing.

"Jade," I called out, "our reservation is in 15 minutes."

"I know," she hissed back.

I was mad, but the three of us headed over to the restaurant overlooking the ocean. The tables had red tablecloths, white linen napkins, and lanterns as centerpieces. There were lights strung overhead, and the waiters wore black and white uniforms. It was lovely but still no sign of Jade.

I asked Brian to go and tell her to leave the game. Jessi and I sat and waited, and it was as if a brick were sitting on my heart.

"I can't believe you made me leave that game," she said when she finally showed up.

"Jade," I reminded her, "you were the one who wanted to eat here."

She ignored me. A plate full of rigatoni in tomato sauce, one of her favorites, sat in front of her, and she refused to touch it. Brian, Jessi, and I ate in silence while we listened to the waves coming up to the beach, the sun sinking behind the horizon. The sky darkened, and the almost full moon cut the sky with a dreamlike quality. But it did little to change the somber mood at the table. I was dumbfounded, heartbroken, and plain sad.

The next day, Jade showed up at the breakfast buffet with a huge smile on her face. "I can't wait to get to the beach," she said, "Jessi, hurry up and eat so we can get down there."

I was disturbed but at the same time didn't want to discourage her enthusiasm. Jade had always been unpredictable; my mother used to call her our drama queen, but this was a whole new level and getting beyond my ability to handle. Later, I found out that Jade had brought Xanax with her and was high half the time we were in Mexico. I was under the impression she was sober for the week, so when we got home, I thought for sure our lives would settle down. My need for control led to my continued denial.

I recently found a note I had written on a hotel notepad while we were in Cabo. In scribbled notation it reads:

> *My 17-year-old daughter is in crisis. How do I help her when I do not understand her up and down emotions? One minute she is on top of the world, the next, crying hysterically. This is not an exaggeration. She will speak the words of a saint, telling everyone she meets "to have a wonderful day" but with her family she can be the cruelest of cruel.*

CHAPTER 22
Game of Charades

As Brian and I entered Lili's tiny office at Boulder Prep, Jade moved as far away from us as she could even though the room was barely the size of a large closet. Scooting her plastic chair into a corner, Jade sat below a poster that read *Books Are the Secret to the Soul*, where she gazed at the industrial gray-blue carpet, the distance between us a huge chasm someone could fall into forever. The headmaster leaned forward from behind her cluttered desk, taking the time to make eye contact with each one of us before she cut to the chase.

"Jade," Lili said, looking at my little girl who was hiding behind a curtain of sun-bleached blond hair, "on a scale of one to five, with five being the highest, how much do you want to use cocaine on a daily basis?"

Not looking at us, Jade studied her chewed fingernails for a second before she answered, "four," and all four walls officially closed in on me.

I had no idea how far gone Jade was when Lili called that morning, asking us to come in right away for a family conference. "I was hoping she'd come back from winter break refreshed, anew," she'd explained on the phone, "but instead she came back worse." *Why didn't I see it coming*, my internal voice asked. Her volatility in Mexico alone should have been a signal.

When we arrived at the school, Jade met us out front, a vacant stare on her face. This was not the same person I'd said goodbye to just a few hours earlier. Behind her, a panoramic view of the snow-capped mountains beckoned me to run away. When Jade delivered "four" in Lili's office I saw the Front Range again in my mind's eye, and just wanted to seek refuge in that sanctuary.

I did everything I could to remain present and available by grounding myself in that room rather than mentally sprinting away. I sat on the edge of my chair, pushed the soles of my feet into the carpet, and made eye contact with whoever was speaking as we discussed the options Jade faced.

Lili made it clear Jade could not come back to school until she got sober. At this point, it was as if Jade woke up from her stupor as she very clearly laid out the possible programs she could go to.

"I know of this one place Mandy went to for 30 days and it totally helped her."

To this, Lili responded, "Jade, you know Mandy is still having some serious issues."

"Well, then, I should just go to Centennial Peaks in Louisville," she said, "Mom, you need to make an appointment for me."

As I struggled to keep my composure, I asked, "You can do that?"

"Yes, Mom, Amanda and Harrison both have been there, and they told me all about it."

When we got home, Brian went back to work. Jade went to her room, and I called to make the appointment. They told me they had a bed available, so I scheduled her session for noon the next day. Soon after, Nora came over to help Jade pack.

"Don't worry, Vicki," she said to me. "I know exactly what Jade needs to bring." Turns out Nora had also spent time there. They went downstairs and when I heard giggling, I was struck by the absurdity of the situation. Jade was getting ready to go to a mental health institution as if she were going to summer camp.

Jade recently clarified that she was not excited about the prospect of going to this facility, rather she was sick and tired of feeling so horrible and just wanted it to stop. Nora, at the time, was able to lift her spirits temporarily.

As soon as Nora left, Jade reverted to her moody self. Jessi had a basketball game and, although we didn't give her a choice, Jade wanted to go as well. That threw me off again—how can she be an addict who's miserable and still want to watch her sister play? At the game, Jade cheered for Jessi as she always did and I wondered, *Is this all even real? Is she pretending to have a drug problem?*

After the game, she waited for Jessi to come out of the locker room, while Brian and I stood at the front of the building. Then we all walked to the car together, but Jade wouldn't talk to Brian or me for the entire ride home. It was a puppet show and Jade was pulling all the strings.

The next day when I left for my run, Jessi had already left for school and Brian was eating breakfast. Jade was still in her room. As I made my way through our neighborhood to the trails in South Boulder, I conjured an image of Jade when she was about 2 years old. We were visiting my mom in Florida. We had taken Jade to a nearby park while Mom shopped in Delray Beach, then we walked back toward town, the main street full of upscale shops and cafes. We located the store where my mom had told us she would be, and while Brian and I waited, we sent Jade in on her own as we watched from the doorway. Jade walked right up to Meema, who was talking to one of the salespeople, tugged on her skirt and held her arms out to be picked up. I can still hear Mom's shriek of delight when she looked down to see her grandbaby dressed in a one-piece romper looking up at her.

I wanted to recapture the innocence and pure love from that moment and wrap it up and hand it to Jade so she could remember how loved she was.

Jade and I left the house around 11:45 a.m. On the car ride, she was sullen and looking out the window or down at her lap—anything to avoid me. One of the counselors would talk to her upon arrival, and depending on what Jade said, a determination would be made as to whether she would be admitted. All I could think was, *They have to take her, I can't deal with this another minute.*

So I asked her what she was going to say to them.

"I want to hurt myself," she responded, with eyes cast downward, hair hanging in her face, and shoulders slumped forward.

"I don't understand," I said. 'How long have you felt this way?"

"Of course, you don't Mom," she blurted back at me. "You've never been depressed a day in your life."

And then it all clicked. She was depressed, just like my mother, and she was self-medicating. This made so much more sense to me than attaching the identifier "addict" to her. For most of her life, I had an image in my mind of the light-hearted, carefree Jade from her early childhood. I never wanted to see the sad side that was lurking there. Brian insisted she had an addiction issue, but I pushed back because it didn't jive with my view of her.

We arrived on time, and as we pulled into the parking lot in front of a nondescript, one-level building next to Avista Hospital, I realized I had never noticed it before, even though I had driven by countless times. We entered the facility which was eerily empty. There were no magazines or vending machines, just rows and rows of chairs and not one person. The counter where a receptionist should have been was vacant. I could see two sets of doors going in different directions, like what you see in a hospital corridor. I wondered if we were in the wrong building. Just then, a woman came out from behind one set of the closed doors. "Can I help you?" she asked.

"We have an appointment for Jade Hunter," I said.

"Oh, wait here and I'll get someone," she responded.

It wasn't long before another woman came out and introduced herself as Leslie, one of the social workers on duty. "We tried to call you," she apologized. "The bed we had for Jade is no longer available."

I had been in such a rush to get us there that I didn't look at my messages before we left. However, they could still do the intake so, thinking I had no other option, I agreed. Jade didn't argue, and I think she also thought she had no choice. Besides, she was in pain and just wanted it to stop. Leslie walked us through the other set of doors that opened to a much larger lobby area. This one had lots of activity with people going in different directions. The social worker took Jade through yet another set of doors and told me I should wait while they did the intake interview.

There was a cafeteria off to the side, and I could see people, who I assumed were patients, many of them around Jade's age, dressed casually, wandering in and out. As I sat there, I started thinking about the rest of my day—first going to the pool, and then getting some errands done, confident I'd be leaving Jade there shortly.

After 20 minutes, Leslie came out and asked me to join her in the back where Jade was waiting in a small conference room. "Based on what Jade told us, we need to put her on a 72-hour hold."

Jade was sitting in a chair, leaning over the table in front of her, resting her head on her crossed arms. I couldn't see her eyes but could tell from this posture she was overwhelmed.

"What does that mean if you don't have a bed for her?" I asked.

She looked at me, in her business suit attire, hair tied back in a taut ponytail, and with a condescending tone replied, "We're trying to find a facility that can take her."

"Can I take her home until you find something?" I asked.

"Oh, no, she's suicidal, and state law requires we keep her until we can transport her to another hospital," she spat back at me.

They couldn't admit her, and they wouldn't release her. Jade started to cry. I felt like I was in a nightmare of my own making. Just a couple of hours earlier, I'd been looking forward to dropping Jade off at a facility that would take care of her and give me a respite from her problems. But now it seemed I was being punished for that wish.

It became a waiting game while they searched for an alternative hospital and an ambulance to take her there because I wasn't allowed to drive her. The caseworker told us there were two choices: Highlands Behavioral Health Center in Denver and West Springs Hospital across the state in Grand Junction.

The latter triggered a slight panic as the mere thought of driving eight hours round trip just to visit was overwhelming. Between work, Jessi's games, and even food shopping, on top of basic needs like eating, sleeping, and bathing, I knew this would mean forgoing some runs. The unease this caused, even though it hadn't been confirmed yet, made my heart pound and my chest ache even more than it already did.

Meanwhile, we were taken to a tiny room with two chairs, a ratty carpet on the floor and nothing to do—no magazines, no television, nothing. Thinking I'd be dropping her off, I hadn't brought anything to distract us. Jade and I alternated between trying to get comfortable lying on the floor and sitting in the incredibly uncomfortable upright chairs planted in the middle of the cubicle-like space. When Jade attempted to lie on the floor to sleep, she'd moan and cry at the same time. "I can't get comfortable," she whined.

"Jade," I said, "I know this sucks, and I'm sorry, but we have no choice right now and there's nothing I can do." She just started crying harder. I was angry at the situation and myself. Why didn't I think of another option before we got stuck like this? I'd always been able to control problems by coming up with a strategy before things got out of hand. In this case, the wheels were moving too fast, and I was just hanging on.

Although I had called Brian to tell him the situation, he was still at work, and I was drowning under the weight of holding it together. He'd said he would get there as soon as he could, but he needed to take care of a few things first. I checked my watch every 15 minutes. Jade had gone from crying uncontrollably to curling herself into a ball on the floor.

Every so often, Leslie would come in to check on us but had no news, which made the clock move even slower.

At 3:11 p.m., Brian arrived, and I fell apart. I took one look at him, in his khaki pants and polo shirt, and fell into his arms. For the first time that day, tears rolled down my cheeks as I tried to make sense of what was happening. He did his best, trying to make us laugh by being silly, but it didn't work. Then he'd offer to go to the vending machine and get whatever Jade wanted, but she continued to sulk while I did some Foundations. The classic pose called the Founder opens the back line of the body and doing the decompression breathing at the same time can reset your nervous system. It was helping me cope.

Around 5 p.m., Leslie, her beige skirt now wrinkled and her make-up dulled, came in to tell us the Denver facility had a bed for her. I let out a sigh and started to breathe fully for the first time in hours. At the same time, the thought of her going to a mental hospital we knew nothing about made me nauseous. In addition, she told us we now needed to wait for an ambulance to transport Jade to the facility.

"How long will that be?" I asked.

"As long as it takes to find one that's available," she responded. I couldn't believe the absurdity of this, knowing that Brian and I could have taken her that very moment. So even though I knew the answer, I asked if we could drive her there ourselves.

"Absolutely not, the state requires that she go by ambulance," and it was clear by her tone she was sick of dealing with us.

We went back to our dungeon to wait two more hours for the

ambulance to arrive. At least now we saw an end to the torture of the day, but that was layered by the unknown of where Jade was going. Those two hours stretched into an eternity, but finally, a little after 7 p.m., the ambulance driver and his partner came into the facility with a stretcher and said they were ready to take Jade.

"Is that necessary?" I asked, pointing at the gurney.

"Yes," one of them said, "she needs to be restrained in the ambulance." Now, I really did want to throw up. Jade hovered beside me, waiting for the next step. Her eyes welled up and a few tears rolled down her face.

"It's going to be OK," I told her.

CHAPTER 23
Worst Day Ever

I gaze out the window of the ambulance, politely nodding my head and pretending to be listening to the driver going on about his family, but really, I'm screaming in my head, "Shut up!"

Boulder is receding in the rearview mirror. As we travel along back roads to the hospital in Denver, the reflection of the blue snow-tipped mountains gets smaller and smaller. I wonder why he's taking this route because it seems to be taking way longer than it should.

I keep my mouth shut and pray it won't be much longer.

I try to peek at the stretcher behind the screen in the back. *Please let her be OK. Please let her be OK. Please let her be OK.*

I had to sit up front with the driver while Jade was in the back of the vehicle with the other paramedic. I could barely see her through the divider. I thought she was asleep, but she later told me she was awake and mortified to be strapped down.

As horrifying as it was at the time, I'm now grateful for that day and for the strict requirements in place. Before Jade and I showed up at Centennial Peaks, I think Jade thought it was going to be like a mini-vacation. The subsequent torture of waiting all day and then having to be transported by ambulance drove home that this was no game.

By the time we got to the Highlands facility, it was 9 p.m. Brian parked in the lot and met us at the back of the ambulance where the two paramedics unloaded Jade. The driver said they would let her walk in with us. They unstrapped her and she moved to my side as if the ambulance itself was on fire. The driver came inside holding a clipboard.

As we entered, I knew this was a place for serious cases. There was no one in the entryway, and a locked gate stood just inside the front doors. The driver pushed a call button and once inside, orderlies and nurses in white met us from the end of a long corridor. *Is this the Cuckoo's Nest?* I kept thinking. But they were as kind as could be. The driver got a signature from one of the doctors and left. I didn't even have a chance to thank him.

Within 15 minutes of arriving, we were saying goodbye to Jade. She mumbled goodbye as I tried to hug her, but she wouldn't let me get close enough. I just told her I loved her.

Brian stood nearby and as she walked away, he told her the same thing. We watched as two nurses accompanied her down the long corridor and got in the elevator without turning around before the doors closed.

We were left to fill out some paperwork and find out details about the next few days. We were told visiting was only allowed on Monday, Wednesday, and Friday during the week and Saturday and Sunday. This was Wednesday night, which meant we couldn't come the next day even if we wanted to. The thought of this on the drive home allowed my body to melt into the seat. All the tension in my neck and back slipped away.

I had my first good night of sleep in months. My run Thursday morning, even though it was just on the bike path around our neighborhood, made me appreciate more than ever the escape it provided. It was a chilly morning, but the sun was shining, and I slipped into the numbing sensation that can happen from the soothing, rhythmic motion of one footfall after another. It was all I needed to momentarily forget what was happening.

When I got home, I was happy to have no one around, especially Jade. Did I feel guilty? Yes, but the weight off my shoulders for that one day was enormous.

I spent the rest of the day on the phone with rehab programs and specialists. I also spoke at length to the psychiatrist assigned to Jade. He told me that he was giving her a dual diagnosis of depression and addiction which officially qualified her for a residential treatment program. In addition, he was recommending she go on antidepressants. Grasping at straws, I agreed we should try medication. But Jade ended up refusing to take anything. I'm still not clear how this transpired. I only know she was adamant about not taking prescribed drugs.

When we discussed it later, she said she'd seen too many friends become dependent on pharmaceuticals and she didn't want to do that since drugs were such a problem for her. In her own words from a recent conversation, "It felt backward for me. I was using anything and everything, and to be prescribed drugs felt like signing up for failure."

I know this is controversial, that many people benefit from antidepressants, and to this day I still don't know if it was the right decision. At the time, I was proud of her for making this choice. I thought it showed strength of character and her will to get better on her own. It signaled to me that she was moving in the right direction.

How could I continue to have this rose-colored view of the situation? I don't have a great answer except I just refused to believe she wouldn't get better.

But Brian wasn't convinced and continued to voice his concerns that she was going to need months in a treatment center. "Vicki," he said to me on Friday as we drove down to see her, "she might die if we don't do the right thing here. You've been in denial for too long, and this happened because you refused to see it."

"So it's my fault?" I shouted. "You're the addict—she got this from you." Then I said, "Just stop talking, I can't listen to you right now."

I refused to adopt a fear-based approach. This had been a sticking point for us for as long as I could recall. Brian was an optimist in general, but not about our girls. He worried they would make the same mistakes he did. I understood his fears, but I also knew it didn't help anything to operate from that place. The girls knew how he would react if they did anything he didn't approve of, so they hid stuff from us, Jade more so than Jessi, but they both did it. As a result, I often acted as the buffer.

Later, I reminded him that he had gotten sober without going into treatment. So had his paternal grandfather, who according to the stories, almost died driving home drunk from his own retirement party. When his wife, Brian's grandmother, threatened to kick him out if he didn't stop drinking, he proceeded to go cold turkey. Perhaps, not only addiction runs in the family, but perseverance.

The weeks to follow were full of ups and downs. But like being submerged in water with my head just above the surface, struggling to breathe, the constant effort was exhausting. I look back now and realize that Jade and I were reliving the trauma we both experienced while she was in my belly. Brian, on the other hand, knew firsthand what it meant to be an addict, and he had no illusions. In his mind, there was only one way for this to play out: she needed to get sober by any means necessary.

On Friday, Brian and I arrived at the facility for visiting hours. We checked in at the front desk and waited for an orderly to come through the locked doors to take us upstairs to the residential area. Getting off the elevator, I saw several teenagers milling about as if it was a typical high school. Kids were talking or playing cards in a group room we passed, and I had to keep reminding myself this was a hospital. We were taken to a private room with a whiteboard and a big table in the center.

A few minutes later, the door opened, and in bounded Jade, a huge smile brightening her face. She was animated and started telling us about some of the friends she'd already made. She didn't make any effort to hug us, but she couldn't stop talking. She called us over to the window to show us the outdoor area where they could get some fresh air.

"So, you feel better?" I finally managed to say, although it was more of a squeak that came out of my mouth.

"Oh yeah," she replied. "So much better! But you need to get me out of here. It feels like prison. They watch everything we do, and I can't even exercise."

I was holding my breath and wondering if she was trying to manipulate us again. Brian didn't say much and just sat at the table looking from Jade to me. To understand better, I feebly asked about the outdoor space. "Can't you exercise there?"

"Not really," she said. "We can toss a ball around, but I can't actually run or anything."

I couldn't help but wonder why running was suddenly a priority when she hadn't ever consistently been a runner. Was it because she knew this would appeal to me?

Jade then told us she had an idea. She proposed going to stay with Aunt Linda while we figured out where she would go for rehab. We all believed a residential program was the best option for her, and Jade shared our concern about her coming back to Boulder and being close to the friends she'd been hanging out with and the temptations they represented. I think she thought of Linda because she knew she lived near the Highlands facility, and she felt safe with her. Currently, there were few people Jade was willing to be vulnerable with, and Linda provided that security. The bottom line though was she simply wanted to get out of Highlands, so she was proposing a solution she thought could happen soon.

"It's a lot to ask," I told Jade. I was worried it would be too much for Linda to take on. All I could think about was that Jade would need to be closely supervised, and Linda was used to being on her own. Both of her adult children lived on their own, and her husband, Jim, had passed away years before. But I agreed to talk to her.

A social worker came in soon after we had this discussion and introduced himself as Adam. Middle-aged and graying at the temples, his facial hair didn't hide the kindness of his smile, and his laughing eyes put us all at ease.

"Jade," he said, "how are you doing today?"

"I'm great!" she replied.

He then turned to us and asked if we had any questions. We asked about what treatment Jade had received so far and as he started to answer, Jade interjected.

"Mom," she said, "tell him about my idea."

"I will," I told her. "But first, I want to hear a little more about what has gone on here the last couple of days.

He told us that he and Jade had spent quite a bit of time talking about what had brought her there. He also spoke about her group therapy sessions. He told us he was impressed with her desire to get better.

I then presented Jade's idea of going to Linda's while I continued to search for a suitable residential program. He didn't dismiss it, but he said he had some concerns.

"Jade," he said, switching the focus, "how did you afford so much cocaine?"

I realized he was referring to her initial intake interview, and I saw what he was getting at, something I had yet to consider. In my head, a horror movie began to play on the screen where I watched Jade slipping in and out of men's cars in dark alleys. But before the nightmare could completely unfold, thankfully, she adamantly denied ever having sex for drugs or drug money.

"I believe you," Adam said, "but you still haven't answered my question. Where did you get the money?"

"Different places," she said as she sunk into her chair and looked down at the table. "Sometimes I stole money from you guys. I used all my birthday and holiday money to buy stuff and other times, people just gave it to me." My inner dialogue was doubting the possibility of all of this, but I pushed those thoughts to the back of my mind and decided I needed to believe her. The alternative was too grim.

We continued to talk about the risks of Jade leaving the hospital too early.

"I'm worried," Adam reiterated, "that if she leaves now, she won't get the full benefit of what we can offer her here."

"I know I need to work on stuff," Jade replied, "but I think I'll do much better if I'm with Linda and have space to myself. I'm suffocating here. At Linda's, I can run and exercise and focus on myself."

When I heard her say those words, I wondered if my own strategy of using exercise to cope had somehow rubbed off on her? I wanted to believe this was the case. I'll admit, I also hated the idea of her being so constrained. Brian agreed that going to Linda's could be a good intermediate step but he wanted her to have treatment in a residential center—that was still the plan.

I left Brian and Jade in the room while I went outside to call my sister. Linda knew what we had been dealing with and graciously said Jade could stay with her with the understanding that it was temporary while I tried to find a suitable place for her to go.

Jade had to remain at the hospital for another 24 hours to meet the 72-hour hold. Brian and I drove home, shell-shocked by the idea Jade would be released so soon. It was Friday afternoon, so we went to Kundalini that evening.

Somehow the universe aligned, and Brian and I were the only ones there, allowing Karuna to focus on us. We had already shared what was happening with Jade, so the space was there for us to let go. Brian and I sat on our mats next to each other with our blankets and bolsters and chanted *ong namo guru dev namo*, the chant used to tune into your higher self. We both wept. There were moments during the class where I lost myself in the mantras and poses, but my mind kept coming back to whether I'd be able to fit in my Saturday morning workout before leaving to go pick up Jade.

Ego-driven Vicki was breaking through the meditation, terrified she'd lose control once again.

CHAPTER 24
Running for My Life

I woke up Saturday morning in overdrive, my nervous system fully in sympathetic mode. I was in fight or flight, running for my life. I never was the type who froze.

During the workout with my running buddies, I felt like I had an engine attached to my legs. I ran the fastest time on our course that I had in months. I told myself I needed to run fast to get back to the house so we could leave for Denver—as if a minute faster on a three-mile course was going to make any difference.

But my steps felt light as feathers, recalling that day I raced shortly after my father passed. It occurred to me how loss—or the thought of it—can fuel something deep inside my being. The heavy weight of grief channeled the light in me.

As much as I loved to run with this group of men, most of them at least a decade older than me, I was hesitant to share my turmoil. I didn't feel secure enough to share the trauma that was my life at that moment, even as Tom commented, "Wow, Vicki, something got into your legs today! You were flying over the course."

"Ah, Tom," I responded, "I'm just trying to keep up with you." And we laughed as I made an excuse for my quick departure.

On the drive back to the house to meet Brian and Jessi, I was fired up, worried that we were making a mistake taking Jade out so soon, and yet eager to get her on a path to recovery.

When we'd dropped Jade off at this mental health hospital just days before, she was strung out and in a bad way. Visiting her on Friday made me think much had changed since then and I was expecting her to be happy when I saw her. Brian and Jessi waited by the car while I went inside to sign release forms. Jessi, I can proudly say, handled it all remarkably well. Even at 15, she was very aware of Jade's problem and her need for help. She's a good sister.

As I got off the elevator with one of the nurses, Jade was there with her head hanging low and little animation in her voice or body. Where was the energetic being who had come dancing into the conference room just the day before? I even wondered if they had given her a sedative. She wouldn't hug me, which was nothing new—it had been years since she'd shown me any physical affection besides the quick hug or peck on the cheek.

It didn't take that long for the discharge, and as soon as she saw Jessi, Jade smiled. She took Jessi by the arm and dragged her away from the car, saying she wanted to show her something. All I could see was the two of them walking into the grass toward a ditch with their arms around each other's waists. I have no idea what they spoke about, but my heart was full as I saw Jade lean her head on Jessi's shoulder.

It was my idea to stop at Whole Foods to pick up some things before we went to my sister's. I thought Jade would want some of her favorites, like gluten-free pumpkin bread, salad bar, and chips, and she was pleased, at first. As I was talking about trying samples they had in the back of the store, Jessi approached me.

"Mom," she said as I stuffed a cracker with goat cheese in my mouth, "we need to get out of here, Jade is losing it." She was right. Jade was pale, her eyes glazed over, the lights, sounds, and crowd clearly too much, too soon.

Once again, I was caught off-guard as to how far Jade had strayed from my perception of who she was. As we drove into Linda's subdivision near Chatfield Reservoir in a suburb of Denver, I heaved a huge sigh of relief. Outside her house, Linda greeted us as she always did, with a smile and laughter saying how happy she was to see us. Both girls gave Linda a hug.

We unloaded the groceries and made small talk. Linda told Jade she could take her stuff to the guest bedroom, and Jessi went with her. Brian was busying himself in the garage helping to unload some heavy boxes with pet supplies Linda needed to be removed from her car. This gave Linda and me a chance to speak.

"Do you think she'll try to get drugs while she's here?" Linda asked.

"Honestly, no," I replied. "I really think she's determined to get sober." And I did believe this even though I knew the statistics. Addicts will manipulate and lie and often have relapses. But, in my heart, I still doubted whether Jade was a true addict. My motherly instincts told me she was using drugs to self-medicate and that she would recover. Maybe, I just wanted to believe this so much I refused to see any other possibility.

I spent the next five days on the phone with every possible program I could find in Colorado and even looked at some out-of-state options, although that was something we wanted to avoid if possible. The dual diagnosis of depression and addiction qualified her for a residential treatment program, but as I started researching programs it became obvious we were in a difficult position because Jade was about to turn 18. If she entered a juvenile program, she'd age out before the program was over. On the other hand, she was too young for an adult program. I saw a glaring hole in addiction treatment for young adults aged 18 to 21. I was frustrated to say the least. Meanwhile, I was speaking to Linda each day.

"Vicki," she asked on the third day, "are you making any progress in finding a place for her?"

"I'm trying," I responded, "but it's not easy."

"Well," she said, "I hope you to find something soon."

"Why?" I asked, "Is she being difficult?"

"Not really," she replied. "She requires a lot of attention, and I'm worried about her."

At this, my heart sank, because I saw the limited options, and I wasn't ready for Jade to come home. I was relishing not having her at home. The lack of tension was a gift I wasn't ready to give up.

Linda and I arranged to meet on the fourth day so we could all see each other, and I could assess how Jade was doing. Brian, Jessi, and I met Linda and Jade at a puppy drop-off in Denver. My sister helped with a dog rescue at the time, so every week she managed the transport of stray and abandoned dogs from neighboring states. The van was late getting there and since we were in the parking lot of a mall, I suggested going into Marshalls. Jade agreed, so she, Jessi, and I went in while Brian waited in the parking lot. Linda was busy talking to the volunteers who had come to foster one of the incoming dogs.

Once inside the store, Jade was short with me, tense, and reactive to anything I tried to point out like a cute top I thought she might like. "Mom, that's not my style, and besides, I don't need anything."

After a few more attempts of trying to cajole her into a better mood, I gave up. "Let's just head back out and see if the van has arrived," I said. She shrugged her shoulders and headed out the door five steps in front of me. Jessi looked at me with sad eyes and then caught up to Jade and they walked back together.

The dogs arrived soon after and I stood aside to let Jessi and Jade play with the animals. Both girls lit up at the sight of the dogs, especially the few puppies that happened to be in this particular load. As they held the baby animals and walked them around the lot, the air around us felt lighter. But my concern over Jade's well-being was causing me to want to control things that were clearly out of my hands. It had become apparent there were few programs suitable for Jade's situation, and the idea of her coming home was overwhelming me.

By this point, I had found a couple of programs that I thought would be great. There was one fairly close by that focused on outdoor activity, but when Jade learned it was four months long, she gave it a resounding no. Since being at Linda's she had decided her goal was to come back and finish her senior year. "Mom, I want to graduate with my class at Boulder Prep, and I want to finish hairstyling this semester."

Upon hearing this, part of me was encouraged, but part of me thought she was crazy. How could she possibly come back and do all of this while trying to get sober? Both Brian and I tried to convince her the most important thing was her health; she could finish high school later and complete the hairstyling program any time, but she was adamant. This was January, and she had missed a full week of school and a full week of hairstyling hours, which was huge because the hours were carefully mapped out, and time away was going to be hard to make up.

Over a week had gone by since the mental hospital ordeal, although it may as well have been a year. Now it was time for Jade to come home. Over the phone, Brian, Jade, and I agreed on what it would look like. Basically, we designed our own rehab program. She would be under our constant supervision unless she was at school. Boulder Prep agreed to let her take the rest of the quarter to deal with her recovery which meant she would start back there in early March. The school had taken major pains to stop the availability of drugs on campus since Jade's revelations that day in Lili's office. Hairstyling was another matter and we set up an appointment with the principal and Jade's teacher to discuss a plan.

I will never forget going to the technical high school, where Jade took the hair course. The receptionist buzzed us into the office and told us Principal Bludhorn would be with us shortly. A minute later Joan Bludhorn walked out to greet us and invited us back to a conference room next to her office. We all sat down at a table that had room for eight, to wait for Jade's teacher. Jade had already experienced conflict with her in the fall semester. I had chalked it up to the teacher being a hard-ass, which she was, but I now realized Jade had been using and most likely acting poorly in class.

As we waited, Principal Bludhorn made polite small talk with Jade and told us she expected the teacher any minute. Jade sat on her hands in the uncomfortable bucket seats, and we watched as the clock's hands continued to move. At 10 past the hour, the teacher strode into the room, and with a big huff sat down.

Jade, in a trembling voice, explained what was going on and apologized for her past behavior. "I know the drugs I was taking affected me, but I'm committed to getting sober and completing hairstyling." She went on to ask for some leeway as she attempted to make up the missed hours and assignments.

Principal Bludhorn was supportive and helpful throughout the meeting suggesting possible ways Jade could make up the work. On the other hand, the teacher was outright rude. She came up with every reason why Jade couldn't meet the requirements.

I finally spoke up. "But she's only missed a week of this semester so far," I said, using my eyes to plead with her, but she wouldn't even glance in my direction, keeping her gaze on Principal Bludhorn. Interestingly enough, she never mentioned the fall trip to Paris.

"She can't complete the hours and assignments," she hissed back. "She's already too far behind, and I will not spend any extra time supervising her."

With the principal's support, we finally got her to agree to a set of five assignments Jade needed to do for the missed work, and then she stormed out of the meeting before we formally finished. The principal was kind and agreed to help in any way she could, even offering Jade the use of her office after school to make up some of the hours. I was grateful for Joan Bludhorn and later wrote to her to say thank you. But I left there thinking Jade's teacher shouldn't be in that profession.

Thus began several months of constant vigilance around Jade's activities and her health. If she wasn't in school, either Brian or I was with her. We drove her everywhere and monitored everything she did. We implemented a strict schedule that worked around her hairstyling course. She had to exercise regularly; she had to keep up with school and chores; and most importantly, she had to attend Narcotics Anonymous meetings with Brian.

He never acted like this was a burden and would suggest different meetings around town until she found one where she got to know some of the people attending and felt welcome. She went daily for a while, and this seemed to make a huge difference. This continued for months, but the meetings became depressing and unproductive as she recognized how often the stories remained the same, with so many people relapsing. After a year, she stopped going. I think Brian and I both wished she had continued, but we realized we couldn't force her.

Another condition of her release from Highlands was that she receive counseling. I did some research and found a therapist in Boulder who specialized in teens with substance issues. Jade saw her once a week for about eight months. I would drive her there and pick her up; not once did we discuss the sessions or what was said. I was beyond curious, but the therapist had told me at the outset that everything Jade told her would be held in confidence and that she would not share anything with me unless she felt Jade was a danger to herself or others. Jade never volunteered any information, so I have no idea what they talked about.

But I saw improvement right away and wanted to believe she was getting over the hump—my impatience made me push her sometimes. I wanted her to be well so badly, I pretended everything was back to the way it was and she had to remind me it wasn't. Early on, I'd suggest we go for a run or go to yoga, and she'd often say, "Mom, I just need some time," and I'd realize what we were dealing with.

What I didn't understand then was that "patience is a form of action." That's a quote I recently found attributed to Auguste Rodin—the very same sculptor whose museum my family gifted to the city of Philadelphia a century ago.

Collectively, our family came together and supported Jade. Jessi, perhaps, is the one who had to step up the most. She was in ninth grade, adjusting to high school and playing basketball. She was there to support Jade, but she continued to do what she needed to do. She was selected MVP that basketball season. The whole family went to all her games, but we'd always done that—Jade always the loudest one cheering her on.

At one of the first games we went to after Jade came home from Linda's, I sat on the hard bleacher seats looking around at the other families, the noise of the gym reverberating in my ears, and thought, *they have no idea what we're going through.*

I felt alone in our story, but also knew that some of these families had struggles of their own. That knowledge didn't make me happy, but it made me let go of any victimhood I might have taken on otherwise. Being at the games gave us the sense we were a family again. Brian and I kept working, attending to our own personal needs by continuing to exercise. But we were all there for Jade 100 percent.

For about a month everything seemed to be going smoothly, so when Jade asked if she could go to a concert at the Boulder Theater with Jessi and some friends, we had a dilemma on our hands.

Brian was not on board. He was sure such an environment where people would certainly be partying was too tempting. As always, he anticipated the worst while I trusted she'd be fine. The addict's brain is different: Brian automatically knew how he would respond in the same situation, and he expected Jade to do the same. But she convinced us, or at least me, that it would be OK.

"It's all ages, so it won't be bad, Mom, and I'll be with Jessi and her friends," she cajoled.

At the concert, Jade got news that the mother of one of her close friends from Prep had ODed. Beside herself, she accepted some oxy from a friend. Jessi told us later she'd seen Jade in the lobby curled up in his arms and hadn't known why.

The good news is Jade told us as soon as they got home that evening and was truly remorseful. She cried as she confessed and said that she was just so sad that this mom, whom she'd had a close relationship with, couldn't get her act together. "It makes me want to get sober even more," she said.

We simply pointed out to her that this was the kind of trigger she needed to be most cautious around, and then I said, "It's time to move on."

I'll admit that Jade's reaction was another piece of her journey that I realized I had missed. While I knew of the boy whose mom had died, I had no idea Jade had developed such a close relationship with her. I won't lie, it hurt that she had this other life I was just beginning to witness. It hurt that she wouldn't let me hold her when I literally ached to do so and she found surrogate mothers in the mothers of her friends, women who appeared to have a multitude of their own problems.

Other information started to surface during this time. Jade admitted that when she first started dating her ex-boyfriend, Nora's brother, he was dealing cocaine and she started using with him and helped him deal. I wasn't surprised by this, but I was horrified to learn that the mom knew and never bothered to tell Brian and me. This truly made me furious but also helped me feel vindicated for not insisting that Jade work off those hours to pay for the Paris trip.

By March, Jade was sober, back in school full-time, and playing golf. The next few months were like a whirlwind, with her at its epicenter. Everything was geared toward helping her succeed, but it was her determination that carried her through. She busted her butt to complete her hairstyling hours while finishing her senior requirements at Prep and becoming the No. 1 golfer on the Boulder High team.

To this day, I am amazed by her fierceness in meeting all her goals. I think she was motivated by people telling her she couldn't do it, like the middle school teacher who told her she'd never graduate high school and the hairstyling teacher who never came around and, in fact, did all she could to thwart Jade's progress. One day in mid-March, I picked Jade up from hairstyling, and on the way over to Boulder Prep, she told me, "My teacher is making me do the hair color experiment twice."

"Why?" I asked.

"She said I need to do twice as much as everyone else since I missed the first week of the semester," she responded.

"That's ridiculous," I said. "We agreed on what you had to complete with the principal right in the room. I'm calling Joan and telling her this isn't okay."

"No, Mom, I'm going to prove I can do all of this. I don't care what she thinks."

In the end, she did it. Jade basically said, "Screw you!" to everyone who'd ever given her the message she was worthless.

Boulder Prep held its 2016 graduation at The Chateau at Fox Meadows, an elegant reception facility not too far from Boulder. We drove up to the manicured grounds surrounding a gorgeous, white, two-story building. Linda met us in the parking lot, and we all walked into the building together where a spiral staircase twisted upward from the center of a large room set up with rows of chairs. Jade and her classmates were running up and down the steps, getting ready to make their entrance. When Jade saw us, she smiled and came over to us, giving Linda a big hug while giving Brian, Jessi and me, perfunctory squeezes. She had just seen us that morning, so I wrote off her casualness to that. She went back to her friends, and we found seats in the middle rows and waited for the ceremony to begin.

The graduates entered by walking down the staircase and took their place at the front. Jade entered, smiling, holding hands with one of her classmates. She had taken enormous care getting ready. She'd straightened her long blond hair so it flowed over her shoulders and down her back and also did her makeup. She wore an off-white shift with slinky heels. She looked like a woman, not a little girl, and her smile erased the hardships of the last few years from my memory, at least for the moment. She was proud, and I was overcome with emotion to see her taking ownership of how far she had come.

There were 16 graduates, each one introduced by a teacher. They all took turns speaking to the audience. Jade's favorite teacher, Leah, spoke of Jade's courage and determination before calling her to the podium.

Jade looked out at the audience smiling from ear to ear, and then, with the strongest voice I'd heard from her in recent times, began, "Four months ago, I never thought I'd be here today." Brian squeezed my hand, and I could see tears in his eyes.

"Frankly," Jade continued, "I didn't think I was going to make it past my 18th birthday," and my heart dropped just in time for her to revive it with, "I am so grateful to be here."

As she spoke of the roller coaster of heartbreak, emotion, loss, and addiction, all those days flashed across the stage of our shared past, and I kept having to bring myself back to the moment, to my first-born, standing tall and speaking her truth. "Crazy ups and crazier downs," she said.

Looking up again, she continued, "I would never have made it this far if it weren't for my sister, dad, and mom. Jessi, thank you for being a pain in my ass. Mom and Dad, thank you for always pushing me to do my best and supporting me no matter what. I want to thank my Aunt Linda for letting me stay at her house while I was transitioning out of rehab." With that, Linda looked at me and smiled. Jessi put her arm around me as Jade gave us all a nod as she returned to her seat amid applause.

I think Jade knew she was on a path of self-destruction but did not know how to get off the roller coaster until it was almost too late. Having a support system of unconditional love around her was the parachute she needed. While we helped her find her footing back on this ground called life, she is the one who orchestrated the landing. She returned to herself.

Two years after Jade's graduation she was leaving on a road trip to Moab, Utah, and I walked out to her car to say goodbye. As she made the final checks on the Tepui tent on top of her Subaru, she paused, gave me a hug, and held on for more than an instant.

As we stood in that embrace, I realized it had been about seven years since she'd last let me really touch her. Jade had started withdrawing from the family in middle school, and along with this went her desire to be close to us physically. When I would go to hug her, she'd pull away. I tried not to let it bother me, but it always hurt. I would see her hug the mothers of her friends and flinch inside. Again, I wrote it off as part of being a teenager. But now I realize she was hurting, wrapping herself in a cloak of protectiveness so tight it would keep out anyone who might reveal the truth: that she was worthy of more; that she did not need to self-harm; that she could have a partner who treated her well. But now the cloak had lifted and she was seeing the light and being the light.

That hug was the best gift she could ever give me. And as I hugged her back, I let go of my past fears, trusting she wouldn't shrink away from me this time.

January 12, 2019, almost three years to the day that we took her to Highlands Mental Health Hospital, almost three years since my mother's death and my broken arm, and just shy of her 21st birthday, Jade summited Mount Kilimanjaro.

She had been volunteering at the orphanage in Kenya where my nephew Brian lived and worked. Ever since Brian went there six years prior, Jade had wanted to go. When she first spoke about it, I assumed it was a passing thing, something she wanted to do because she looked up to her cousin. But Jade's will and desire to travel and make a difference in the world are just a part of who she is. I love the light I've seen in her now that it's not dimmed by drug use or depression.

Jade was able to call me from a satellite phone to give me this incredible news once she got back to base camp. As I looked out on our backyard, snow covering the ground, she said, "The trek was the hardest thing I've ever done, Mom. It was so cold, there was a snowstorm on summit day and my hiking boots were digging into my feet and they went numb. I didn't think I would make it, but then I started chanting *sat nam, sat nam* to help make those final steps."

As I parent, I question whether I could have done anything differently to avoid the path Jade took as a teenager. Could I have been more present? Did she need me more than I was aware? I know that I tried to find a balance providing safety and security, while also encouraging independence.

When Jade was 5, she begged me to let her go to gymnastics class by herself. She didn't even want me to walk her to the entrance of the enormous recreation center where she would have to walk through the halls by herself to the gym on the opposite side of the building. The protective side of me screamed, *No!* The word echoed in my head, but I acquiesced and let her go into the building by herself. I had Jessi with me, so we followed at a distance without her knowing. While she did know I would still come to watch, as I never missed a gymnastics class for either of them, it was important for her to know that she could get there on her own.

When Jessi and I arrived a few minutes after class started, I saw her, head held high with a huge smile on her face. She looked over at me and almost winked, as if to say, *See, Mom, I can take care of myself.*

But the stakes get higher as they grow older, and starting in middle school, I let go of the reins quite a bit. That was how my mom parented me and I thought to myself, *I came out OK.*

When I found out Jade was experimenting with alcohol and marijuana, I said to myself, *I did all of that at her age and I figured it out.* But Jade's experimenting went way further than I ever imagined. I still have an argument in my head about whether she is truly an addict or if she abused substances to deal with emotional issues she couldn't control. This is ongoing as it's hard for me to truly understand how her brain works. I want to believe she has control and can stay sober because she chooses to. The reality is I can never know for sure.

What is now understood about childhood trauma is that the effects last way into adulthood. Most children experience at least one adverse childhood experience (ACE), and most overcome one or two of these. But when it's more than three or four, the risk for educational failure, addiction, and depression increases.

If we include the car accident while Jade was in the womb as one ACE, her clubfoot as another, and her parents' addictive behaviors as one more, Jade had obstacles stacked against her from the beginning. We will never know for sure how much the accident affected her. I have seen her triumph over the negative feedback she has gotten in life, and I hope that she can continue to be strong and reach her full potential. ACEs can be devastating, but they do not have to be definitive. Many people overcome poverty, abusive parents, homelessness, and so much more and go on to live highly successful lives. But it's also true that many of them will suffer the consequences of being born into horrible circumstances, out of their control. Jade is one of the fortunate ones. She has a supportive family with the financial means to have provided the support she needed.

As parents, Brian and I did our best to create a loving and safe environment, but at a certain point each person needs to take charge of their own life, and even the children of the wealthiest, most loving families don't always make it.

Brian is very open about how and when he started drinking. He was 8 or 9 when he started raiding his grandparents' liquor cabinet. He and his younger brother would mix all the drinks together to make a concoction and then challenge each other to drink it. Brian and his brother saw all the adults drinking at family gatherings, including their dad who drank at least a six-pack of beer every night. I also know his dad was tough on him, but he doesn't attribute his drinking and drug use to that. In fact, Brian maintained a good relationship with his father, who passed away in 2021. In no way does he blame his father for his addictive tendencies. However, he recognizes that he most likely inherited these from him.

Brian also says that he struggled in school, although he worked so hard in ninth and 10th grade that he made the honor roll. But once he started going down the path of harder drugs and more drinking, it helped him escape his frustrations. Plus, in his words, "it felt good." There's much research out there to support the idea that alcoholism is inherited, so perhaps Brian was doomed from the start. But I also know that when he was 18, he decided to get sober. Yes, his mother gave him an ultimatum, but he had to do the work. And he did.

He has been sober for 38 years, never relapsed, and has worked his entire life. So, yes, you can beat the odds, but you need to want it and have the commitment to stick with it.

The truth about parenting is that it's a mixture of the good and the bad, the beautiful and the ugly, and we need to accept it all. Recently, Jade and I were talking on the phone as she now lives on her own. "Mom," she said, "I'm so thankful to have you as a parent. So many of my friends have parents that are so controlling and judgmental. The more I'm on my own, the more I realize how lucky Jessi and I are."

I paused for a moment, "I always tried to let you be who you are," I replied, "and to have open communication, but sometimes I think I failed you."

"Mom, you did an amazing job, but after all, you had a daughter who was practically cooking crack in your basement."

My life has been guided by my passions: running and learning. The word passion is derived from the Latin term, *patior*, which literally translates to *suffer*. Anything worth striving for entails effort, and as a result, we derive satisfaction from the pursuit of our goals. I wouldn't trade the injuries and disappointments I've experienced trying to achieve certain ends because they have contributed to who I am. They've led me to where I am now.

But passion without discipline can lead to overuse, abuse, and negative outcomes. Learning to balance my passion for running with the discipline to know when I need to back off has been an ongoing challenge for me. I strive for balance while leaving time for family and other pursuits.

I'm thankful to be here every day, and every day, I know I can be better. I can be a kinder, more aware person, and that's what I am striving for now. Every morning, I take a few minutes before jumping out of bed to do some long, slow breathing. I don't hesitate to stop during a run and take a moment to notice my surroundings. Just the other morning, I paused on the dirt road by Boulder Reservoir to observe an eagle perched in a tree. If I have an opportunity to have a conversation with someone, even if I am on my way to something else, I take the time to chat.

Recently, Jade and I were hiking in the Rocky Mountains, outside of Estes Park. On the way up to the summit point, we passed several groups of people, as well as one elderly gentleman, using a walking stick, hiking on his own. He was particularly friendly, joking with us as we passed him. "Wow," he said with a laugh, "I know I can't keep up with you young ladies."

"Oh, that's my mom," Jade replied. "I need to be on my toes with her." We all enjoyed the moment, pausing to look over the edge of the trail at Estes Lake far below us. Then Jade and I made our way up to Kruger Rock, where we climbed through the space between two massive, slanted slabs. We arrived at the summit where a gorgeous view of the Rocky Mountains awaited. We started to run back down but slowed as we came upon the same gentleman, slowly making his way to the top. He started to talk to us, and Jade and I both stopped. He then told us that he was coming back from a major heart attack just six months prior, and now he was on a solo hiking trip across the West. We spent several minutes with him sharing his joy at being able to do what he loved. Jade and I both agreed it was the highlight of our day.

I've learned that you never know what you might learn during those in-between spaces—the ones you didn't plan for.

Afterword

"There are years that ask questions and years that answer." —Zora Neale Hurston

The year 2016 was a year that asked, and I have spent the years since trying to find some answers. I'm still searching.

I wonder about addiction and whether it's inherited or just part of the human condition. I believe everyone has the potential to become an addict to something. Life is full of challenges and heartache, and it makes sense that we would seek a way out of the pain caused by those disappointments. People find refuge in different places: work, food, exercise, drugs, alcohol, sex. The ability to navigate the downs of life often translates into how resilient a person is.

Everyone will experience trauma, but it's how the moments after those events are managed that will determine how we navigate life. Acknowledging the negative can be the first step in recovery.

It can be argued that addiction is a response more than a disease. Human beings naturally seek equilibrium, and if we're dysregulated by trauma, which can take many forms, we might seek to find balance through substances or other methods. I think this is why so many people have lives that end up feeling out of sync. We work too much, exercise too much, eat too much, sleep too much. On the opposite end, but for similar reasons, some of us can't hold a job, can't sleep, can't eat, and can't find the energy to exercise. Either way, it's a lack of balance, often caused by being overwhelmed by life's challenges.

After my car accident, I had a choice. I could dwell on the horrific nature of the accident, my injuries, and the possible impact on the baby growing inside of me, or I could accept what happened and move on. I'm not saying it was easy. I had many days when the pain was almost unbearable. But I made a conscious decision to feel the pain, emotionally and physically, and then do what I could to get better. I had to go through a process of mental acceptance during my physical recovery so that I could move forward. I also had to let go of my identity as an invincible runner and go through a mourning period as well as a rebirth. I still had to do the physical work of recovery, but my mind wasn't fighting it by wishing it had never happened or giving up entirely on getting better. Instead, I embraced it and took it on as a challenge.

I believe that we pass on certain traits and tendencies from generation to generation. But I also believe that by bringing those tendencies to the surface, talking about them, and questioning their influence on our lives, we can help alter those patterns. Even in my recovery, I still had the trait of impatience that swept over me. I wanted simply to move on. After Jade was born, I went back to my old habits of trying to do as much as possible. Running, of course, was my main outlet.

The why of this might seem complicated to an observer, but to me it comes down to the fact that running settles me. After a long run, my nervous system is calmer, and that's a sensation I'm continuously seeking. I want that feeling of joy, calm, and satisfaction that I get from running. The problem is, it doesn't last. So, I need to run, again, and again, and again.

My mom got the same feel-good sensations from food as well as pharmaceuticals. But that never lasted, either, so she went through a vicious cycle of over-eating or over-medicating.

Jade used various drugs to make herself feel better and to escape the pain she endured trying to find her place in the world.

We all suffered from anxiety that led to the impatience of wanting to just move on to the next place where maybe we'd feel better. We'd find it temporarily, but eventually, we'd be faced with reality. My mom would overeat and feel sick to her stomach. I'd run too much, not stay in the moment, and get injured. Jade found cocaine as her primary drug of choice, which at first, allowed her to stay functional until it didn't.

Impatience is a learned trait and I got it from both my parents. I, unwittingly, passed it on to my kids. I want to help them leave that behind. I want to give them the gift of being in the moment.

We have no idea how long we have on this earth, so treasuring the now is all we have. I'm still working on this and hopefully, I'll never stop. But I know I've made progress when I can stop in the middle of a run and observe the beauty around me, or when I can say "no" to a planned run because my body says it's not a good idea.

Diana Brewer, a scholar on Judaism, was asked to articulate what the notion of running and returning means, and she writes, "The one who knows she is susceptible to a fall at any moment, who is striving to live a life of justice, and to connect through heart-opening truth."

This quote speaks to me because I have tried to avoid falling throughout my life to escape the pain I thought I'd feel if I let myself go. But it was the opposite. By running away, I just kept falling.

Run and return. We do it every day, running toward or away from something. Returning to comfort and safety wherever we can find it. My dad's family was running from oppression when they left Russia for the United States. Once here, they ran toward the accumulation of wealth. My father wanted more meaning in his life, so he became a teacher instead of going into the family business. My mother's family ran away from their Jewish heritage seeking a different life by assimilating. My mother spent her life trying to find love to make up for the lack of it she felt as a child.

The process of writing this book has also been one of run and return. When I first started to put pen to paper, six years ago, I wanted only to share my story of recovery from my car accident. I was proud that I had overcome the physical trauma of my accident and wanted to tell other people how I did it. I thought it would take me a year to write the book, and it held the same urgency becoming a mother had when I was in my early 30s. Little did I know where this would take me and how much patience I would need. I found editors and writing teachers who pushed me more than I thought possible.

It has been painful at times. I didn't want to go to the places that brought back sad memories and hard times, but the more I wrote, the deeper I had to go. The truth is, you can't run forever. This book has been my return to my parents and to myself.

Listening to ourselves and others and being fully present is essential to overcoming the obstacles we encounter in our everyday lives. I hope to continue to make that a priority. It all starts with loving ourselves. Only if we truly love ourselves can we be in a true relationship with others. I wish my mom had learned this earlier in her life so that she could have used food to nourish herself instead of punish herself. I am thankful I have learned to be kinder to myself and can now make better decisions. I know that Jade is on her way to finding her true self, and I hope she continues to grow in light and love.

This book is really just a snapshot in time, and as I move on to the next stage I hope that I continue to learn. I have compiled some of the research and resources I've collected, and they can be found in the following appendix.

Appendix

To Heal, You Must Move

Human beings were meant to move. The modern sedentary lifestyle is not sustainable for a healthy life.

Take my mother. Once she became an adult and started having babies, she basically stopped moving her body. By the time she was in her 50s she was out of shape and resistant to exercise. When I compare my life as a 60-year-old to hers, it makes me sad. She could have avoided so many of her health problems and likely eased her lifelong issues with depression if she'd developed some sort of movement routine.

My husband Brian, in contrast, never stops moving. Even when he's hurt, he finds a way to get his dose of motion. When our kids were young, Brian broke his ankle trying to do a wheelie on his mountain bike. He had gone to the mountain town of Breckenridge with some of his buddies for the day. I was looking forward to some time alone as the girls were with friends. I had just finished my run and was coming back to our house in Boulder when I saw Brian in front of our house. It was only 11 a.m., so I couldn't understand why he was back so early.

"What happened?" I started to ask but then stopped as I could clearly see he was hobbling, not putting any weight on his right leg.

"We were at the trailhead," he answered, "and I was just goofing off on my bike when I did a wheelie and the bike came out from under me, but my pedal didn't release so my ankle kind of got twisted." Then he showed me the aftermath which was an ankle that didn't look like it belonged to the same leg. I realized we were in for a long day at the hospital. He couldn't do anything with his legs for a while, but it didn't slow him down. He managed to get hold of a specially made hand bike developed for paraplegics. Until his ankle healed, he rode that thing all over town.

I remember one cold, rainy day, I had a long run planned, and he wanted to join me on the hand bike. As we got further from home, the sky darkened, and I asked if he wanted to keep going on the 12-mile loop I had mapped out. He nodded his head yes and continued into the freezing wind, pedaling with his gloved hands. I managed to stay relatively warm because I was running, but on a bike, not using his legs, Brian was getting colder and colder.

As the sleeting rain pelted us, he finally turned to me and surrendered. "My hands are so cold I can't grip the handlebars anymore," he said. "I'm going to head home now." An hour later, I found him underneath the covers in our bed, trying to get warm. He was still shivering, but it had never occurred to him not to go with me.

The key for athletes used to relying on movement for a feeling of well-being is to also develop a practice of mindfulness, stillness, and calm. When an unavoidable accident happens, the athlete who has prepared mentally to be fine with stillness will do better than the person who cannot quiet their mind without moving their body. Finding a balance between movement and stillness is the beginning of an enlightened way of living.

Our bodies were built to move. However, our bodies also need rest. One without the other leads to disequilibrium, both physically and mentally. I know the difficulty of this, as there's usually a constant conversation going on in my head. In the past, it took running for hours to silence those voices. But recently, I've managed to find ways to get to a place where the critical voice gets quiet and I remember I'm enough as I am. Instead of always running, I can simply return to who I am at my core.

For Brian and me, moving is a key part of our worldview—it molds our daily lives. When we're healthy and it's summer, it's not unusual for us to run in the morning, swim at noon, and stand-up paddle later in the day. In winter, it might be cross-country skiing and snowshoeing. When physical or emotional trauma interferes with the routine, we find alternatives and try new therapies and practices that might help. This has always gotten us back to a movement routine. I recognize the privilege we have in being able to afford the time and expense that some of this requires. The world is not a fair place, and my words sound hollow to those struggling to get food on their kids' plates. I recognize the bias in my favor.

I was born into a class that has allowed me the luxury to pursue my dreams. I can only hope and dream that someday the world is a place where everyone has this opportunity. I can only write of my experience, though, so my hope is that people, even those without the same resources, will heed the message that we must take better care of ourselves. By doing so, we can heal our wounded selves. Furthermore, I call on those who have equal privileges to mine (or more) to be motivated to share their wealth in ways that make it possible for those who can't afford to do everything from practice yoga to getting massages.

This emphasis on activity isn't only best for athletes. Everyone can benefit from movement and the new catchphrase, "sitting is the new smoking," is not without merit. It doesn't have to be three workouts a day, but being active can do much to prevent injury, disease, and delay some of the effects of aging. We lose muscle mass as we age, so any movement will help slow that process down.

Most of us, at some time or another will need healing, whether the cause is illness or injury. While this often means rest or physical therapy as the first steps, that should be considered only a beginning. Full recovery requires commitment to consistent movement, and it helps greatly if that commitment is there before the need to heal arises. I am proof of this as the doctors told Brian after my car accident. The fact that I was in such good shape most likely saved both my life and Jade's.

My recovery, 24 years after my car accident, is still a work in progress. Not a day goes by that I don't think about the accident and how lucky I am to be alive. Today, I'm completely pain-free and can compete in races from 5k to 50 miles in my 60s. However, this is a result of continuing a recovery plan even though I'm technically recovered. I now use a maintenance strategy that reminds me to pay attention, to be mindful everyday of what my mind and body need to stay true to myself. I must notice my tendency to run away so that I can avoid the anguish and trouble I've suffered in the past by not listening. Metaphorically speaking, it's all about staying in corpse pose at the end of a yoga class, slowing my breath down, relishing in the architecture that is my body. It's stopping to appreciate the beauty of the natural world.

There's no shortcut to staying pain-free. Just like there's no short-cut to beating addiction. It's a life-long journey that must be practiced every day by the choices we make and continue to make. It's about remembering to return to the present moment when the past tries to draw us back or the future begs us to hurry up and get there already.

I've used many modalities over the years. I've already discussed most of them but here I further explain their benefits in the hopes you will find something that resonates and brings you joy and healing, something that helps you return.

Movement for Prevention and Recovery

Water Running

Water running has been my salvation more times than I'd like to count. Now I use it almost daily as a preventive tool. It combines flexibility, strength, and cardiovascular conditioning for a whole-body workout. It simulates running better than any other exercise I've tried, and even if running on land is uncomfortable or not permitted by a doctor, water running may appeal to you and be a safe option.

As a preventive tool, as little as 10 minutes can provide benefits. Most recreation centers offer sliding scale rates, and if you're eligible for Silver Sneakers, it's free. Anyone with a bathing suit can try this.

Although I started water running due to an injury, I continued to make it a part of my regular training routine. To this day, I water run four to five times a week for 30 to 60 minutes. I always get in the water after a long or hard run for at least 10 minutes to unload my legs. This reduces the fatigue I might feel from the pounding of running. I recommend using some sort of floatation device, so you maintain proper form. Belts designed for aqua jogging are easy to find, and many pools even provide them at no extra cost. I've created an instructional video that can be accessed through my website: www.vforcepro.com

Swimming

Though I never saw her do more than bob in the ocean during beach vacations, my mom believed everyone needed to know how to swim. She loved the water, and she passed that on to me as a child. Before I learned how to water run, I swam regularly, and I still do. I started doing masters swim workouts in my 20s and continued for many years. Now, I mostly swim on my own or with Brian, but it's part of my exercise plan regardless of where I am. I love the fact that swimming is no-impact and that I'll be able to do it as long as I can breathe.

The fact is that physical activity like swimming improves mood by stimulating the production of endorphins—natural opioids in the brain—as well as dopamine and serotonin, neurotransmitters that affect how we feel.

Foundation Training

Foundation Training is a postural corrective program developed by Dr. Eric Goodman. It involves a series of postures designed to strengthen the posterior muscle chain and to counteract the effects of gravity on the body. The compression our bodies endure from daily life can be a contributing factor to injury and pain. We live in a culture that loves to sit, but sitting, by its nature, is not conducive to health. Using breath and movement, Foundation poses help decompress the spine and realign the body so it can move more efficiently. The scapula pain from my car accident lasted 16 years, and I did not find lasting relief until I discovered Foundation Training. I found it so helpful, I became a certified instructor.

It doesn't take long to reap the benefits, even five to 10 minutes a day is beneficial. There's no special equipment needed, so you can do it anywhere. When recovering from my broken humerus, the simple act of arm tracing restored range of motion to my shoulder and elbow joints. Arm tracing involves pulling your thumbs up from your hips to your armpits, leading with your elbows. This was one of the first exercises I practiced, and it proved to be one of the most effective. You can find free videos online to see if this interests you. There are certified instructors all over the world. Find one at www.FoundationTraining.com.

Pilates

I started taking Pilates classes over 15 years ago. Pilates is a system of exercises developed by German fitness pioneer Joseph Pilates in the early 1900s to help correct muscular imbalances and improve posture. While imprisoned in an internment camp in England during World War I, he came up with a unique apparatus (now called the reformer) that used bed springs to help his fellow bedridden prisoners stay in shape.

Pilates is complementary to Foundation Training due to the emphasis on breath control and strong posture. In fact, Pilates originally called his program Contrology. I like to challenge my body by giving it different kinds of movement on a regular basis. If we get used to doing the same movements over and over, the body adapts and stops progressing.

I vary how often I do Pilates but try for one to two times a week. Joining a studio is probably the most economical strategy, but look for punch passes and discounts for multiple classes. You can also find lots of free videos online, and I recommend trying different ones to see if this is an activity that works for you.

Strength Training

My recovery from the car accident did not follow a linear path. I had many setbacks along the way. When Jessi was less than a year old, my body once again seemed to be failing me, this time in the form of knee and foot pain. Craniosacral work and massage helped, but I knew I needed to get stronger, and that I needed help to do that. I found that in Jeff Hoobler, a strength trainer I met at RallySport. I worked with him for 18 years to develop a much stronger, well-balanced body. I owe much of the racing success I had in my 40s and 50s to him. Jeff helped me to work on my upper body strength, something that most runners, including myself, tend to ignore. I'm thankful I developed some of this prior to breaking my arm as it certainly helped my healing.

The cost for strength training varies, but it can be done relatively cheaply by using an at-home program with some makeshift weights. Even lifting heavy things like rocks or logs can serve as weight training, just be sure to use proper form when lifting. Don't bend at your waist—learning how to hinge at your hips is crucial for lifting anything, from your child to a heavy box.

Brian has always hated going inside to exercise. When we lived in the mountains, he would chop wood and fill a wheelbarrow with the logs. Then we'd take turns pushing the wheelbarrow up our driveway as part of our strength work. When they were small, we bought the girls a mini wheelbarrow so they could join in on the fun.

Kundalini Yoga

Kundalini yoga is the yoga of mindfulness, and the postures are meant to prepare the physical body for the stillness of meditation. There are over 4,000 Kriyas (a series of postures, breath, and sound), so no class is ever the same. It can even be silly, like playing patty-cake or humming (which has been shown to have healing effects on the body). But that's part of the joy of it—returning to our child-like selves.

This focused "slowing down" has been critical to my recoveries. I've always told myself and others that running is a form of moving meditation, and I believe this. It's helped me calm my nervous system and channel my anxiety. But there's something different, and equally beneficial, about sitting meditation.

The act of sitting is the opposite of running, so even though this may seem obvious, it's precisely this difference that can help a runner or any athlete cope with injury. Although as humans we tend to identify ourselves through our physical selves, the body is only a container for who we are. Having to sit with that can make the difference between acceptance and denial of whatever life is dealing us—even injury.

Kundalini is hard because it makes you face yourself. The main chant, *sat nam*, means "truth is my identity." There is no escape in Kundalini— that's the beauty of it. When Jade said she used this mantra to help her make it to the summit of Mount Kilimanjaro, the impact of the practice on my life came full circle.

This practice can also be accessed with free online tutorials and videos and there are classes everywhere. There are many other types of yoga that can be explored. Most studios will offer discounts to those in need.

Slow, Steady Progression

All my life I have been organized, and this has served me well when it comes to training, exercise, injury prevention, and recovery. Writing down what I do daily has been a consistent part of my life—I have running journals dating back to 1976.

Recording a run in a journal makes the act feel concrete, but it also forces honesty. Bad or good, if it's written down, you can go back and see what went right and what went wrong and learn from it. Some people use online methods to keep track of their workouts. But for me, the act of writing in a journal brings the activity to life and gives me a sense of satisfaction. It's another way I have practiced the art of returning.

Training for a marathon usually involves a plan that can last several months and includes weekly components such as a long run, hill sessions, intervals, and rest days. When I started to seriously train for a marathon with the goal of qualifying for the Trials, I was lucky to have elite athletes as my mentors who didn't charge me a cent for their advice. I was unaware at the time, but they were using a training method based on the legendary coaching of Arthur Lydiard. I am such a believer in his principles that I went through training to become a certified Lydiard coach.

The key is to make each workout count. Even easy days matter and must be a part of the schedule. Picking a goal is important, whether it be to break three hours in a marathon or run a first 5k. Work backwards from your goal to build your plan.

Improvement requires progression. It's not a good idea to go from sitting on the couch to running a marathon. It takes time to get strong, and progress comes with consistency. The other important principle is adaptation. The body will adapt to incremental changes and increased load, but ramping up too quickly will inevitably lead to injury or illness. Following some sort of plan helps the athlete stay on track

In the same way, incremental, deliberate progression, and having a plan will help you recover. Everyone must find their own mix of exercise and recovery. It's an ongoing juggling act as life stresses, age, work, and family dynamics all change regularly. It's easy to get stuck, either doing too little or too much, and the trick is to keep reworking the balance. To find resources on the Lydiard method go to www.LydiardFoundation.org

Bodywork

Many people assume that massage is a luxury, but it has helped me heal from hard workouts, falls, and injuries. I've been lucky enough to have a fabulous body worker, Lori Kucyznski, work on me ever since I was pregnant with Jessi and experienced sciatic pain. Not only does it feel good, but it also contributes to an overall sense of well-being. Humans need to be touched, and touch deprivation is an actual syndrome that can lead to depression. I get massages regularly and see Dr. Nuzzi for craniosacral work. I believe both have been integral to maintaining my physical and emotional health. I believe that if more people got regular bodywork, health care costs would go down and societal mental health would be improved dramatically.

Acupuncture is another method I have used over the years. After the car accident, my practitioner prescribed an herbal tea that smelled and tasted horrible. I drank it, though, because Ming said it would help the baby. I use acupuncture now whenever I feel the need to restore my energy balance.

Most massage and acupuncture schools provide low-cost clinics so students can practice.

Breathwork

There are many types of breathing practices one can follow. The one I do the most is decompression breathing from Foundation Training, followed by the Wim Hof method, otherwise known as breath withholding. This type of breathing stimulates the nervous system and can be very energizing. Wim Hof's personal story of healing from trauma is inspiring. He started seeking answers to his feelings of despair when his wife, who was mentally ill, killed herself and left him with four children to raise on his own. He found breathing and cold therapy as his way back to the world. Today, he offers teachings and courses on his method and a free app you can access on your phone to guide you through the process.

There's a lot of literature on the importance of breathing well, and it's something we, as humans, often take for granted because it is autonomic. In other words, we don't need to think about breathing, our body does it automatically. But, to breathe well, we do need to think about it. One of the simplest changes you can make is to only inhale and exhale through your nose. This alone can change many imbalances in the body.

The best thing about breathing is it doesn't cost a cent.

Counseling

A key component in my process of healing has been talking about my problems. At different times, this has meant seeking out professional help. There are so many types of specialists, including, but not limited to, psychiatrists, psychologists, counselors, and social workers. There are also alternative forms to choose from such as yoga therapy, art therapy, music therapy, mindfulness therapy, and many more.

As painful as it has been, talking has been the starting point for moving through the trauma. Sometimes, it's enough to have a friend or family member you can trust to talk things through. But I recommend going to a trained therapist if you continue to struggle. Sometimes, the clinical role of a therapist is needed to allow for total honesty.

The methods presented here are simply ways I have found to maintain a sense of balance and health in my mind and body. They're only suggestions. Each person needs to find the right menu for them. A recent study, led by University of Colorado assistant professor Colleen Reid, reports less depression and anxiety during COVID for people exposed to the outdoors. Further proof that my childhood self was on to something wanting to be outside most of the time. My hope is that my story helps encourage people to find a path toward their best selves and supporting their communities in return.

One other simple way to contribute to your own healing is to help others. It's a known fact that volunteering or just doing a kind gesture for someone else increases one's sense of self-worth and happiness. Helping others leads to better self-esteem and a feeling of wellness.

Below are some organizations that help those in need gain access to sports and resources. You can also check in your local community for groups needing support. Nonprofits always need donations and volunteers. Some of my favorites include:

Blackgirlsrun.com

Trailsisters.net

Womensportsfoundation.org/the-equity-project/

Trackgirlz.com

Risetowin.org

Backonmyfeet.org

My Block/My Hood/My City (https://www.formyblock.org/mission)

For more resources and access to the research I've compiled, please go to www.vforcepro.com/book-resources.

About the Author

Vicki Ash Hunter is a writer, runner, coach, and retired university instructor. A lifelong athlete, Hunter found respite in running as a teenager in the 1970s and has since relied on it to satisfy her competitive nature and keep her body and mind healthy and strong. Her running resume is stacked with races ranging from 5K to 50 miles, including the 1988 Olympic Marathon Trials and the Pikes Peak Marathon a dozen times. She still competes, and in 2021, at age 60, ran the Boston Marathon in 3 hours, 30 minutes.

Hunter's running career is dotted with accidents and injuries, however, and some of them were life-threatening and life-altering. Most significantly, she came back from near-death after a car accident in 1997, when she was pregnant with her first child. She credits her own fitness and fortitude; her will to deliver a healthy baby; running; and the care of specialized and alternative practitioners for her and her daughter's survival, recovery, and return to real life.

Hunter, who retired from the University of Colorado, where she taught political science, is now a running coach certified in Foundation Training and the Lydiard method. She is a movement specialist who works with athletes of all levels and abilities and is particularly attuned to the needs of ultrarunners. Influenced by her own experience recovering from injuries, she is passionate about and dedicated to helping people move better.

Hunter holds a Ph.D. in political science and is the mother of two grown daughters. She and her husband live in Boulder, Colorado, and Kona, Hawaii. *Running and Returning* is her first book.

CPSIA information can be obtained
at www.ICGtesting.com
Printed in the USA
LVHW081606220622
721875LV00015B/530